**Someday I
May Find
Honest Work**

Other Books by Sam Venable

An Island Unto Itself

A Handful of Thumbs and Two Left Feet

Two or Three Degrees Off Plumb

One Size Fits All and Other Holiday Myths

From Ridgetops to Riverbottoms:
A Celebration of the Outdoor Life in Tennessee

I'd Rather Be Ugly than Stuppid

Mountain Hands: A Portrait of Southern Appalachia

Rock-Elephant: A Story of Friendship and Fishing

You Gotta Laugh to Keep from Cryin':
A Baby Boomer Contemplates Life beyond Fifty

Someday I May Find Honest Work

A Newspaper Humorist's Life

Sam Venable

Illustrations by R. Daniel Proctor

The University of Tennessee Press / Knoxville

Copyright © 2007 by The University of Tennessee Press / Knoxville.
All Rights Reserved. Manufactured in the United States of America.
First Edition.

Most of these essays originally appeared as Sam Venable's columns in the Knoxville *News
Sentinel.* They have been edited for book use and may differ somewhat from their original
form. Used with permission.

This book is printed on acid-free paper.

Library of Congress Cataloging-in-Publication Data

Venable, Sam.
Someday I may find honest work : a newspaper humorist's life / Sam Venable; illustrations by
R. Daniel Proctor. — 1st ed.
    p. cm.
Collected columns.

ISBN-13: 978-1-57233-600-1 (pbk. : alk. paper)
ISBN-10: 1-57233-600-5

I. Title.

PN4874.V46A25 2007
070.4'4—dc22   2007002855

For Kim and Max, the two newest loves in my life

Contents

Chapter 3.

Chapter 4.

Chapter 7.

Chapter 8.

Chapter 9.
Loose Screws and Other Leftover Parts   191

Introduction

Clocking in at the Word Factory

The title of this book is adapted from a line I often use in my newspaper columns and standup comedy routines. Forever amazed that publishers and audiences actually pay for my drivel, I keep promising, "Y'know, I *really* oughta find honest work one of these days."

It just might happen. But, hopefully, not anytime soon.

Since January 3, 1968, I have been employed by three Tennessee newspapers—first at the old *Knoxville Journal* (now deceased), then at the *Chattanooga News–Free Press* (now the *Chattanooga Times Free Press*) and, since 1970, at the *Knoxville News Sentinel* (still going strong under the same name, minus the once-prominent hyphen between *News* and *Sentinel*).

Note I said "have been employed by" as opposed to "have worked at." There's a vast difference. In my mind, "work" conjures up a scary image of odious tasks. Irksome responsibilities. Sweat-of-the-brow labor. I've never considered any of that to be a part of my job.

Yes, writing a newspaper column can be difficult, sometimes frustrating, often pressurized. The nature of this craft requires that the juices flow even when the pipeline is clogged. The only time I ever sat down with the late Atlanta humorist Lewis Grizzard and had a one-on-one about our silly occupation, he called it "creativity on demand." That's a perfect description.

Writing a column is the best way to enjoy this nutty, mysterious, yet marvelous experience called life.

Is it exasperating at times? No doubt about it. Try approaching deadline when your computer is down or a must-have phone call won't come through.

Occasionally gut-wrenching? Of course. Not everything I write is humorous. You ever attempted to pry quotes from someone who's headed to jail or has just buried a friend or is picking up the pieces of a demolished house or any other tragic episode of human drama?

Exhausting at moments? Naturally. Frequent mental exercises are supposed to be good for the brain, but you can only go to the well for the right noun, adjective, or catchy phrase so many times a day before you're fried.

Scary sometimes? Sure. Happens whenever you're staring at a blank computer screen and realize that 112.26 lines of text (by digital count, trust me) must magically appear—and you're not in a particularly creative mood.

Fun factor low every now and then? Join the club. There's not a truck driver or heart surgeon, carpenter or dentist, preacher or teacher, firefighter, coach, farmer, salesclerk, mechanic, secretary, or lawyer anywhere in American who hasn't occasionally clocked in for the day wistfully thinking, "And I actually *chose* this?"

Never-ending? Yeah, that one's right on the money. It could be the one vocational quirk shared by newspaper columnists and assembly-line workers. Just when you finish one piece—or twist a bolt, as it were—another one comes along. Then another. And another and another and another. Day after day. Week after week. Year after year.

But thankfully, the dark spells flee quickly. Mostly you're grinning inside, blissfully repeating, "Man! This sure beats workin' for a living."

One of the most frequently asked questions for people in my occupation is, "Where do you come up with ideas?"

I always reply, "Hells bells! Anywhere you look!" I don't intend that to be rude, curt, or cute. It's simply a statement of fact. This world is so hilarious, ideas often come dripping down like rainwater out of a leaky gutter.

Years ago, while doing research for a book about Little Pecan Island in southwest Louisiana, I interviewed Lucille Duplechain in Lake Charles. As a young woman in the early 1920s, Lucille and her family lived on Little Pecan, a tiny ribbon of "high" ground (six feet above sea level) snaking through the desolate marsh. They had no electricity, no telephone, no car, no refrigeration, no modern convenience of any description. Yet they feasted at every meal.

"You just went outside and held out your pan," she told me. "Food was everywhere. My husband and I had a garden and a milk cow. Daddy butchered twice a month. There were turtles, fish, and crabs in the lake. Or else I'd take Daddy's shotgun and shoot coots, ducks, or rabbits. We ground our own coffee and made our own bread. There never was a whole lot of money, but we sure didn't go hungry."

That's the same theory I have about newspaper columning. Just hold out your notepad. You ain't ever gonna get rich, but the ideas are plentiful enough to keep food on the table.

In many respects, there's no real difference in what I do and you do—except I charge for it and you give it away. We both get tickled at something we see or hear. We both get peeved about the latest political nonsense in Nashville or Washington. We both coin one-liners and exchange jokes. You do it for free around the office coffee pot or at home, at church, at the hardware store, or while standing in line at the supermarket. Then you go your merry way. I scribble it down and get a paycheck. In the meat industry, this is known as making baloney—or creating chicken salad out of chicken, uh, feathers.

I'm not going to lie to you. Writing humor is fun. So is performing humor on stage. As any class clown or office ham will attest, making people laugh is quickly addictive. This is our drug of choice, and we crave it like a junkie. I'm not a psychologist (thank God), so I can't say whether this quirk indicates a genetic defect, a self-defense mechanism, or simply the inability to think deeply. I'm not going to spend a whole lot of time worrying about it, either.

Writing equipment sure has changed since I started in this business. When I was a cub reporter—and for many years thereafter—every word was composed on paper with manual typewriters and set in metal type, a process virtually unaltered for more than a century.

Then the computer age dawned. Thus began a roller coaster ride of learning new technology, then forsaking the new technology for newer technology, then forsaking the newer technology for the newest technology—which will be outdated by the middle of next week.

Big deal. As much as I fuss about high-tech woes (there are several examples in the following chapters), the process really doesn't worry me. As long as people read, I figure I'll always have a job. In fact, I'm sure I will because our personnel department (I refuse to say "human resources," as if people were coal or lumber) has just devised a self-evaluation system for rating my production.

I'm serious. I hold a copy of the form as we speak. It wants me to grade myself. Where was this system when I was in college, for Pete's sake? I'd have a doctorate by now.

I won't bore you with all the bureaucratic mumbo-jumbo and my responses. Just a few of the highlights.

Under the category of career goals, I wrote: "Staying off everybody's radar screen."

Under the category of my skills: "A master in the field of bovine scatology."

Under the category of administrative and interpersonal: "Huh?"

But I saved the "additional comments" line for my finest and most truthful observation: "Anybody who can squeak by so long doing so little clearly is a genius. Double this man's salary immediately!" What an astute judge of journalistic talent I am.

Let me wipe the smirk off my face for the remaining paragraphs in this introduction, then I promise not to express another serious thought for the rest of the book.

There's an important distinction between playing off of a news event and outright fabrication. My stock-in-trade is to let the news function as a straight man. All I do is supply the spin and grin. But there has to be an element of honest-to-gosh fact to begin with. Newspaper columnists who forsake this cardinal rule and drift into unadulterated fiction should—and often do—find themselves ushered to the door and unceremoniously drop-kicked into the street.

What's more, credit must be given where credit is due. That's not only professional courtesy, it's the law. Sadly, plagiarism seems to be rampant these days—in schools, corporations, and government as well as newspapers.

Allow me to convey two pieces of advice to writers who feel compelled to shoplift their lines.

The first comes from mothers and Sunday school teachers everywhere: "Be sure your sins will find you out." Given the ready availability of electronic phrase-tracking devices, anyone would be a fool to knowingly heist previously published text and call it their own. Yet hardly a day goes by without revelations that another high-dollar author has been caught with his or her hands in someone else's sentence.

The second bit of advice comes directly out of Journalism 101: Cite your sources of information. Tell where you got the stuff. Then you'll be on solid footing for further elaboration. Geeze. How hard is this to understand?

One other somber thought before I take a cold shower and get my mind off seriousness and into frivolity.

I do worry about the future of the newspaper business. Seems like the bottom line drives *every* decision these days. Editorial department staffs are shrinking, as is the space dedicated to news. Strict divisions between news and advertising are eroding. Superficial fluff tends to take precedence over hard-core investigation. All this may please the stockholders, but it spells bad news for readers in the long run.

Industry analysts worry about these trends, too. In an attempt to identify readership, they create charts and spreadsheets. Marketers keep experimenting with gimmicks to entice nonsubscribers to buy newspapers. I suppose this has been going on since Gutenberg was tinkering with moveable type, but it's disturbing nonetheless. In my antiquated mind, the product ought to be good enough to sell itself.

All I can hope is that we keep doing something right. And that consumers want us. And that there's always a need for hired help down at the word factory.

Chapter 1

Take Two Forms and Call Tech Services in the Morning

Just my luck. About the time I'm flirting with the notion of retirement, I discover I should have studied medicine and science rather than journalism.

Not for a career, mind you. Journalism was, and continues to be, immense fun. I can't imagine any other vocation.

Instead, I should have spent more time analyzing medicine and science so I can attempt to comprehend what's going on around me. Many of us codger-in-training baby boomers are in the same situation. The fields of medicine and science have completely dominated our lives—yet we're still mentally stuck in the '50s, enjoying pot roast with Ward and June Cleaver.

Take medicine. When I was younger, you went to the doctor if you were sick. He—doctors were always "he" back then—treated whatever ailed you and sent a bill, which your parents promptly paid.

These days, you visit teams of doctors to, theoretically, keep from getting sick. These practitioners debate your potential ailments, prescribe a battery of preventative pills, and refer you to specialists. Then the entire lot of them sends dozens of bills to your insurance company, which charges you outrageous premiums for jamming the system with paperwork and, ultimately, refuses payment. This is called progress.

It's even worse on the scientific front. I am not a techie, not in the most remote of fictive senses. I am easily baffled by the simplest of wizardry. Even today, I can think back to those cheesy James Bond movies of the '60s and still marvel at the wondrous special effects.

I take notes with paper and pen, not a Palm Pilot. I listen to an FM radio in my pickup truck, not an iPod. I eat blackberries, not text-message on them.

Still, I have a bizarre attraction to weird science. Especially strange numbers. The more oddball the set of numbers, the more I enjoy poking fun. When scientific stories involving numbers come rolling down the pike, I can't wait to sit down at my computer—even if I don't altogether trust the computer to perform as requested.

For example, you may not have realized it, but at the start of 2006, a dollop of extra time was added to our clocks. It was called a "leap second" by timekeepers of the world, who are guided by ultraprecise atomic instruments.

As was reported in *National Geographic News:* "Earth's rotation is ever so slightly slowing down, but atomic clocks remain unwaveringly consistent. The planet's slowing is mostly due to the friction of tides raised by the gravitational pull of the sun and the moon. In fact, a day is now about two-thousandths of a second longer than it was a couple of centuries ago."

I was most surprised to discover this wasn't the first time we received a leap second. Far from it. This was the twenty-third leap second added since 1972. We last got one in 1998.

Think about that. We've had all this excess time on our hands and never realized it. So I immediately set about to spend mine wisely.

But how? By sleeping an extra second longer than normal, perhaps? Doing more "field research" (translation: hunting, fishing, or goofing off when I'm supposed to be working)? Traveling? Picking up fallen limbs in the back yard? Cleaning out my closets and bedroom drawers? Straightening desks at home and the office? Paying bills? Preparing my tax return? Exercising?

None of those options sounded good. You see, I wanted this to be something special. Something memorable. Something that would allow me to wring every glorious ounce of joy and excitement out of my extra second.

Then I remembered! It was the perfect solution for filling every action-packed instant of the bonus time! I don't know why I didn't think of it sooner! I used my leap second to spend my most recent pay raise. Each lasted exactly as long as the other.

Another batch of weird figures fell into my lap one day when an Australian astronomer announced he and his fellow researchers had counted the number of stars in the heavens.

This exercise was a bit more intricate than "one potato, two potato, three potato, four." Indeed, it involved long hours at the telescope coupled with high-level calculations. Also an immense amount of practice writing zeroes.

According to their findings, the star population of the universe shakes out to be seventy sextillion. Which is a seven followed by twenty-two zeroes.

A *sex*tillion? Well, whataya know. All along I assumed stodgy mathematicians never had any fun. And to be perfectly honest, I always thought the official name of seven and twenty-two zeroes was a gazillion. Or maybe a gobullion. I'm forever fuzzy in matters of math because I laid out of college classes any time numbers were on the agenda.

It's never been a problem, though. As a newspaper columnist, I never have to worry about any number more complicated than, oh, $14.27.

Up-sized Rodents

Here's reason number 3,587 why it's better to be living Right Now instead of Way Back Then: There are no mice weighing three-quarters of a ton.

If you've been keeping up with the latest scientific news, you know what I'm talking about. Seems that in South America, researchers have discovered the bones of a giant rodent that roamed—make that "thudded"—through the region eight million years ago.

Archaeologists have been calling this thing *Phoberomys pattersoni*. There's no mention of what Fred Flintsone and Barney Rubble called the beast, but I suspect it was something along the lines of "Holy $@&*%! Run!" That's because *Phoberomys* had a long tail, huge gnawing teeth, and stood about the size of a modern-day buffalo.

There are a number of geographical and physiological reasons why this animal became extinct—not the least of which is the fact it was too large to dig a burrow and too slow to flee when pursued by predators.

(Which brings up reason number 3,588 why it's better to be living Right Now instead of Way Back Then: In East Tennessee, there are no predators large enough to feed on rodents the size of a buffalo. But I digress.)

Ever since I heard about this discovery, I've been wondering about the trouble Fred and Barney had with such humongous rodents. Or maybe "wondering" isn't the best choice of words. "Pitying" is more like it.

It's one thing to discover BB-sized mouse doots in your pantry. I daresay the effluent left by *Phoberomys* was more along the size of basketballs. Definitely not something you would sweep into a dustpan.

I'm rather sensitive to this subject because I'm constantly at war with mice. This comes with the territory when you live in the woods. The mice were there long before I built my log house, and they seem to resent the fact that I moved into the neighborhood.

They show this resentment by nibbling anything remotely edible. Of course, "remotely edible" in mouseze encompasses any material that is animal, vegetable, or mineral. You expect mice to munch their way into sacks of bird feed stupidly left beside the garage door. You do not expect them to chew through life preservers inside the storage locker of your bass boat.

Furthermore, the mice around my place show their resentment by appearing at odd times. You expect mice to scamper across your boots when you're unloading firewood from the log pile. You do not expect them to scamper across your soapy feet when you're standing, buck nekkid, in the shower stall of your boat shed.

Thus we battle.

I have trapped enough of the pesky things to make my wife a fur coat. I have caught them on sticky pads. I have, uh, "tapped them lightly" with sticks. I have even plinked several with a rifle.

At last count, the mice were winning. I suspect they will continue to prevail as long as I'm in the neighborhood.

Still, it's comforting to know they are, well, mouse-sized. If they weighed three-quarters of a ton, I would have—to quote Fred Flintstone—"yabbba-dabba-doooed" out of there a long time ago.

A Shaky Truce

I don't hate computers like I used to.

This turnaround has not occurred quickly. But if peace can come between the United States and Russia, anything is possible.

Computers entered my world in the form of word processors. I was certain they were tools of the devil. Writers were supposed to perform their craft on typewriters—manual typewriters, of course—that clacked violently or softly, depending upon the writer's disposition, and frequently required a change of ribbon.

It was bad enough, in the mid-1970s, when the newspaper switched to electric typewriters. Electric typewriters have no soul. They sit there, rat-tat-tat-tatting, spitting out letters with all the emotion of a wart. But at least they are typewriters, using real, honest typewriter paper.

Then we went all the way, and my life as a writer has never been the same.

I vividly remember my first session in wordprocessology. I felt like an Old West stagecoach driver who suddenly found himself at the controls of a Boeing 747. I was perfectly content with simple, manual functions like the space bar and margin release, but this thing had a blinking light and about ten thousand foreign keys.

One of the keys was labeled "Go to Head." Since I had just drunk four cups of coffee, that's precisely where I went. Unfortunately, the people in charge of training found me cowering there and ordered me back into the classroom.

As the years went by, my bitter resistance to computers began to wear down. I started to realize how easy it is to "think" on a word processor. Also switch from one story to another, move paragraphs around, correct errors, and save text for future reference.

There is a psychological explanation for this type of behavior. It is called the Stockholm syndrome. It's an erosion of personal values often occurring in kidnap victims. The Stockholm syndrome is what made Patty Hearst join her captors on bank robbery sprees.

Be that as it may, I initially refused to work on a computer at home. I composed more than one hundred magazine articles and one entire book manuscript, including three complete rewrites, on a typewriter. We purists have our principles.

But a few years later I started working on another book manuscript. And, my hands quake at the admission, I started using computers in earnest.

The first home computer we bought was not an advanced piece of equipment. Its software—I still don't understand that word—was developed during the first presidential administration of Ronald Reagan. Certain commands on the keyboard were in different locations than the keyboard I use at the newspaper, causing me to hunt and peck with cramped hands. The monitor occasionally went blank, but I learned to bring it back to life with a series of sharp slaps.

Through the years, we purchased new computers for home, and I learned how to operate them. In all honesty, each generation has been more user-friendly. We've actually begun to coexist in peace.

I signed up for one of those 800-number drugstore services. It's fast and efficient. But there's something that worries me every time I call to refill a prescription.

The automated voice on the other end seems only vaguely interested in establishing my identity. All it ever asks for is the prescription number and my ZIP code. No name, no address, no doctor's name, no drug name, no nothing.

But then when I key in my credit card number, the digitized voice repeats it back to me, demands verification, asks for the expiration date on my card, and demands verification a second time.

No offense, Doc Digital, but it does bother me that you blow off the pharmaceutical portion of our "conversation" in order to concentrate on the color of my dough.

Yes, there have been occasional moments of tension, but no permanent harm has been done. I am even starting to feel comfortable with these high-tech things.

But like Teddy Roosevelt, I believe in the Big Stick theory. I still own a manual typewriter. I even bought a fresh ribbon not long ago. Just in case.

Daylight Saving Technicalities

After four days of trying, I'm about to adjust to Daylight Saving Time.

At least the biological transformation is pretty well complete. My internal clock—the one that regulates important daily events such as lunchtime, happy hour, and bedtime—has accepted this new standard.

The technical transformation, however, is progressing more slowly. As it always does.

Just when I think every timepiece in the house has "sprung forward" or "fallen backward," depending on season, another one rears its evil head. Meaning, of course, I have to summon my wife to push the right buttons in the proper sequence and bring the recalcitrant clock into compliance.

Some people are not meant to understand technology, and I am Chief Dunce in Charge. I was weaned on watches and clocks with moving hands and stems that twist whenever their time needs changing. I don't do buttons.

It doesn't matter how many times Mary Ann patiently walks me through the process because it's different with every clock. Thus something invariably goes wrong when I attempt the job solo. I reverse the A.M. and P.M. cycles, or else I miss a step and cause the hateful thing to blink the incorrect time incessantly. In the case of car radio clocks, I somehow manage to mess up the station selections. Either way, I'm confident this is why God invented hammers.

The VCR and computer clocks in our house change time automatically. They tick along until the first Saturday night in April or the last Saturday night in November, and then at the appropriate hour, *ker-ching*, they spring forward or fall back without being told.

(Well, no, they don't actually say "ker-ching" like a 1947 cash register or other respectable piece of machinery. They make no noise whatsoever. They just sit there, smugly chuckling under their digitized breath about what geniuses they are and what an imbecile I am. Which is another reason to distrust them.)

Foolishly, I asked Mary Ann the same question Lewis Grizzard once posed about a thermos, which keeps cold things cold and hot things hot: "How does it know?"

Now that cell phones are capable of taking photographs, have you ever been tempted to pick up a camera and call someone with it?

Major mistake. Nontechnical people should never ask a technical person to explain anything. That's because technical people feel obliged to start these discussions at the dawn of creation, connecting every scientific advancement since fire like so many link sausages, until the nontechnical person's eyes glaze over—a feat usually accomplished in twenty-six seconds or less.

"Point to an empty area of the task bar on your desktop," she began.

"I don't want a lesson," I replied. "I just want to know how the $#@% computer is smart enough to know how to change its %$#@ clock."

"The computer doesn't know," Mary Ann said calmly. "Someone had to program it to change. It begins with . . ."

I cut her off with my customary "Arrrgh!" and stormed out to cut the grass.

I must have finished the job precisely at high noon, because when I glanced at the garage clock, it was blinking "12:00." I considered it a case of perfect timing.

Doctor Feelgood's Diagnosis

Doctor Feelgood's Sure-Cure Clinic is open for business, and today he's delighted to reveal the number one secret for enjoying a lifetime of excellent health: Don't ever get sick. Otherwise, you might as well trot on down to the jailhouse or the mortuary for a new suit of clothes.

Doctor Feelgood has come to this conclusion after perusing recent news on the medical and legal fronts.

First, there was the flu shot shortage caused by tainted vaccine. Folks who normally lined up for their annual injection were told to forego the experience for one year unless they were "at risk."

Doctor Feelgood wants to know "at risk" for what? Coming down with the flu or catching some hideous other disease from bad vaccine? Either way, the prospects weren't exactly promising. As a result, people plunged into the depths of the sickness season with nothing more than hope to keep them free of aches and pains, fever and chills.

> *What are you supposed to do if your cardiologist insists you always take the stairs instead of the elevator because your heart needs the exercise, but your orthopedist insists you always take the elevator instead of the stairs because your knees require rest?*

In the meantime, what happens if you wind up getting ill? Do you swing by the neighborhood drugstore and round up a sack of remedies?

Heavens, no. Not unless you want to spend the rest of the winter being hounded by the cops. You think it's bad enough sneezing, wheezing, coughing, and hacking in the privacy of your own home? Then try doing it at the crossbar hotel.

In case you haven't kept up with current events—or haven't come down with the crud—you may be surprised to learn many popular over-the-counter cold remedies are now subject to strict control. This is especially true of decongestants containing ephedrine and psuedoephedrine, which can be "cooked down" into the highly addictive and illegal drug methamphetamine.

Meth labs are popping up in the rural south faster than mobile home parks. Hardly a day goes by that law enforcement agencies don't bust a new one. Among the tip-offs that lead the cops to pay dirt are large purchases of cold medicine. So unless you want the snoops on your tail, Doctor Feelgood recommends suffering in silence.

Actually, be thankful all you have is the sniffles. It could be worse.

For instance, if your aching back and throbbing knees start to act up, do you reach for that ol' reliable prescription medication, Vioxx?

Not on your life. That's one of the "Cox-2" painkillers recently taken off the market. Researchers believe their long-term use leads to a higher incidence of heart attack and stroke. It's not just the prescription stuff, either. Even some over-the-counter painkillers have been yanked.

All of which leads Doctor Feelgood back to his original premise: If you want to stay healthy and pain-free, don't you dare get sick.

That'll be two hundred dollars, please. Cash. Doctor Feelgood appreciates your business.

Nobuttatall

If you're in the market for a new car, have a seat.

I mean that literally. Sit down. Take a load off. Rest your backside.

If what I've been reading about changes in automobile design is accurate, folks are paying more attention to butt comfort than fuel economy, horsepower, color, and other boring details.

If you've been shopping for a new car, you're already aware of this fact. For that matter, if you're shopping for a new car, you just won the Powerball or patented a cure for the common cold or were smart enough to choose rich, short-lived parents. The rest of us can only imagine.

At least five foreign brands—Toyota, Honda, Mercedes-Benz, Subaru, and Mitsubishi—have followed the lead of domestic manufacturers by making their seats wider.

According to the NPG Group, Inc., a market research firm, this change was necessary because Americans are growing tubbier by the decade. More than 60 percent are now considered overweight or obese. In vehicular circles, this is known as "seat-covering the spread."

Not that it matters to me, of course. For two reasons.

First, I acquire new wheels on the same relative cycle that Tennessee wins national football championships. With any luck, my next purchase will come equipped with one of those groovy eight-track tape decks.

But the main reason this automotive innovation doesn't interest me is because it doesn't apply. I may be a balding, beer-gutted, barely sixty baby boomer, but my beam isn't broad. Never has been. In fact, just the opposite is true.

All my life I've suffered (oh, the embarrassment!) from a rare physical disorder, nobuttatall.

Unlike normal humans, I have only one set of rounded cheeks. They're on opposite sides of my face. Down on the lower forty, there's only a faint, concave collection of skin.

Nurses use nobuttatallics like me for target practice when they're learning to give injections, the reasoning being if they can hit such an itty-bitty bull's-eye under such extreme circumstances, jabbing the remainder of society should be a cinch.

But our biggest challenge is shopping for clothes.

You think a protruding posterior's a pain? Try having nothing but empty space, coupled with vast real estate in the belly region.

People afflicted with nobuttatall can never find a comfortable pair of pants, jeans, or dress slacks. If the waistline fits fine, there are two square yards of wasted cloth in the seat. If the rump is right, you can't button the hateful things without (a) assistance from heavy equipment and (b) serious oxygen depletion.

Holding everything up with a belt? Forget it.

A belt has two requirements for staying in place: belt loops and a butt. If either ingredient is missing, the belt won't work. This is especially true if you bend over more than twice in an eight-hour period.

I'm thinking about forming a victims' rights group like "Nobuttatall Anonymous" to lobby Congress, automakers, and clothing designers for sweeping reforms. We're not going to sit on our nonbuns and take this abuse any longer!

End of the Earth

The world is coming to an end.

I am not lying. I've just finished reading several scientific reports about this unpleasantness, and each of them paints a dismal picture.

The first comes from Donald Yeomans, manager of the Near Earth Object Program at NASA's Jet Propulsion Laboratory in Pasadena, California. He says that on April 13, 2029—not surprisingly, that's a Friday the thirteenth—Earth could be struck by a thirteen-hundred-foot-long asteroid.

He gives the odds as three hundred to one against a direct hit. Nonetheless, he said in a recent Associated Press dispatch, "We can't yet rule out an Earth impact."

However, Yeomans stressed there's no reason to panic: "This is not a problem for anyone, and it shouldn't be a concern to anyone."

Isn't that pretty much what the captain of the Titanic said to passengers as he welcomed them aboard?

I don't know about you, but I'm planning evasive action right now. This isn't something to put off. I guarantee you won't catch Sam Venable sitting around, fat and sassy, on April 12, 2029, sipping iced tea and laughing, "Asteroid-smasteroid. I'll worry about that thing tomorr—AAAIII! DO YOU SEE WHAT I SEE?!?!?"

Well, yes; you're right. Sam Venable may be neither fat nor sassy nor sitting around on April 13, 2029. He may be slim and stiff and pushing up posies. Sam Venable is projected to be eighty-one by then, which would make him the oldest male in his family to ever survive four score plus one. And wouldn't *that* be a fine kettle of fish! You outlive everybody in the clan only to wind up being smashed by an asteroid. Some days, you just can't win.

In any event, here's my recommendation on how to avoid impact: Be *anywhere* besides Atlanta on April 13, 2029. That way, you're sure to miss the brunt of the impact.

I make this pronouncement after having lived in the South all of my life. I know, as does everyone in Dixie, that nothing comes out of the sky without going through Atlanta first. Thus stay away from Atlanta on that fateful day, and you stay away from danger.

Design your travel route away from Atlanta by car, bus, bike, truck, motorcycle, train, or foot. Just don't take a plane or else you'll wind up smack in the middle of ground zero.

(Frankly, if that stupid asteroid is destined to strike in 2029, why must it happen in April? April is a wonderful, warm, exciting month, bustin' out with dogwoods, tulips, and fishing. April is much too special to be ruined by an asteroid. It would be much more fitting for disaster to erupt during a dull time of year. Some cold, rainy day in late February, for instance. At least it would liven up the landscape.)

Even if we dodge a bullet on April 13, 2029, consider what three prominent astronomers from prestigious institutions of higher learning have to say about the distant future: We're toast.

The three—Anne Kinney of Johns Hopkins University, Bruce Balick of the University of Washington, and Howard E. Bond of the Space Telescope Institute in Baltimore—formed their sobering opinion after studying photos from the Hubble Space Telescope.

They say the sun is burning up, and we're going to get scorched in the process.

It ain't gonna be pretty. According to these learned people, the sun will consume all of its hydrogen in a "thirty-million-degree nuclear furnace." Once the hydrogen is gone, the core of the sun will collapse, causing superheated plasma to blow about in all directions, frying the surface of earth like a slice of green tomato. Then the lights go out and we freeze our fricasseed butts off.

Of course, this prediction isn't exactly new. For decades, scientists have been saying the sun will fizzle out and humans will cease to exist. But this time, they've put in on a schedule.

We've only got another six billion years, tops.

Sure, that seems far off right now. I can hear you naysayers: "Oh, good grief! Doesn't Venable have anything better to do? Why does he worry about something that isn't going to occur for a long time?"

I'll answer those questions in the order they were asked.

1. No, thank you. I don't have anything better to do. I am a newspaper columnist.

2. A long time off? Hah! That's what you said last year about Christmas shopping and Christmas card–sending, isn't it? And that's what you kept saying all spring, summer, and fall—yes, right on through Thanksgiving, past the beginning of Advent, plumb up until Christmas Eve itself, right? And then, in a blind panic, you raced to the post office and then to a shopping mall and tried to buy thirty-seven carefully chosen gifts for friends and relatives when the only items on the shelf were half a dozen broken cookies, a sample jar of perfume, and a size XXXL chartreuse sweater, right?

Time's wasting. Start worrying immediately.

Knowing Nature's Signs

People are doing a lot more than talk about the weather these days. They're betting their money on it.

The Chicago Mercantile Exchange is now offering weather futures like any other commodity. The idea makes sense because weather is often the key to success or failure in agriculture, power production, and a host of other areas where investors buy and sell options.

Of course, risky ventures like this require a degree of research. And I can't think of two better sources of information than the late Helen Lane, the "weather lady" from Crossville, and the folks at the Museum of Appalachia in Norris.

Lane, who gained national attention for her native forecasting skills, was a firm believer in woolly worms—those fuzzy critters you see crawling across back roads every fall.

"If they're black on each end and red or brown in the middle, winter will start out bad, turn mild, and then get bad again," she once told me. "Or they could be brown on each end and black in the middle. That means it'll start off mild, get real bad in the middle of winter, then slack off."

Savvy investors need to know how to count, too.

When you hear the first katydid in July, add 90 days and that should portend the first frost in October, Helen used to say. Of course, this is subject to regional interpretation. It's been my experience that 120 days, or four months, is a better indicator here in the lowlands of the valley. I think it always gets cold earlier in Helen's neck of the woods.

Weather speculators also need to count the number of morning fogs in August. This indicates the number of bad snows later on.

Ailene Phillips, who runs the kitchen at the Museum of Appalachia, grew up in Lake City under the tutelage of old-timers who could interpret weather signs. She seconded Helen Lane's motion about woolly worms as the number one key to predicting winter conditions.

"Just remember dark means a bad winter and light means a mild one," she recommended. "You have to find several to get a trend."

Museum founder John Rice Irwin—a woolly worm watcher and fog-and-katydid counter from way back—also believes in corn husks, spider webs, and wasps nests. If the husks are thicker than usual and the wasps build close to the ground, put your money on a harsh winter, he advises. Same is true if the hair on a cow's back is thicker than normal. But if the wasps build high and the spiders build low, keep the Coppertone handy.

Of course, all of these valuable tips won't do one whit of good for the slicks and suits who never venture outside the concrete jungles of corporate America. If they don't have access to woolly worms and cows or don't know what a katydid sounds like, let alone are in position to hear one sing on a summer night, they need praying over for reasons other than financial.

But who knows? These folks might be resourceful in their own right.

Maybe they can count the rings in their latte.

A Bite of Technology

I've got an appointment with my dentist in a few days. It's for routine cleaning. Nothing to get worked up about.

But—and I speak for 99 percent of Americans in this regard—you always grip the chair a little tighter when Doctor Bicuspid starts probing around after the final rinse and grit-spit.

Please-oh-please-oh-please, you're saying to yourself, don't let him (or her, as the case may be) say, "Hmmm."

"Hmmm" is one of the most terrifying words in oral medicine. It is dentist-speak for "Wow! This crater runs halfway to Peking!"

Immediately upon hearing a dental "Hmmm," you have a decision to make. Do you (a) scream, (b) burst into tears, (c) bolt from the chair and leap out the window, or (d) all of the above?

Since there are several more days before my appointment, I'm not going to waste time worrying about the possibility of hearing the dreaded "Hmmm." Furthermore, I've made up my mind about one other potential dental decision.

I'm not going to have a telephone implanted in my teeth.

Not today. Not tomorrow. Not next week. Not in two hundred thousand years.

Indeed, if officials of the telecommunications industry are banking on me to get a phone drilled into my choppers, they're crazier than those goofs who sent WorldCom into the tank. Before I would agree to this new procedure, I'd drink a hundred cases of New Coke and drive a dozen Edsels. I trust this makes my opinion about such an "innovation" perfectly clear.

In England, however, there are two inventors who believe the world is ready to talk, literally, through its teeth.

James Auger and Jimmy Loizeau, students at the Royal College of Art, invented this gizmo and unveiled a prototype at the Science Museum in London. What's more, they have signed up with Media Lab Europe (European research partner of the Massachusetts Institute of Technology) to perfect the thing for worldwide distribution.

No, I am not high on laughing gas. I hold in my hands an Associated Press account of the invention. It talks in glowing terms about the many possibilities. To wit:

"Theoretically, the device would allow spies to receive instructions secretly or athletes to hear from their coaches while on the field. Other beneficiaries could include investors and brokers and sports fanatics who want to be informed the moment their team wins or loses."

The story goes on to describe how this so-called telephone tooth works.

Seems a tiny, wireless, low-frequency receiver is inserted into a back molar. It turns audio signals into vibrations, which are then passed from the tooth directly to the inner ear as audible messages. At the science show, Auger and Loizeau gave demonstrations by speaking through a walkie-talkie and letting spectators pick up the sounds via a plastic cocktail stick gripped in their teeth.

And you thought Ben Franklin was strange for flying that kite in a thunderstorm.

Currently, the telephone tooth only works one way. It just picks up sounds. But the inventors believe it's merely a matter of time before technology to permit two-way conversations becomes available.

How weird is this going to be?

Already, people stand around in restaurants, buses, department stores, and shopping malls gabbing mindlessly on their cell phones. I thought I'd never grow accustomed to the sight and sound of this spectacle. But, sadly, we all have. And now—Lord, give us strength—we've got to get used to 'em doing the same thing with their teeth.

No doubt the techno-bugs of this invention will be worked out. No doubt tooth talk will ultimately become the rage among trendies. No doubt the rules

Knoxvillian Freddie VanWinkle recently ordered a replacement key for his car. Since it was one of those fancy new electronic keys, he figured it would be rather expensive. This was a correct assumption. Including tax, the bill came to $145.

"But when it arrived," he told me, "I noticed the tiny little plate that covers the batteries was missing. I called about it, and they said, 'Oh, yeah. That's extra. It costs $3.28.'"

What did he do?

"I paid the $3.28!" VanWinkle exclaimed. "It was like buying a pair of pants and discovering the zipper was extra!"

I wouldn't know. I've never spent $145 for keys or pants. In fact, that's $20 more than my first car cost—and it came with two keys.

of etiquette will be updated to incorporate ventriloquism skills when conversing in crowds. No doubt old geezers like me will continue to chew our gums in disgust and disdain.

And no doubt the first tooth-talk person who gets a weak signal and starts running around with his mouth agape, frantically turning his head this way and that, will dash into traffic and get flattened by a car driven by someone yakking on a cell phone.

At least he will if there's any justice in this world.

Order Your Baby Today!

It's the year 2100, and Herb and Sally Johnson are making excited plans for their first baby.

"Welcome to Gorgeous George's Genome Warehouse—the home of super-duper kids at rock-bottom prices! We offer the full range of DNA options, up to three billion choices. I'm Bill, and I'll be your sales associate today. What would you folks like for your first selection?"

"Speed," says Herb. "I want Little Herb to clock no slower than 3.8 in the forty-yard dash when he tries out for grass-cutter football. Back when I was in school, 4.4 and 4.5 were OK. But not anymore. The competition for running backs is getting more and more intense."

"You better believe it," says the salesman. "You've gotta keep up with the Joneses, not to mention the Smiths, the Whites, and the Wilsons. I think 3.8 is an excellent selection. I can just see Little Herbie now, racing down the field, his blond hair blowing in the breeze."

"Who said anything about blond?" says Herb. "We want Little Herb to have brown hair. Straight, with only a little bit of wave. No tight curls. And no premature balding, either."

"Sorry," the salesman apologizes. "I got carried away. What's next on your list?"

"Height," Sally answers. "Not a giant. Just maybe six four, six five, something like that."

"I'm thinking six six would be best," the salesman advises. "Little Herbie is going to hit elementary school in six years, and I can tell from our earlier orders that's going to be a good year for height. You never know how the trends will go on these things. Short will probably come back in style, but right now I'd stick with tall."

The salesman scribbles a few notes on his pad, then flips the page.

"Now that we've got the basic parameters outlined, let's get down to specifics," he says. "I'm sure you'll want the standard health package for Little Herbie, right?"

"How much is it?" the Johnsons ask in unison.

"You couldn't have come in at a better time," the salesman responds. "We're running a special this month. The complete package against colds, flu, measles, mumps, chicken pox, smallpox, and polio is on sale for only fifteen thousand dollars. That's a two-thousand-dollar savings over our regular price."

"How much extra for protection against cancer and heart disease?" Herb inquires.

"Depends on the type of cancer you have in mind. Prostate protection is cheap. Just seven thousand. But lungs are a biggie. I'm afraid that runs another twelve Gs—but it's worth every penny. Remember, you're not just buying a child, you're making a lifetime investment."

"Yeah, I know," sighs Herb, "but an extra twelve thousand might blow our budget right out of the water. How come it's so expensive? Isn't this simply a matter of tweaking the genetic codes—pulling out a gene that's cancer-prone and inserting one that's more resistant?"

Edith Williams sent me a flyer that came with one of her prescription medicines. It warned not to take the pills "within one hour before or two hours after antacids, eggs, whole-grain breads, or cereal, milk, milk products, coffee, or tea."

This stuff may not cure what ails you, but you're guaranteed to lose weight!

"Yes," says the salesman, "but it's also a matter of supply and demand. Sorta like it was for petroleum way back in the old days."

"What do you think, Sally?" the hubby asks. "Reckon we oughta pop another twelve? Or do we want to roll the dice on lung cancer, like they did a century ago?"

"Gosh, I just don't know," says his wife. "In fact, this whole selection process for Little Herb is terribly stressful. There are so many decisions to make, so many choices. We haven't even scratched the surface yet and already I'm confused. I'm not even sure if I want a baby boy. Why don't we think about a girl, honey?"

"We've already been through this!" Herb shoots back. "I thought we had made up our minds. There's no way we can afford a girl right now."

"Perhaps you folks might want to browse around the showroom a little longer," says the salesman. "Here's my card. Just look me up when you've settled on a model you like. Oh, yes—and be sure to check out our specials on IQ, cheekbones, and biceps. We're having close-outs in every department!"

Mars Mission Mistake

I've been on some long trips in my life, in a variety of vehicles, and consider myself somewhat of a travel veteran. But there's no way I'd ever sign up for a trip to Mars.

Not that Martian tours are available now or will be in the immediate future, you understand. Even though the rover Spirit successfully touched down on the red planet in 1997, trips by humans are so distant they don't even make a blip on the screen.

But hold the laughs. It's only been a century since two bicycle mechanics managed to coax a rickety "aero craft" aloft for a few seconds off the barren sand dunes of North Carolina. If you'd been standing there at the time and loudly predicted that travelers would fly coast-to-coast in a few years, you'd probably have been taunted for spreading silly gossip.

Going to the moon is one thing. What's it take—six days there and back? That's plenty of chair time. But investing six months just to reach Mars is more than my buns and legs could bear.

I get fidgety enough on airline trips from Knoxville to, say, Dallas or New Orleans. By the time I reach the terminal, it's all I can do to keep from jumping around. If I blasted off in June with no prospect of landing until the following January, my buns and legs would be jelly.

This quirk afflicts more than my buns and legs, come to think of it.

As anyone who has ever ridden with me will sadly attest, I am bladderly challenged. Couple that with my incurable habit of drinking while driving—coffee, I stress—and you get the idea that my notion of "nonstop" travel means Knoxville to Tazewell. Assuming the trip is progressing smoothly, that is. If not, expect tree irrigation somewhere around Maynardville.

Another factor that would nix my journey to Mars is the pinpoint accuracy involved.

Consider the Spirit landing: NASA's wizards hurled a spacecraft more than one hundred million miles into the void and yet missed their intended target by a mere six miles. I shudder to compare this to my own geographic "accuracy" here on Earth.

Once, my brother-in-law, Tony Deaton, and I were attempting to meet at the University of Tennessee's Thompson-Boling Arena for a basketball game. For perhaps fifteen minutes, we discussed our rendezvous point over the telephone, making sure each knew where the other would be. Over and over and over, we described the exact entrance where we would meet. Both of us were iron-clad certain of the location by the time we hung up.

At the arena that evening, we finally found each other shortly before half-time—and spent the remainder of the game fussing with each about who was in the wrong location.

But the number one reason why Mars is not in my game plan is the weather. I quote directly from news accounts of the Spirit mission: "It was a little warmer than expected, about ninety-eight degrees below zero Fahrenheit."

Brrrr to the tenth power!

I know how to dress for the cold. I haven't hung out in duck blinds and deer stands all these winters without learning a thing or three about staying toasty during harsh conditions. But terms like "a little warmer" and "ninety-eight degrees below zero" are mutually exclusive. We are talking a meteorological alpha and omega.

Besides, it'd be just my luck that NASA would lose the suitcase containing my goose-down coat.

Shock Season

At the onset of winter, I start slapping things.

Before I touch a doorknob, I slap it.

Before I insert the key into a car lock, I slap it.

Before I bend over to drink from a water fountain, I slap it.

Before I retrieve a piece of paper from the copy machine, I slap it.

I'd like to slap people before shaking their hands, too. But unlike car doors, water fountains, copy machines, and other inanimate objects, people have a habit of slapping back. So I refrain.

My slapping reflex has been developed over the last twenty or thirty winters. It helps dull the savage bite of a static electricity shock.

Yes, perhaps I occasionally bruise my hands by slapping a car door or water fountain upside the head. But at least my fingertips don't get zapped by 127,352,000 volts.

Even though I've been victimized for decades by static electricity, I've never understood the scientific phenomenon at work. So I consulted the source of all newspaper knowledge, the *World Book Encyclopedia*.

In the *E* volume, under the heading of "Electricity, static," it explained how John Doe loses electrons while walking across a carpet, resulting in a positive electrical charge. Thus, when stupid, predictable, nonslapping John touches a metal object, he receives—this is a direct quote—"a mild shock."

Which, of course, is a bald-faced lie. What John receives is a jolt of juice strong enough to run four hundred Mister Coffee machines simultaneously. Furthermore, *World Book* fails to say what *really* happens after the union of John and the metal object. Namely, that John kicks the metal object while screaming, "No-good $#@*-ing piece of #@%$!" at a decibel level high enough to shatter inch-thick plate glass. At this point, John is suffering from a broken toe as well as third-degree electrical burns to his fingertips. He is doubly irritated with himself because he realizes none of this pain and suffering would have occurred if he had only slapped the metal object first. What's more, the *World Book* fails to point out that static shocks occur more often in cold weather because electrons exit East Tennessee en masse around Thanksgiving, travel to southern Florida, bask on the beach on their itty-bitty electron blankets, and don't return until April.

I've also noticed a marked increase in static shocks since we moved into a spanking-new office building. So have many of my newspaper colleagues.

I think it's because this structure seems to consist of a large metal frame overlain with metal strips and metal sheeting. As a result, anytime anybody touches anything, it's circuit city. Indeed, even blindfolded you could follow the progress of some of my associates as they move about the office. All you have to do is listen for a brisk *zaaaap!* followed by a chorus of "$##@!&!"

If you wanted to find the official name for outbursts like these, you could consult the *World Book Encyclopedia.* Just look in the *L* volume for "Language caused by static shock."

Or ask any static-shocked reporter. Most are fluent in the mother tongue.

The Wonders of Duct Tape

In the wake of the latest duct-tape discovery, I have a question: Throughout the history of civilization, has this stuff ever been applied to ductwork? If so, I'm not aware of it.

I've seen duct tape used for repairs on everything from car windshields to chest waders. I've seen duct tape clinging to book covers. I've seen duct tape used to reinforce the sides of cheap foam ice chests. I've seen it wrapped around ball bats and axe handles. I've even seen it fashioned into clothing. And that only covers approximately one-tenth of 1 percent of the possibilities. For goodness sake, entire books have been devoted to duct-tape alternatives.

Jules Bernard is distraught about the proliferation of digital cameras over the old-fashioned ones that use film.

Not because he'll have to learn new photography skills, you understand. Instead, it's because there won't be any more of those thirty-five-millimeter plastic film canisters.

"They're the handiest things ever devised for carrying fish hooks, sinkers, and reel pieces," he sighed.

But now that this wondrous gray matter has made a medical breakthrough, I suppose it will drift out of the hardware department altogether.

Surely you've heard about recent testing at the Madigan Army Medical Center in Tacoma, Washington. There, doctors successfully used duct tape to remove warts. In fact, the tape method proved more effective than the traditional procedure known as "cryotherapy"—which is a fancy word for blasting the wart with liquid nitrogen and freezing it off.

The doctors said wart removal was effective 85 percent of the time with tape, compared to only 60 percent with the freezing method. In addition, it was cheaper and less painful, although it took upward of eight weeks to work. That's because the tape had to be applied, left in place, then removed at certain intervals, then reapplied.

(When I perused the results of the study, yet another question ran through my beady little brain: "Who th'hell thought of this weird medical procedure in the first place?" This is the same question I pondered years ago when I read where medical researchers had concluded that Coca-Cola, when used as a douche after sex, proved to have certain contraceptive properties. Of course, this was before the introduction of Cherry Coke, Vanilla Coke, Diet Coke, Diet Coke with Lime, and caffeine-free Diet Coke, so more shenanigans—I mean high-dollar scientific testing—is needed. But I digress.)

I can just picture the nation's leading dermatologists sitting around a table, formulating this latest test.

Doctor Smith: "Why don't we experiment with a new procedure to remove warts?"

Doctor Jones: "Excellent suggestion, Doctor Smith. What about a different form of cryotherapy, say, with liquid helium this time?"

Doctor Johnson: "Why it is always cryotherapy? Why not microsurgery for once?"

Doctor White: "Has anybody thought of lasers?"

Doctor Black: "What about arthroscopy?"

Doctor Doofus: "Hells bells, fellows! Do you all realize it's only thirty-five minutes until our tee time? Just slap some duct tape on those warts and be done with it."

And another landmark medical discovery goes into the books.

Of course, this is going to change the way duct tape is manufactured and sold. Right now, your standard (translation: super-duper-econo-magnum) roll of duct tape available at Home Depot, Lowe's, and other retail outlets contains enough material to remove warts the size of Mount Rainier. I suspect we'll soon see smaller rolls on the market, complete with "dots" of tape for more effective dermatological applications.

And now that this genie is out of the bottle, what other medical breakthroughs are we likely to experience, thanks to the miracle of duct tape?

Wisdom-tooth extraction? Childbirth made simple? Hernia repair? Broken bones healed? No more sutures? A preventative for cancer?

Obviously, the horizon is bright. I can only imagine the tingle of excitement pulsing through the medical community right now. It must be the same feeling of accomplishment and awe that was last experienced when Jonas Salk conquered polio.

If there is any fairness in this world, though, duct tape will make its most heroic medical mark in a discovery for the masses, a treatment that affects people up and down the line of humanity—young, old, rich, poor, urban, rural, illiterate, and educated alike: Duct tape and a cure for the common cold.

If that's not a match made in heaven, let alone Wall Street, Madison Avenue, and the headquarters of the AMA, you may scream into my stethoscope.

Child's Play

I'm pleased to announce a medical breakthrough.

It's possible for children to sit on their rumps and still not gain weight. All they gotta do is read magazines instead of watch television.

As anyone with half a lick of caloric sense knows, obesity in children is one of the biggest fears facing parents today. Two generations ago it was polio; today it's a pot gut. I suppose this is progress.

All over our plump country, mamas and daddies are worrying themselves silly because their kids are turning into fat factories. Of course, these same mamas and daddies are worried because the drive-through line at Wendy's is nine cars long, and they're afraid they won't get home in time to catch their favorite *Frasier* rerun while munching a sack full of triple bacon cheeseburgers. But that's neither here nor there.

Like all modern Americans, Mom and Pop want a quick fix for Junior and Suzy. That's why I'm so excited about my research.

We all know that TV ads are supersaturated with grease targeted to children. Between the shills for hamburgers, soft drinks, candy, and ice cream, it's a wonder there's enough time to squeeze in a few minutes for some wholesome sex and violence.

"Why is it," Leon Ridenour wants to know, "people wouldn't think of buying a hearing aid unless it was the smallest, lightest, most inconspicuous model on the market—but they'll gladly walk around with one of those hands-free cell phones dangling on their ear?"

Beats me. It's all I can do to keep from laughing every time I see somebody sporting one of those hideous contraptions. I'm always tempted to walk up and ask sympathetically, "How long did the doctor say you have to wear that thing?"

But I wanted to see what the kids are reading. Since teenage obesity is on the increase, it stands to reason that boys and girls are being unhealthily influenced by print advertising, too. So I trotted over to the library to peruse the latest magazines.

I selected recent issues of *Teen People* and *Seventeen* from the periodicals shelf and settled down to start counting the evil ads that tempt young people to fill their bellies with empty, artery-clogging calories.

Wow! Was I ever shocked!

No, not because the pages dripped with lurid pictures of doughnuts, potato chips, and french fries. Just the opposite. There were hardly any food ads at all.

I'm serious. I had to flip a full sixty pages into *Teen People* before I found the first food advertisement. It was for Hershey's chocolate milk. The only other food spots were for 7-Up, Sprite Remix, plus a generic "Got Milk?" blurb.

Seventeen had a few more sugary enticements, including Lemon Head and Red Hots candy and Dippin' Dots ice cream. But by and large, both publications were devoid of anything remotely associated with junk food.

Oh, both were jam-packed with commercial messages, all right. Page after page after page of 'em. In fact, the table of contents in *Teen People* didn't show up until I had waded through twenty pages of huckstering.

For what products?

Cosmetics. Clothing. Shampoo. Shoes. Skin conditioners. Fragrances. Zit ointments.

Thus I could only conclude that kids who read magazines aren't fat—at least not from caloric intake. It might be another matter, however, if you added up all those layers of pricey makeup, blue jeans, perfume, lip gloss, and skin moisturizers.

Lord have mercy. I'm amazed the little darlings have strength enough to stand, let alone lead active lives.

Keeping Up with the Stars

Coming soon to a school board budget meeting near you: "We need funding for new textbooks immediately! The science series is *sooo* outdated, it still lists Pluto as a planet!"

This is bound to happen. Now that the International Astronomical Union has stricken Pluto from the ranks of the chosen in our solar system, changes will have to be made up and down the line.

I don't understand everything I know about this situation. I doubt 99 percent of humanity does. In fact, I haven't given much thought to it since, oh, around the fifth grade, when I finally realized Pluto the planet bore no relationship whatsoever to Pluto the cartoon dog. I just knew planetary Pluto was somewhere out there in the Milky Way. (Or was it the Mars bar? I always got those two confused, unlike Mounds and Almond Joy or plain and peanut M&Ms.) In any event, I haven't lost must sleep over the IAU's decision to officially separate Pluto from Mercury, Venus, Earth, Mars, Jupiter, Saturn, Uranus, Neptune, and other blobs orbiting the sun.

Frankly, it's about time school kids caught a break. They deserve to have one thing less to remember in science class because they have approximately five hundred more things to remember in social studies.

For instance: Back when we doddering baby boomers attended elementary school, there was a giant hunk of land in northern Europe called the Union of Soviet Socialist Republics. Anytime the teacher unveiled a geography test, all we had to do was write "USSR" across the region—even if we thought it stood for "Uncle Sam's Slick Railroad"—and we were guaranteed a passing grade.

But then the USSR dissolved into a jillion itty-bitty "-stan" countries like Kyrgyzstan, Uzbekistan, Kazakhstan, Custerslaststandistan, Snapbackwithstanbackistan, and Stanthemanmusialistan, and it's been deep pandemoniumistan ever since. Kids could easily run through four no. 2 pencils trying to identify these places on a test—assuming there's such a thing as no. 2 pencils in schools any more. Or geography tests.

The point is, youngsters have a lot more material to memorize than we did. So if their irksome workload can be trimmed by the elimination of Pluto, I'm definitely in favor.

And speaking of memorization, today's kids can forget those stupid mnemonics we deployed to remember the planets in order.

Here's how it worked: You took the first letter of each planet, selected random words, and arranged them into a sentence. Back in the Ozzie and Harriet Fifties, the best our goober minds could concoct were bromides on the order of "My Very Educated Mother Just Served Up Nine Pizzas" and "My Very Early Mother Just Saw Us Near Paris."

If today's kiddies adapt with newer, trendier, hip-hop versions like "Man! Veronica's Expensive Metal Jewelry Sure Upstages Nancy's!" then, by gosh, more power to 'em.

Sore Sight for Old Eyes

If you're searching for an exercise regimen to stretch tired muscles and put spring back into your step, forget about jogging, yoga, cycling, weight lifting, or belly crunches.

Instead, try wearing new bifocals.

First, it'll give your neck and upper torso an extreme workout as you duck, bend, bob, and weave every time you attempt to focus on any object from fifteen inches to one-hundred feet away. Second, you'll rediscover the skill of springing—also ricocheting, tumbling, and stumbling—every time you miss a step in the staircase you're attempting to climb.

Like most folks in the AARP set, I need vision correction. I've worn contact lenses for decades. They take care of my faraway seeing just fine.

But several years ago, I realized how small the type had shrunk in telephone books, dictionaries, newspapers, and other printed materials. Thus I began investing heavily in half-glasses that make you look like a dork and are the perfect size to conveniently (1) fit into your shirt pocket and (2) get lost everywhere.

But when I'm wearing neither contacts nor reading glasses, I need bifocals.

I got my first set five or six years ago. They were the "lineless" variety popular with us aging baby boomers.

Unlike the "lined" bifocals our goober parents wore, these don't have distinctive panels in each lens for closeup or faraway vision. Thus we think we're pulling a slick one over on the Generation Xers and twenty-somethings in the office kitchen—when in reality, the Gen Xers and twenty-somethings are doubling over with laughter while we pour coffee on the cuff of our shirt sleeve.

I thought I'd never get used to that first set of bifocals. I kept taking them back to Doc Cornea, convinced he had made a mistake with my prescription. But Doc wouldn't budge. Just keep wearing them, he insisted; you'll adjust.

By gum, he was right. After a few weeks, my eyes and the bifocals finally began to jibe.

I didn't have one iota of trouble until recently, when Doc Cornea decreed it was time to change the prescription once more. I decided to get new specs altogether—ones with an oval-lens design so the Gen Xers and twenty-somethings would again realize how hip Old Man Venable truly is.

Smugly, I told myself, I've already mastered the art of bifocals. How hard can adjusting to a new pair be? Aren't all bifocals alike?

In retrospect, I realize this was like saying, "One wife or a dozen—how hard can it be to adjust? Aren't all women alike?"

Holy digitized diopters! Every time I drape these new ones across my nose, I'm immediately transported back to the Hall of Mirrors at the carnival. I can't go up or down stairs without wobbling like the town drunk. Whenever I extend a hand to introduce myself, I shove it into the other person's coat pocket. Or else I stand there, stupidly bobbing my head up-down-up-down-up-down like one of those dashboard doggies, trying to find the sweet spot.

And yes, I still provide entertainment for the Gen Xers and twenty-somethings whenever I'm wearing bifocals and approach the coffee pot.

Let 'em laugh. Their day's coming.

Chapter 2

Political Science, Political Correctness, and Other Governmental Gaiety

You want to send a newspaper humorist into fits of depression, not to mention panic? Tell him or her not to write about politics, bureaucrats or anything remotely related to governmental activities.

Ouch. Without politics and politicians, we'd have no security blanket, no immediate go-to topic on a slow day when the creative juices are AWOL.

This field isn't the sole purview of journalism, by any stretch. It is incredibly ripe for comedic commentary for venues throughout the land—in barbershops, around water coolers, at lunch counters, and on TV talk shows. When it comes to cracking wise about "the guv'mit," everybody's an expert. Thank heavens we live in a country where this laughter doesn't result in an ominous knock on the door at midnight.

Partisan readers might disagree—indeed, they usually do—but I like to think of newspaper humorists as equal-opportunity offenders when it comes to the government. We don't care if the subject is a Democrat or Republican, some high-profile commissioner or judge, a mayor, a governor, or a president. Or even an American, for that matter.

Back in the 1990s, when President Bill Clinton was dodging the nickname "Slick Willie" at every turn, I realized he was missing a golden opportunity to cash in on an idea being touted by a Russian named Mentimer Shaimiyev. Then the president of the republic of Tatarstan, Shaimiyev arbitrarily deemed it illegal for any of his fellow countrymen to insult him.

"The president can be criticized," Shaimiyev said in a news dispatch, "but he must not be insulted."

First offenders were subject to a fine of eight hundred dollars, roughly twenty times the monthly minimum wage. Fines for repeat offenders ranged as high as fourteen hundred dollars. Newspapers and magazines that reported an insult could be assessed upward of six thousand dollars, plus have their offensive publications confiscated.

Can you imagine what would happen if this became law in the United States?

We'd have no national debt, that's what. Woosh! It would be gone inside of two months, and the nation's coffers would start gushing leftover funds like an Oklahoma oil well. Once President Shaimiyev's plan went into effect, the United States could set up permanent housekeeping on Easy Street.

Get out your pocket calculator and start figuring how much "Slick Willie" money would have flowed into the Treasury under the Shaimiyev rule. On second thought, forget a pocket calculator. It wouldn't have near the capacity for this type of computation. We'd need something much larger for the job—like the computer Congress uses when doling out mega-billions in pork-barrel projects.

And that's just for one insult. Try to imagine the implications across the board during a presidential election year. Once the two sides started paying to sling dirt at each other, there won't be a bank vault big enough to hold all the money. Not to mention how much more would pile up in gutters and alleys after radio talk-show hosts, the tabloids, and everyone else in the media—"legitimate" or otherwise—anted up. There wouldn't be one red cent left in America!

And speaking of presidential elections, I'm reminded of the fact that the subject of political humor doesn't even have to take human form. For proof, consider "chad."

During the 2000 race between George W. Bush and Al Gore, humorists enjoyed a windfall with this word. Indeed, the phenomenon caused folks all over the land to dust off their dictionaries.

Yes, "chad" truly exists. It was not invented by newscasters in the bungled wake of the Florida vote count. In fact, it has been part of our language for more than half a century. Here's the score, straight from page 223 of my *Webster's Ninth New Collegiate Dictionary:* "Chad [perhaps from Scots, gravel] (1947): small pieces of paper or cardboard produced in punching paper tape or data cards; also, a piece of chad."

I became so chadified in those days, I started actively writing about the word—hanging chad, pregnant chad, the country of Chad, anyone named Chad, here a chad, there a chad, everywhere a chad-chad. Of course, everything that comes around goes around (a phrase, incidentally, that has been hanging around far too long itself.) "Chad" ultimately was relegated back to the vocabulary dustbin, along with "Y2K," "El Niño," "I've fallen and I can't get up!" and "Where's the beef?" And we wordsmiths were forced to return to original thinking, dang it.

Fortunately, there's a plethora of easy political subject matter. When a remake of the old TV series *The Beverly Hillbillies* hit theaters in 1993, the political correctness police went ballistic. Actually, that was somewhat of a pleasant surprise, since rednecks and hayseeds rarely are afforded the same sensitivity as other members of society. Nonetheless, as a proud son of southern Appalachia, I took the opportunity to rewrite the opening lines of the movie's theme song so as not to offend anyone. To wit:

Come listen to my story about a white male named Jed, an economically disadvantaged resident of rural, mountainous America, whose extended family barely existed on a diet high in saturated fats and low in nutritive value.

Then one day, while attempting to participate in the consumptive use of wildlife, he caused a projectile from a firearm, probably unregistered, to penetrate the surface of the earth and uncovered a previously undocumented dome of petrochemicals, resulting in massive environmental damage, albeit one that resulted in tremendous personal economic gain.

I'm still waiting to collect my royalties. Whee-doggies! Maybe I'll earn enough to build me a cee-ment pond.

State of the Union Exercises

I always enjoy watching presidents give their state of the union address.

Not because of the history that's being made, of course. Not because of the championship oratory, either. Nor the hard-hitting social, economic, and diplomatic issues that are raised. Or the heart-warming patriotism woven throughout.

No, no, a thousand times no. You hear one state of the union speech, you've heard 'em all. The only thing any president, Republican or Democrat, really needs to say is, "Despite the mess Congress and I have gotten this country into, it is still alive and kicking. I expect this trend to continue. Thank you and good night."

Instead, Hizzoner drones on incessantly about the unprecedented accomplishments of his administration and the boundless prosperity this country could achieve if only those lousy (take your pick: Democrats, Republicans) would cooperate.

Big deal. The real show takes place in the audience. Watching members of the House and Senate jump through their obligatory hoops as the dog-and-pony show unfolds is more entertaining than a Three Stooges film festival.

Invariably, the applause and standing ovations fall along party lines. When a Ronald Reagan or a George Bush (Elder or Dubya) reports on the status of the nation, the Democrats scowl, sit on their hands, and make snide comments to their colleagues. When a Jimmy Carter or a Bill Clinton is at the podium, the Republicans are similarly stricken mute.

Nonetheless, I will say this for the political bodies at a state of the union speech: They've got to be in great physical condition. All that hand-pounding and leaping-to-feet surely grows burdensome after awhile.

After President Clinton's address in 1996, commentators for ABC News said that during the sixty-one-minute stem-winder, he was interrupted by applause fifty-six times and treated to twenty-seven standing ovations. Even for veterans of the baby-kissing and chicken-dinner circuits, this is a strenuous workout. Perhaps they warmed up before the event with squats, leg stretches, and finger extensions. As any fitness expert will tell you, limber muscles don't cramp as readily as ones that are coiled like box springs.

And who knows? Maybe this is a new career option for members of Congress when frustrated voters finally induct them into the Royal Order of the Boot. It's a natural for the Home Shopping Network: "Get your copy of ex-Senator Bilgewater's new aerobic workout video today! Then you can stay in shape without leaving the comforts of your office!"

One word of marketing caution, though. Politicians travel in different fiscal circles than the rest of us mortals. Even with a special introductory price of twenty million bucks per tape, there might not be many takers.

The Official Word

Have you ever lined up at the cash register to pay your lunch bill, only to open your wallet and suddenly discover that—uuuuhhh-ooooooh!—your wife extracted forty dollars the night before?

Such was the queasy feeling that crept through the halls of Knoxville's government a few years ago. Except in that particular instance, the missing money was significantly greater than forty bucks. Four zeros greater, in fact.

All this came about when the Tennessee Valley Authority sent a letter to the mayor informing him that the agency was ending an annual $400,000 payment for its headquarters in the Twin Towers. The sudden loss of four hundred Gs didn't bankrupt Knoxville, but it did cause no small amount of scrambling down at city hall.

Knoxville is not alone. Cities all across the nation are facing a serious economic crunch. Is there a solution?

Yes. But not from the traditional source of revenue: Washington, D.C. Instead, the answer comes from Cranberry Township, Pennsylvania, just outside Pittsburgh.

Officials in Cranberry Township recently entered into an agreement with the Coca-Cola company to make Coke their official drink. Meaning anytime there's an event on township property where soft drinks were sold or served, they have to come from Big-C. The contract runs for five years and nets the town a tidy thirty-three thousand dollars.

Since whoring out to sponsors seems to be the accepted way of doing business, civic or otherwise, these days, all municipalities might consider jumping on the same bandwagon. The possibilities are as endless as the profits.

You know those plain vanilla cars and trucks every city has in its fleet? Why not sell sponsorships all around town and decorate those vehicles like NASCAR? Have an official car, an official tire, an official battery, an official fuel, an official windshield wiper and an official floor mat.

Don't stop there, for heaven's sake. There's a pile of money to be made. Look over my shoulder as I run down city offices in the blue pages of the telephone directory.

What about an official ladder for the fire department? An official gun, not to mention an official line of ammunition, for the cops? An official ink for the print shop? An official ball, official jock strap, and official swimming pool chemical for the recreation department? An official shovel for pothole repairs? An official pen for parking ticket writers? An official paint for the sign shop? An official fertilizer for horticultural services? An official apple for school administrators? An official vitamin and official laxative for the senior citizens center? An official flea powder for the zoo?

Cranberry Township already has the jump on everybody, so there's not a moment to waste. I implore every municipality in this great country to move as quickly as possible to nail down lucrative sponsorships before other cities try to horn in on the action.

Laugh if you will. But when the budget surplus overflows, you can thank me.

Sure, there are a few potential flies in the ointment—not the least of which is the mountain of bovine scatology certain to envelop city hall when lobbyists, telemarketers, advertising executives, and other shameless hucksters gather with politicians to choose these exclusive sponsorships.

Thus, for the welfare of the citizenry and preservation of the environment, the first order of business should be to select the official air freshener.

Memo to the Tennessee Wildlife Resources Agency: Stick to fish and wildlife matters. Forget calendars.

Anybody who ever received one of these calendars (the agency publishes them for hunting- and fishing-license buyers) immediately notices a difference from the ordinary: The year does not cycle from January through December. It runs from August through July, roughly following the ebb and flow of outdoor seasons.

OK. I can live with that. But the factual errors contained therein are getting downright ludicrous.

The July 2004 sheet, for instance, contained only thirty days, prompting some woods and waters enthusiasts to wonder if they could apply the missing day to vacations later on.

It didn't get any better for the October page. According to TWRA's calculations, Daylight Saving Time ended one week early.

Just wondering: If a hunter got arrested for violating the sunrise or sunset laws anytime that week, reckon he could haul one of these calendars into court and prove his innocence?

A Law-Abiding Citizen

I just spent a week on the beaches of North Carolina, and for the most part I avoided breaking any laws.

I did not shoot fireworks. Well, yes, I watched some fireworks that were being shot, but as I had no part in the purchase, placement, or ignition of these devices, I claim complete innocence in the matter.

I did not drink beer in public. Assuming that the front porch, side yard, and grilling areas in and around a beach house are not considered "public" places.

I did not speed. Except when necessary to get around slow-poking interstate idiots who should never have been granted a driver's license in the first place.

I did not violate fishing regulations. Indeed, my surf-fishing ventures resulted in no exploitation whatsoever of the Atlantic Ocean's vast resources.

I did not bring glass containers to the beach. With the itty-bitty exception of the morning I carried a ceramic coffee mug, full of smokin'-hot joe, onto the sand while I was on dolphin patrol.

Yet there is one North Carolina law that I absolutely, positively did not break, or even bend. I did not curse in the presence of a dead body.

Thank heavens, I learned about this law just a few days before I traveled to Tar Heel country. Can you imagine how embarrassing it would have been if I was walking on the beach one day and a dead body suddenly washed ashore at my feet and I jumped back in surprise and said, "Holy #$@!" and the cuss cops came running out of the sea oats and slapped cuffs on my wrists?

Members of the North Carolina legislature, who apparently are as dedicated to public service as their counterparts on the western side of the Smoky Mountains, are responsible for this rule. They recently amended an existing statute to make it illegal to utter "profanity, indecent or obscene language in the presence of a dead human body." Furthermore, they decreed a human corpse may not be transported in the open bed of a pickup truck or other vehicle where the body is visible.

On one hand, there is a compelling reason why laws like these are so wonderful. It proves conclusively that legislative lunacy is not restricted to Nashville and Washington. Just when you think the only skills politicians possess are dribbling the tax ball and chasing interns around the bedroom, along come bold initiatives like these to refresh your faith in America.

But on the other hand, they set a number of dangerous, freedom-restricting precedents. For Pete's sake, you can't even give Bubba one last spin in his GMC before the undertaker arrives.

And, oh, how I pity the millions of decent, honest, hard-working North Carolinians, standing in funeral parlor lines in the future, when they realize they're forbidden to converse in the traditional manner.

No more can they exclaim, "You mean Rufe was only sixty-eight year old? Why, hale far, I give him to be at least ninety!"

No more can they reiterate what a rhymes-with-witch Aunt Myrtle was throughout most of her wretched life. No more can they tally up all the good deeds they did for Uncle Floyd "and that tight-wadded sumbitch had better remember me in his will, too."

Makes you appreciate how fortunate we Tennesseans truly are. Our lawmakers are concerned only with important, cutting-edge legislative debates— like whether or not we should wash our hands after using the bathroom.

Lending a Helping Hand

Talk about a bunch of ingrates!

You try to lend the folks at the Internal Revenue Service a helping hand, and what do they do? They turn you down flat, that's what.

This happened a few days ago when I was on the telephone with Dan Boone, a public affairs officer with the IRS in Nashville. Yes, Dan Boone is his real name. Actually, it's Daniel, but he gets enough double-takes and wisecracks with Dan.

In any event, I had called to see if I was one of the 1,054 lucky Tennesseans who are due a total of $423,431 in refunds from last year. Nationwide, the figure stands at $50 million for 96,000 taxpayers.

Not that I had a refund coming. My memory may be slipping, but you better believe it remembers things like this. Nonetheless, if Uncle Sam can misplace a $500 kajillion satellite in outer space, who's to say a refund check, planned or otherwise, can't slip through the cracks?

Alas, there wasn't a Venable anywhere on the refund list. There was a Vanosdale, also a Vandeventer. I tried to convince Dan Boone that people sometimes misspell Venable that way, but I don't think he bought it.

Then he told me some of the dollar amounts involved, and I nearly fell over. One woman in Nashville is due $32,842.

"You mean there is someone walking around in Nashville, and the U.S.-By-Golly Government wants to cross her palm with thirty-two grand, and she doesn't have the decency to claim it?" I asked.

"We're trying to find her," he replied.

I told my ol' buddy Dan—we were on a first-name basis by then—that I traveled to Nashville frequently and would be happy to take care of the chore for him.

I said, "You folks send me the $32,842—cash will be fine—and I'll drive to Middle Tennessee in a week or so and look around for awhile and do my dangdest to find her."

Dan said thanks for the offer, but no thanks.

I even volunteered to do some sleuthing in Knoxville. Dan told me there is an individual right here in River City whose name is on a refund check for $5,084. He would not, alas, offer any details. Rats. If I don't know who this person is, how can I get my hands on the mon . . . I mean, how can I assist my country?

"Of course, those are on the high end of the scale," Dan said. "Some of these amounts are only for one dollar."

One buck or one thousand, how can people simply vanish when Uncle Sam is chasing after them, money in hand?

"A variety of reasons," he replied. "Sometimes they move and leave no forwarding address. Maybe they've had a name change or their name is illegible on the tax return or there's a wrong digit in their address. I remember a case last year where a guy's mailbox had been knocked down on the very day the post office tried to deliver his refund check. It came back to us, and we had to track him down."

They didn't take any volunteers along to help out, either. Is it any wonder people are leery of the federal government these days?

I say we should hark back to those soul-stirring words: "Ask not what your country can do for you, but what you can do to line your pockets."

That was John Fitzgerald Halliburton, wasn't it?

A Story That Really Smells

Uncle Sam wants you! (If you can stink up the joint, that is.)

In a bold move certain to delight members of the Sophomoric Noxious Noise and Potty Humor Society—yours truly, president—the U.S. government has launched an all-out search for the worst-smelling substance known to humankind.

The Pentagon wants to develop a nonlethal "odor bomb" to disperse crowds and has contracted with a company in Pennsylvania to conduct the research. Cross my heart. The American Chemical Society's newsletter, *Chemical & Engineering News*, describes the project in detail. Among the immediate possibilities being investigated—I'm quoting directly here—are "human waste, rotting animal flesh and garbage."

"We are going for odors that every culture has experienced and the experience is negative," said Pamela Dalton, a spokeswoman for the Monell Chemical Senses Center in Philadelphia.

Arrrgh! Talk about clearing the ol' sinuses!

Do you suppose these scientists sit around in their lab, comparing notes and talking shop like wine tasters?

Bob: "You really must try this Grease Trap '99. Finest I've sampled in weeks. It's a full-bodied little number, assertive yet balanced. It has wonderful depth with a very appealing finish."

Dave: "Perhaps, but it can't compare with Sweat Sock '92. We all know '92 was a very good year for socks in general, but this one is head and shoulders—or should I say 'heel and toes'? tee-hee—above the rest. Quite complex: tart and sharp but also velvety to the nose."

Alice: "Athlete Armpit '98 is another competitor. It really creeps up on you. At first, it seems rather tired—then, bang, the bouquet all but overwhelms you. It's the zestiest entry I can recall since Pinto Bean '87."

Herb: "Can't forget Trash Dump '01, either. Even if it is relatively young, it has a seductive approach. There's almost a buttery texture to it. What's more, it displays good legs in the container and . . ."

Bob: "C'mon, Herb. You can do better than that. Any fool can see the buttery texture comes directly from a Bluebonnet margarine tub. And it's not the aroma that has legs. It's that old chicken leg down in the bottom of the Dumpster."

Herb: "Ooops. My mistake. But I still insist this is a winner."

How do you train for a job like this? Do you have to be voted Worst B.O. in your senior class at high school? Are there scholarships available from meat-packing plants and paper mills? Does a promising stink assessor get his or her nose insured in college to protect against career-ruining injuries?

It may be presumptive for a rank amateur like me to offer suggestions, but having spent much of my lifetime in hunting and fishing camps and athletic locker rooms, I do have a decent track record in smellology. I not only have been present when some of the most ghastly, visceral odors have been unsheathed, but I also lived to tell about it.

Yet I'm not sure we humans can lay claim to the all-time grossest smell. We've got a long way to go to beat the fishes.

Not just any fish, of course. A freshly caught trout, crappie, or bass exudes a most pleasant aroma, certainly nothing even remotely vile. But ratchet on down the species list to carp, and you've got a contender.

Not just any carp will do. It needs to be a good-sized one. Eight pounds, minimum. It's gotta be four or five days beyond dead. It's gotta be perfectly positioned on the river bank: half-way in the water, half-way on shore. Oh yes, and bloated to the size of a Volkswagen. For full effect, all of these ingredients must come together in the direct sunshine of a ninety-eight-degree August afternoon.

I can save the folks from the Pentagon a lot of time and money in this regard. If they would like to accompany me to Fort Loudoun Lake sometime this summer, I'll show them the mother lode of raw materials, free for the taking.

Surely they know to bring gas masks and rubber gloves.

Don't Worry about Old Age

We've been going about this health business completely bassackward. Instead of trying to keep folks alive and well and active for as long as possible, we need to do just the opposite.

Kill 'em off like flies—or, technically, let people kill themselves off. Not only will this solution assuage any nagging worries about overpopulation, but it will make millionaires out of the survivors.

That's the conclusion I reached after reading about a cost-of-smoking study that was released the other day. The project was funded by Philip Morris, which—*cha-ching!*—fills its cash register every time somebody lights up. But don't let that minor detail cloud your thinking. You and I both know Philip Morris has only the most honorable of intentions in its dealings with human beings.

A reader named Roger McCown has a suggestion for the CIA, the FBI, and U.S. armed forces in their relentless pursuit of terrorists.

Forget conventional intelligence, he says. Put snoops from the U.S. Department of Agriculture in charge of the hunt for Osama bin Laden.

"They can track down individual cows and their offspring," says McCown. "Just imagine how good they'd be at tracking down people."

Then again, the mission might result in udder failure.

This particular study was conducted in the Czech Republic, where smoking is quite common. The researchers concluded that because smokers, as a group, kick the bucket faster than those who abstain, they save their government millions of dollars annually.

Specifically, the "indirect positive effects" of these premature deaths (savings in health care, pensions, housing, and other costs associated with those blood-sucking societal leeches known elsewhere as "old people") amounted to a $146 million net gain to the Czech government, all thanks to good ol' tobacco.

Gosh. Why didn't someone point this out before? Aren't we grateful to those wonderful humanitarians at Philip Morris for showing us the way?

If the annual benefit to the Czechs is $146 million, imagine the windfall this would be in America!

The first thing to do is get rid of those wasteful anti-smoking campaigns—especially the ones aimed at children. The little urchins need to be hooked faster than ever.

I say start shoveling free packs of cigarettes into every kindergarten in the land. Encourage smoking in class by first or second grade. Fire any administrator who doesn't include smoking etiquette as part of the curriculum. Punish any goody-two-shoes students who refuse to cooperate; we'd be better off without those radicals, anyway.

That's just for starters. If smoking can save us mountains of money, why not look into other untapped gold mines, like nutrition?

No more fiber, green veggies, "good" cholesterol, and other costly dietary nonsense that keeps people alive longer than absolutely necessary. In their place, let's draft a more modern set of basic food groups: grease, sugar, alcohol, and preservatives.

As for exercise? Outta here. Thanks to Philip Morris's bold new way of thinking, I now realize those thin, sweaty, nimble fools you see in gyms and on running tracks are selfishly trying to prolong their lives—and stealing money from everyone else at the same time.

Yes, this is a 180-degree turnaround. It's going to require some adjustments. But Americans never fail to rise to a challenge, and I'm sure this will prove to be no exception.

If we all work—and smoke, pig-out, and couch-potato—together, we can knock a good twenty to twenty-five years off the average life expectancy in no time at all, freeing up billions and billions of dollars in the process.

The new and improved Great American Dream: Millionaire by age sixteen, dead by twenty-one. That's what I call efficiency.

A Rolling Wheel Gathers Much Tax

In a legislative-economic move I've yet to understand, the Knox County Commission recently approved a "wheel" tax that has nothing to do with wheels, per se. Instead, it's the vehicle rolling atop those wheels that's being taxed.

Whether you drive a Boss Hawg "dualy" pickup truck with six knobby, mud-grabbing tires or a pipsqueak VW with four wheels the size of a salad plate, the tax will cost you the same. While I'm not leaping with joy at the thought of digging deeper into my pockets, this isn't loathsome. The way gasoline prices fluctuate these days, you can easily fork over an extra twenty or thirty bucks any time you stop at the pump. What's more, this levy is earmarked for a good cause: pay raises for teachers and county patrol officers.

Nonetheless, the name—"wheel" tax—scares the bejabbers out of me. It has the potential to grow into a sure-nuff monster. What if the county commission actually starts taxing *wheels*? Nobody except Bill Gates could afford to live here.

I took a quick stroll around my house a couple of nights ago and inventoried my wheel supply. Immediately I realized the dire implications, for in no time I tallied dozens of them in all sizes.

For starters, there was my pickup truck and my wife's car. They've got four wheels apiece, a spare apiece (Mary Ann might get a reduced tax since her spare is one of those dinky "doughnuts") and a steering wheel apiece. That's a total of twelve.

I also found four two-wheeled carts (eight total), two utility carts with four wheels each (eight), four rolling suitcases (eight), a vacuum cleaner (four), two fertilizer spreaders—there's an abundance of b.s. at our place—(four), a pair of old roller skates (eight), two garden hose reels (four), two plant stands (seven), two boat trailers (seven total, including spares and the steering wheel on my bass boat), three garden bins (six), a wheelbarrow (one), a lawnmower (four), a charcoal grill (two), two garbage carts (six), a spinning wheel (one), and a little red wagon (four).

That was the easy stuff. I didn't even take into account the bazillions of small plastic "wheelettes" that roll on tracks inside cabinet drawers and folding doors.

On the plus side, I thanked my lucky stars I had previously removed the four wheels on the legs of my workbench, ridding myself of yet another potential source of payments. I also discounted the pulley wheel on my extension ladder because the rope broke twenty years ago and I never replaced it. What's more, Mary Ann and I sold our bicycles back in the early '90s, so we don't have to worry about forking over moolah for those wheels.

The entire exercise got me thinking that society might be better off if the wheel had never been invented and we just pulled heavy items along behind us.

Not that it would help, of course. You know as well as I that the politicians would simply pass a new rope tax.

The Evil Swamp Fly

Umpteen years ago, back when our kids were not much older than toddlers, a friend of the family took my wife aside and broached the subject of foul language.

"I'm afraid your husband might have brought some of his newspaper talk home with him and has been saying it in front of the children," the woman began. "Just today, I heard Megan use an ugly term."

My wife's mouth flew open in shock. What kind of crude oath had spewed from the mouth of her baby?

"Well," the woman confided, lowering her voice so as not to be overheard, "she called another one of the children a 'stupid idiot.' Do you think she might have gotten that from her father?"

Mary Ann's mouth flew open again, wider than before. But it was from laughter this time. In fact, it took her several seconds of hoo-haaing before she regained her composure.

"Megan must have picked it up from one of her playmates," she said. "Sam's not guilty. He would never have taught his children to call someone a 'stupid idiot.' Maybe '%$#@' or '#@#&.' But 'stupid idiot'? Never. The man has his standards."

I couldn't help but recall that ancient vignette of family history when I read about an attempt in the Israeli parliament to curtail the invective being hurled from one side of the chamber to another.

A rookie lawmaker named Colette Avital is behind the move. She is chairwoman of the Knesset's Colleagues of Ethics Committee. Recently, Avital circulated a list of sixty-eight insults she wants banned from legislative discourse.

The Associated Press dispatched a list of these verbal affronts. After looking it over, I feel like Mary Ann did way back when. That's because the majority of these "epithets" are the most hilarious things I've ever read.

For example, one of the top contenders for banishment is "swamp fly."

As mad as I've ever been at someone or something—I mean torqued up to TNT level on the expletive explosion chart—I've never shouted, "Swamp fly!" Nor have I ever heard anyone else use this term.

Closest I can think of is "swamp rat," which is what they used to call Dewey Warren when he was a quarterback for the Tennessee Vols in the mid-1960s. But it wasn't an insult. It was a complimentary nickname, harkening to his home in the Georgia lowlands near Savannah.

Now try this one on for size: "gut-ripper."

This is an insult? You've got to be kidding. As a lifelong teller of jokes, I can think of no higher honor than to hear my latest offering was a real "gut-ripper."

"Eye-gouger" also made the list. So did "nincompoop."

Frankly the more I read, the more insulted I became. Not only is this the most vanilla assortment of coarse putdowns (by the way, "coarse" also made the list) I've ever seen, it was a slap in the face to three of my all-time heroes.

I speak, of course, of Moe, Larry and Curly, the greatest eye-gouging nincompoops to ever corrupt (another listed word) the youth of America.

(Da-doink!) What a woiseguy this Colette Avital is. Nyuk-nyuk-nyuk.

And you can quote me on that.

ID Cards All Around

Noble intentions notwithstanding, does anyone in America believe the new identification law is going to keep young people from smoking?

In case you missed it, this federal regulation requires persons between the ages of eighteen and twenty-seven to produce a photo ID before purchasing cigarettes or chewing tobacco.

(Of course, if they want to puff an Antonio & Cleopatra cigar or some Sir Walter Raleigh, they can pass through the line without hassle, since stogies and pipe tobacco are exempt from the law. I guess it never dawned on federal regulators that youngsters—who are already deft enough to roll joints of mari-juana—can figure how to transform a pouch of pipe tobacco and some papers into a handful of cigarettes. But, hey, who am I to question the intelligence of bureaucrats?)

Although this rule might make sense in theory, its practical application is downright laughable. It'll probably be observed about as closely as 55-mile-per-hour speed limits on desolate highways.

But you never know. The Food and Drug Administration is already gearing up to send undercover agents into stores across the land to snare miscreants who would dare let a twenty-six-year-old father of preschoolers buy a pack of Camel Lights without showing a card.

I can only imagine what's next. Fat cards, mayhaps?

You walk up to the counter, plop down a bag of Cheetos and two packs of Ding Dongs and reach for your billfold.

"Not so fast, mister," says the clerk. "I need to see some ID."

"Beg pardon?"

"Your fat card. Let's have it."

"What on earth are you talking about?"

"It's the new federal law. Anybody with a body fat content greater than 47 percent is prohibited from buying junk food. No fat card, no sale."

Or what about, say, a tooth card for the purchase of chewing gum? It must be authorized by a dentist, proving you are cavity-free and thus are qualified to drench your choppers in sugar juice.

"I'm sorry, ma'am, but I can't sell you this Doublemint."

"How come?"

"Your tooth card has expired. Obviously, you haven't been to the dentist in the last twelve months."

"I've been meaning to go. Honest. I've just been too busy."

"Sorry. No exceptions. We let a few folks sneak by last month and got busted. I've got to see a valid tooth card or else you've got to settle for Carefree. It's sugarless."

In restaurants there might be diet cards to prove we have not exceeded our personal caloric intake.

"May I take your order?"

"Yes, waiter. I'll have the meatloaf special with mashed potatoes and gravy, green beans, and rolls, please."

"Sorry, sir. Says here on your diet card that gravy is off limits."

"Gimme a break, will ya? I haven't touched the stuff in weeks. I won't put sugar in my tea or butter on my rolls. I'll even jog back to the office to burn it off."

"OK, but just this once and only because you're a regular customer. Don't let the word get out that I'm easy, or else this place will be crawling with cops."

Scary? You better believe it. But before we dismiss all of these protecting-us-from-ourselves regulations, consider just one more.

The fashion card.

You'd have to produce it to purchase any type of garment—slacks, dress, suit, socks, shoes, shirt, sweater—to prove you know how to mix and match fabrics, colors, and patterns.

Then again, maybe not. As well intentioned as this law might be, half the folks in Tennessee would wind up going naked.

Quartergate

Poor ol' Tennessee. When it comes to money, we can't get anything right.

In the first place, our state budget is busted flatter than a 'possum in the middle of Interstate 40.

Yes, I know. That's old news. Tennessee's budget is often busted. One year, the Legislature "fixed" the problem—insert horselaugh here—by spending our once-in-a-lifetime money from the tobacco settlement. This duct tape and bailing wire scheme was about as farsighted as a mole. A year later, the budget was busted again, and there was no tobacco cushion to fall back on. Yee-ha. Welcome to the Edjukashun State.

But Tennessee's most current fiscal woe has nothing to do with the budget crisis in Nashville. It's a funny money problem that is national in scope. Uncle Sam goofed with the Tennessee quarter.

Got one of those new twenty-five-cent pieces in your pocket? Take it out and give it a look. See those three stars on the back? They stand for the three grand divisions of Tennessee—East, Middle and West. Next, check out the musical instruments. There's a fiddle to represent East Tennessee's bluegrass, a guitar for Middle Tennessee's country music scene, and a trumpet for West Tennessee's delta blues.

Clearly, the U.S. Mint believes in the theory that it takes money to make money.

The agency recently announced that, for the first time in history, the cost of manufacturing both the penny and the nickel exceeded the value of the coins themselves. It now costs 1.23 cents to make a penny and 5.73 cents to crank out a nickel.

But I'm not worried. Surely Uncle Sam will find a way to make it on volume.

Now, look real close at the trumpet. If you're my age, you'll need a pair of drug store cheaters, maybe even a magnifying glass. Quarters aren't as big as they used to be. Nothing is.

Notice anything out of kilter? No? Then you're not a trumpet player. But if you do know trumpets, the mistake will be apparent if you study just a bit. See it now?

The horn on the quarter is put together incorrectly. It's backward. They don't make trumpets like that. Never have, according to musicians I have talked to.

"It has to do with which side the mouthpiece and lead pipe are on with respect to the bell," says Steve Voorhees of Oak Ridge. "There is no such trumpet like that."

Steve suggested I seek a higher authority for proof. So I contacted Ray Stone. In terms of musical experience, you can't get much brassier. Ray grew up here, graduated from Knoxville High School, spent a career as a professional musician (big bands during the early '50s, then sixteen years as a member of the U.S. Air Force's Airmen of Note jazz ensemble) and now sells horns for Lunsford's Musical Instruments.

"No doubt about it," he said after close inspection of the coin. "It's incorrect."

For good measure, I went to *News Sentinel* art director R. Daniel Proctor, who played trumpet in the University of Alabama (a crime I have yet to forgive) marching band. Dan'l eyeballed the quarter intently, checked a reference book to be certain, and then concurred with the others.

"This is what you might call a 'left-handed' trumpet," he laughed.

That ain't all. An obvious omission is the absence of a bow to play the fiddle with. But Charlie Klabunde, another Oak Ridger, has spotted something even more intriguing.

"The 'f-holes' in the fiddle's front have slipped quite a way down from the correct location," he says. "In a real fiddle, the little cross bar in the middle of each 'f' marks a line on which the bridge should sit. The bridge, which supports the strings, is one limit of the 'bowable' portion of the strings, the other limit generally being the end of the fingerboard. The middle of that bowable section is in the middle of the narrowest part of the middle of the instrument—thus providing the most clearance for the bow to saw on each string without touching the fiddle's body. Probably this artistic license was taken to permit these tiny details to be seen at all, rather than disappear in a blur."

But wait; there's more. There are also problems with the guitar. Several readers and callers pointed out that it has six tuning pegs but only five strings. Indeed, this disparity has been lampooned by *Coin World* magazine.

How come all the errors made it into production? Beats me. I spent the better part of one afternoon on the telephone—on hold, actually—with bureaucrats in Washington. I called the U.S. Commission of Fine Arts, which approved the original design. They bounced me to the U.S. Mint, which makes the coins. Nobody returned my calls.

Unofficial translation: Oops.

No, this isn't an earth-shattering goof. It's certainly not on par with NASA's failure to convert English measurements to metric on the Mars Climate Observer program back in 1999. That little miscalculation sent a spaceship fizzling off into the void to the tune of $165 million.

These quarters will still spend. And for all I know, there are design mistakes on some of the other state quarters. Still, it irks me that Tennessee's contribution to the national coin series is flawed.

Maybe there's a lucrative way out—for everybody. Maybe the federal government could reissue the Tennessee quarter with proper instruments, meaning all those incorrect ones will suddenly escalate in value. They could be sold to collectors and the proceeds given to Tennessee so we can fill the gaping holes in our budget.

I expect this to occur at roughly the same time everyone in the IRS schedules a vacation during the first two of weeks in April.

The Sweet Taste of Tax Laws

I've been trying to understand the state's definition of food, but all I get is a bad case of indigestion.

Ever since the new sales tax went into effect, the Tennessee Department of Revenue has been issuing edicts about what constitutes "food and food ingredients." Yet the more clarifications I read, the more confused I become. I can only imagine the angst this situation has created among butchers, bakers, and hot-dog makers from Memphis to Mountain City.

Not that any of us should be surprised, of course. Given the fact that these regulations were cobbled together during the thick of a state shutdown, it's a wonder the entire food industry hasn't passed out.

You may recall that when the 1 percent increase was passed by the legislature, "food" was exempted. Sounded simple enough. But as usual, this is one of those things that works better in subcommittee than at the checkout line. Or as they say down at the mess hall, "Did you want chopped steak or hamburger on that shingle?"

I hold in my hands several revenue department guidelines about this matter. Feel free to read over my shoulder. Just be sure to clean up your crumbs.

The vittles exempt from the new levy are "substances, whether in liquid, concentrated, solid, frozen, dried or dehydrated form, that are sold for ingestion or chewing by humans and are consumed for their taste or nutritional value."

But just because you ingest or chew for taste or nutrition does not get you or your taste buds off the tax hook. That's because "prepared food" is subject to the extra tax.

What is "prepared food," you ask? Read on: "Food that is sold in a heated state or food that is heated by the seller; food where two or more food ingredients are mixed or combined by the seller for sale as a single food item; food sold with eating utensils provided by the seller such as knives, forks, spoons, glasses, cups, napkins or straws."

(The fact that chopsticks were not included in this list makes me think the Department of Revenue could use a lesson in cultural diversity. But I digress.)

OK, so we're ready to sit down to the ol' dinner table and separate our chow between old tax and new tax, right?

Heavens, no. We have only begun to slice and dice. Where's a Vegamatic when we really need one? For instance, we haven't even broached the subject of candy, which more or less falls into the "prepared food" category. More or less, I reiterate.

According to the state's official sweet-tooth advisory, candy is "a preparation of sugar, honey or other natural or artificial sweeteners in combination with chocolate, fruits, nuts or other ingredients or flavorings in the form of bars, drops or pieces. Candy does not include any preparation containing flour and must require no refrigeration."

Thus M&Ms and Mr. Goodbars are candy. But Kit Kats and Twix bars are not because they contain flour. (Kids: Don't try this argument on your parents. Unlike the government, they know authoritatively what is candy and what isn't.)

And if you think that's crazy, get a load of the fine print regarding refrigeration. "If an item requires refrigeration, it is not candy," the official state guideline specifies. "For example, Popsicles and ice cream bars require refrigeration so they are taxable as 'food and food ingredients' at the lower state tax rate."

It gets worse. You can buy a cake at the lower rate. You can also buy food coloring at the lower rate. But if you buy baking chips or cake decorations, they are deemed candy and thus are taxable at the higher fare. Is this nuts or what?

Oops, did I say "nuts"?

Please be advised you can buy peanuts (which actually are legumes) and other nuts all day long at the lower tax rate. But if you have a yen for warm nuts, fork over the extra 1 percent. Same if you want honey-roasted nuts, which officially are "candy."

Alas, we have only begun to churn this strange stew. In the eyes of the state's dietary tax collectors, potato chips, corn chips, chip dip, and popcorn are "food." (Translation: low tax.) But cough drops and lozenges are "candy," and vitamins and minerals are "dietary supplements." (Translation: high tax.)

Gird yourself, Tennesseans. I've got a queasy feeling this thing's gonna come back up faster than week-old chili.

Cold Cash

It was with sadness and dismay that I read the latest news of alleged corruption in Washington.

According to the FBI, U.S. Rep. William Jefferson, a Democrat from Louisiana, accepted a one-hundred-thousand-dollar bribe. Federal agents said they videotaped the transaction. Later, authorities said they raided Jefferson's home and found most of the dough in his freezer, wrapped in aluminum foil.

I'm shocked.

Not that another politician has been accused of being on the take. Ho-hum; same-old, same-old. This happens with such regularity, newspapers oughta start publishing a standing box—you know, like we have for lottery results—listing the names of politicians arrested during the previous twenty-hour hours.

Instead, what I'm so surprised about is the method of preparation Jefferson supposedly used.

Aluminum foil? Geeze. That's *sooo* old school. Nobody freezes with aluminum foil any more. It doesn't have anywhere near the permanency of other vessels.

Your Uncle Frostproof knows whereof he speaks in this matter. I've done more than my share of food prep for the freezer, and I can tell you from experience foil isn't the way to go.

Yes, aluminum foil still has many household uses. It's great for retaining moisture in meats and veggies as they cook in a conventional oven. (Not in a microwave, of course, unless you enjoy pyrotechnics.) Aluminum foil also excels as a handy, pliable sealant for bowls, cups, plates, and other containers filled with leftovers.

There are a number of unusual applications, as well. A wadded-up section of foil makes a Jim Dandy scraper for cleaning the backyard grill. You can also tie a piece of it to a string and let it flutter in the breeze to scare birds off your ripening strawberries and away from your picture windows.

But ever since the advent of thick, self-sealing plastic bags and vacuum systems, aluminum foil has been eclipsed as a medium for freezing.

Frankly, I'm amazed that someone smart and resourceful enough to get himself elected to the U.S. House of Representatives wasn't aware of these innovations. We expect our political leaders to stay ahead of the curve.

Self-sealing bags are good in and of themselves, but they require you push out as much air as possible before zipping them shut. A far better option is one of those permanent air-removal systems that are the rage among homemakers these days. Just ask any gardener, hunter, or fisherman who freezes vittles for future consumption.

They're not necessarily cheap. I made a quick check of some Internet sales sites and found that a decent home-vacuum system will run anywhere from $150 to $200. You can go on the cheap for $50 to $75 or blow the budget with fancy models costing more than $300. No matter which one you select, another $40 to $50 will keep you in extra bags for months.

Three hundred bucks isn't chump change, by any means. But you'd think anybody who can turn a one-hundred-thousand-dollar profit for a few minutes work could easily afford the best.

Chapter 3

Pedaling Slowly in the Fast Lane of Life

One day Og and Ogette were sitting in front of their cave, casually munching a brontosaurus burger, when Ig, the genius from the other side of the jungle, approached. He was pushing something round.

"I've just made a new discovery," Ig said proudly.

"You and your dadblamed inventions," Og scoffed, spitting out a piece of gristle. "Aren't you ever satisfied with things the way they are?"

"Hey, cut Ig a little slack," Ogette snapped at her husband. "A lot of times he's onto something. You enjoy fire on a cold winter's night, don't you? We never had that until Ig figured out how to capture sparks. Fire sure makes meal preparation easier, too."

"Yeah, right," Og replied sarcastically. "Makes it easier for you to burn everything. You know I like my meat rare."

"Don't listen to him," Ogette said to Ig. "He's just an old grump who never appreciates the marvels of modern living like the rest of us. Tell me about this new invention, Ig. What's it called?"

"A wheel," Ig answered. "It makes stuff easier to roll around."

Og burst into gales of laughter. Eventually his hoo-haas and hee-hees grew louder until he fell to the ground, wiping his eyes and grasping his sides. Finally able to catch his breath, Og said, "You take the cake—or at least you would if there was such a thing as cake. What the hell are we supposed to 'roll around,' as you call it?"

"Anything that's too heavy to carry," Ig said.

Og rolled his eyes again. "Wha'samatter? You got something against arms and legs? Listen to me, Ig. You start puttin' these 'wheels' on anything that's a burden to carry, and it's going to mark the end of civilization as we know it. Why, I can just see the young kids now, spinning around willy-nilly when they oughta be grunting and groaning with the rest of us. Wheels? Bah!"

Surely Og was one of my ancestors—maybe just a few generations back. In our way of thinking, the status quo doesn't require constant tinkering. The more gadgets and widgets that come along, the more complicated life becomes.

Oh, sure. I use modern tools. As we speak, I'm typing on a space-age computer. I drive a motorized vehicle. I ply lakes and streams with an aluminum boat instead of a dugout canoe. I hunt deer with a high-powered rifle, not a hand-thrown spear. But that still doesn't keep me from poking fun at technology, inventions, new customs, changing times. In short, I'm at my happiest when griping about this crazy world in which we live. Comes with the territory in this business.

Some years ago in our old newspaper office, they finally ripped out the worn, tattered carpet we had been complaining about forever. So what happened when they started to lay down a new rug, a job that required everyone to box up their belongings for a few days? We complained even louder. As my colleague Tom Chester noted, "It's our mission as journalists to bitch unceasingly."

Fortunately, I get to vent in print. Hardly a day goes by that I can't find something about modern life to spin into a column. Thanks to Great-Granddaddy Og, all I have to do is think about the wheel and my creative juices start perking—I mean rolling.

Like what happened when the fancy-pants folks who make Lincoln cars decided to enter the pickup truck business.

A Lincoln truck? Heaven help us. What has happened to the lowbrow, laid-back, white-socked, truckin' neighborhood of yesteryear?

It was bad enough when automakers coined the term "sport utility vehicle" and began creeping into the exclusive territory of pickup trucks. It got worse when they started filling the roadways with knobby-tired skyscrapers whose primary "off-road" duties involve carrying kids to the mall on snow days. And then life as we know it virtually ended when Cadillac and Lincoln joined the SUV fray.

Throughout this madness I stood idly by and said nothing. But as a thirty-year owner and driver of pickup trucks—honest, dented, hard-working, ass-kicking, paint-faded, gear-shifting, cracked-glass, rifle-carrying, deer-hauling, bass boat–towing, four-wheel-drive, caked-with-mud-and-cow-manure, filled-with-firewood pickup trucks—I can remain silent no longer.

I have nothing against progress. I know we must change with the times. Pickup trucks have certainly advanced beyond the rolling shoeboxes they were in the '50s. I can live with that. And although I think pickup trucks with extended cabs and four doors look sillier than a boar hog with mammary glands, I can live with that concept, too.

But a Lincoln truck, one that sells for the same price as a house? Sorry. It simply doesn't compute. No way would I buy one, even if I hit the lottery tomorrow and could afford a fleet. I know the ghost of my frugal father would rise from the grave and spank me.

If this is reverse elitism on my part, so be it. I am guilty as charged and proud of it. It's an east-is-east/west-is-west thing, and I'm quite content to stay on my side of the fence.

Lincolns are cars. Fine, elegant luxury cars. More power to the people who drive them. But Lincolns belong at the country club. Pickup trucks belong in the country—out where the fescue is baled, not manicured for people who wear silly clothes and swat little white balls.

There's nothing more pathetic than a hillbilly dressed to the nines in polyester fashions and putting on airs like some big shot—unless it's a blueblood wearing creased designer jeans, alligator-skin loafers, and a starched white shirt and yearning to blend in with the good ol' boys by attempting to speak rural tongue. In both instances, they come off looking and sounding like frauds. That's precisely the case here.

A Chevy is a Chevy and a Ford is a Ford, no matter how shiny the paint and how high the sticker price. Conversely, a Lincoln is a Lincoln, no matter if it's carrying coon dogs and mired to the axles in mud. Some things just ain't supposed to be.

Thankfully, I am not the only person who shares this view.

"Since they sold more trucks than cars last year, I assume we'll see a Rolls Royce dualy soon," Knoxvillian Michael McGuire recently e-mailed me. "Where will it end? And what would you do if, at 3 A.M., your friend showed up to take you hunting in a Lincoln pickup truck?"

Probably ask for an old Grey Poupon mustard jar to spit my tobacco juice in.

Now that I've lashed out at the automotive industry, it's only fitting that I conclude my tirade with one of those faster-than-the-speed-of-light legal messages you hear on the radio. Let me take a deep breath and then you listen carefully:

"Allopinionshereinarestrictlythoseoftheauthoranddonotreflectanypolicy officialorotherwiseof the *KnoxvilleNewsSentinel* orUniversityofTennesseePress. Readerassumesallresponsibilityforanyconclusionsreached.Ifyou'restupidenough topayaking'sransomforanoverpricedoversizedgasguzzlingtruckthat'syourbusiness. Butwhatthehey.Ifyou'vegotthatkindofmoneyyououghtabuyseveralcasesofSam Venable'sexcellentbooks.(Stocknumber011802.Taxtitleandlicenseextra.)"

How do they train announcers to speak so fast? Is there anyone in America who can understand such nonsense? Who do the auto sellers think they're kidding?

But that's all grist for the future. For now, just turn the page and start wading through more mysteries of modern living.

Og and I won't join you. We'll be back at the cave. We've had enough progress for one day.

Pocket Change

Money doesn't buy much of anything these days. Especially money of the coin variety.

All it does is set off alarms at airports and chew holes in the pockets of your pants. Unless you happen to be carrying four pounds of dimes, nickels, and quarters—meaning you walk to the tune of a steel-drum band—you can't even scrape enough together to buy a vending machine soft drink because the bill-feed doohickey will be on the fritz.

And now we have new one-dollar coin, the Sacagawea.

Even though these things have been in circulation for awhile, they don't seem to be universally recognized. Not long ago I plunked one of them down, along with a fistful of paper bills, to pay for my gas at a twenty-four-hour store. The clerk eyed the coin suspiciously. She gave me the same look.

"It's a one-dollar coin," I said.

"From what country?" she replied.

"The United States. You know, the ol' red, white, and blue. Us'uns. That coin spends just like a paper George Washington."

Apparently I have an honest face. The woman finally shrugged her shoulders, rang up the sale, and deposited the coin in her cash register. "Just wish somebody hadda told me about it," she commented as I headed for the door.

Clearly, this clerk has not been watching TV lately. Otherwise, she would have seen evidence of the government's forty-million-dollar ad campaign to acquaint Americans with the Sacagawea dollar—which is named for the Shoshone Indian woman who helped guide the Lewis and Clark expedition in the early 1800s. Not that it matters, but the forty-million-dollar advertising budget is roughly three times what the U.S. government paid for the Louisiana Purchase that Lewis and Clark were exploring in the first place. I guess that's what you call inflation.

The U.S. Mint has taken great pains to make certain this coin doesn't suffer the same fate as the Susan B. Anthony dollar. The Sacagawea is a different size than any other U.S. coin. It's made from a manganese alloy on a copper base and is finished in gold.

Whether or not society at large accepts this design, however, I predict there is one small group who'll shout, "Alleluia!" I speak of church ushers and church treasurers throughout America. If that statement causes you to scratch your head, you've never helped take up, or count, the offering on Sunday morning. Otherwise, you'd know the trouble paper money can cause.

Church money—were talkin' the loose stuff here, not checks or offerings tucked into tithe envelopes—comes in two styles: silent and noisy.

Preachers and building fund directors are partial to the silent type. It adds up quicker, and can be spread substantially farther, than the other. But ushers and treasurers would rather handle the noisy kind because it's easier to count. Anybody who's ever dumped the plates onto a table in the church office—and I have—understands these differences.

Many parishioners, for reasons known only to them and Gawd Hisself, feel compelled to fold their bills into teeny, tiny, itty, bitty, tightly compacted shapes.

Laid on a flat surface, paper money stacks easily. Unfortunately, paper money rarely shows up flat in a collection plate. Instead, it usually is presented like a rose bud that must be unfurled, one petal at a time.

Another popular shape among the bill-folders is what I call the "toothpick" or "cigar." This is created by tightly rolling, or folding, the bill from one end to the other. The newer and crisper the bill, the tighter it can be compressed. I swear I've extracted "toothpick" bills from a collection plate that could be stood upright on a two-by-four, struck sharply with a hammer, and driven in like a nail.

Still other worshippers are prone to exotic creations. No doubt they are students of origami, the Japanese form of paper art. Over my years as an usher, I've unfolded everything from crude dinosaurs to birds.

But perhaps pew-side creativity will diminish after the new coin gets into circulation. Even the most innovative contortionists should have trouble folding this baby.

Unless, of course, the sermon is a stem-winder of the fire-and-brimstone variety.

Not Your Mama's Beauty Parlor

If someone you know gets the latest hairstyle, one thing's for certain: You aren't going to see it. Not unless he or she is a *very* close friend.

That's because the latest hairstyle doesn't take place on the head. Instead, it's a bit farther to the south. Somewhere below the belt and above the knees. A rather private region.

Yes, I'm talking about Way Down Yonder.

This hairstyle is called the Flair-Do. In Knoxville, it is performed at a business called Ideal Image. And it's all the rage.

"You'd think it would just be teenagers and college students," Heather Martinez responded when I telephoned for information. "But it's people of all ages, especially women. We have women come in here who are very conservative. You'd think never in a million years would they have this done."

Martinez is office manager at the Knoxville store, one of approximately fifty Ideal Image franchises in the United States. The company specializes in laser hair removal on just about any part of the body.

"We work on ear hair, nose hair, facial hair, eyebrows, backs, underarms, arms—anywhere there's hair besides the scalp," she told me.

Yes, including Way Down Yonder—down there among the jungle that never sees the light of day unless maybe you're taking a shower or you're at the doctor and he says, "Turn your head and cough."

"It's very popular in Europe and has now come to the United States," Martinez said. "We stencil in a design and then laser the hair around it."

What kind of design?

"Oh, squares, triangles, flowers, hearts, just about any kind of shape," she responded. "We've even done the Playboy bunny, a dog bone, and the Tennessee Power-T."

Technically, the Power-T is trademarked. In any other application, I daresay the University of Tennessee's copyright police would want a cut of the action. Given the real estate involved, however, this would probably be ruled a case of splitting hairs.

Martinez said the procedure takes about forty minutes. It doesn't hurt "any more than a small rubber band snapping over and over. We offer numbing cream, but most people don't even need that."

However, you will notice excruciating pain in your billfold. The cost of a Flair-Do is $1,520.

All of which brings up the obvious question: Why?

"Because it's something popular, something different," Martinez replied.

(Note to self: There's nothing wrong with unpopularity and the status quo.)

If you are contemplating a Flair-Do, though, keep this in mind: It isn't shaving or waxing. It is permanent removal of all hair around the design. Once it's done, there's no going back, except to alter or shorten the original outline.

In other words, if you're a woman and your boyfriend's name is Fred and you want him memorialized Way Down Yonder, you and Fred should never break up. If you do, try to find a guy named Red. And if that relationship ends, your only option is Ed.

Up in Smoke

I don't know why I keep checking out the cigar counter in supermarkets, convenience stores, and specialty shops. I haven't smoked in more than twenty-five years and have no inclination to restart the habit. And even when my lungs stayed permanently fogged, cigars weren't my nicotine delivery system of choice.

Maybe it's because I'm amazed people will fork over more money for a single cigar than I used to pay for a whole carton of cigarettes. I'm not only nostalgic, I'm also cheap.

A few months ago, I was startled to discover a new brand of cigarillos called Al Capone had hit the market. Yes, the same Al Capone who was Public Enemy Numero Uno back in the 1920s and '30s. Do you suppose three-quarters of a century hence a new brand of cigarillos called Osama bin Laden might become popular? Or maybe Saddam Hussein?

But as I was walking out of one store the other day, I naturally drifted by the cigar rack and stood there, dumbfounded, in front of the latest rage.

Flavored cigars.

No, I don't mean rum- or cognac-soaked cigars. They've been around awhile, purveying both hooch and tobacco in one convenient package. Is this a great country or what?

The ones I saw offered a veritable smorgasbord of flavors, including honey, coconut, peach, chocolate, vanilla, and two types of berry: strawberry and regular berry (which I suppose could mean rasp-, black-, blue-, goose-, huckle-, boysen-, cran-, elder-, Halle-, and others of their ilk).

I poked around to see if there was a Neapolitan combination of chocolate, vanilla and strawberry, like ice cream. Finding none, I assumed this flavor had not been invented, or else it's exceedingly popular and was sold out.

I mentioned this discovery when I got back to the office and was met with a chorus of "Where have you been?" from the cigar smokers, like I'd just walked in and announced, "Hey! Did you know they make a device called a Tivo that'll record TV programs when you're away from home—and eliminate the commercials, too?" One aficionado who orders high-dollar smokes from a catalog said he'd been seeing ads for the flavor parade for several months.

Occasionally I glimpse a bit of Storm Week on the Weather Channel. Some of the home videos depicting the raw, unbridled violence of hurricanes and blizzards are eerily spectacular. But I'm continually dumbstruck by the idiocy of professional TV meteorologists who walk into the teeth of these storms just to report—ta-dah!—how bad the conditions are. A typical broadcast will show the goof, dressed in the obligatory rain suit, holding onto a metal railing with one hand while clutching a microphone with the other.

"As you can see, the wind is whipping like a chain saw, and the rain is falling in torrents! Trees and power lines are dropping all around me! This is a very dangerous situation! Authorities have evacuated everyone! No one should be here! Do not venture out!"

So why are they there?

Far be it from me to question the rationale of tobacco that tastes like a Hershey bar or coconut cream pie. Indeed, the words "rationale" and "tobacco" tend to be mutually exclusive. If someone wants to puff a stogie that tastes like a pomegranate, have at it. Just as long as we aren't in the same room.

But for the life of me, the notion of fruity cigars doesn't square in my head.

You remember Clint Eastwood in *The Good, the Bad, and the Ugly?* You remember those closeup shots of his chiseled, stubbly face when he drew deeply on a cigar? You remember how he squinted his eyes so menacingly and delivered a fearsome soliloquy without saying one word?

Now imagine him doing it with a cigar that smells like a strawberry parfait.

Hmmm. On second thought, maybe that's precisely the kind of cigar Eastwood was smoking all along. If so, it sure would explain the soundtrack's nauseating *waaa-waaa-waaaaa.*

A Matter of Perspective

With the price of gasoline rising by the day—make that by the hour; oops, I mean minute—it's time for every red-blooded, patriotic American to take action.

Get out there and blame somebody.

As any talk-show host will tell you, this crisis clearly is the fault of money-grubbing Republicans, money-grubbing Democrats, money-grubbing automobile designers, money-grubbing OPEC members, money-grubbing petroleum refineries, money-grubbing petroleum haulers, money-grubbing petroleum wholesalers, and money-grubbing petroleum retailers. Not to mention uninformed, shortsighted consumers who think MPG means Mindlessly Pumping Gas.

I, personally, blame the nation's money-grubbing sign makers.

Think about it: If there weren't signs at every service station advertising these ridiculously high fees, drivers wouldn't be forced to pay them. That's my theory and I'm sticking to it.

But since high prices are apparently here to stay—did you ever think you'd wax nostalgic about two bucks a gallon for regular?—we might as well make the best of the situation. As your momma used to say, keep on the sunny side.

Well, yes, now that you mention it, all that exposure to the sunny side back in '56 has contributed to your precancerous skin condition today. But let's not quibble over petty details.

This thing is simply a matter of perspective. I did some shopping the other day and realized that gasoline, compared to certain other liquids, is a bargain.

At my neighborhood liquor store, for instance, one liter of Jack Daniel's Black Label whiskey sells for $29.00. Or approximately $110.20 per gallon. From that vantage, gasoline seems cheap as water.

Want even more encouragement? Then start thinking of gasoline in terms of mass measurement instead of liquid.

A gallon of gas weighs roughly 5¹/2 pounds. In Knoxville these days, the average cost of this unit of regular grade runs around $2.79.

But to buy 5¹/2 pounds of turkey meat, you'll spend more than $8. For 5¹/2 pounds of bacon, the price jumps to $16.50. The same amount of pork chops runs $22. And if your taste turns to rib eye steak, you're looking at $55.

Mind you, that's just for the raw meat. Unlike gasoline, which comes right out of the pump ready for use, the meat has to be refrigerated, cut, cooked, and served.

OK, so you're vegetarian. To buy 5¹/2 pounds of top-grade baking potatoes, you're going to fork over $5.45. The same amount of bread will set you back $8.80.

See what I mean? Don't you feel better? Doesn't this make you grateful for today's unbelievably inexpensive fuel?

Me neither. But since we're on the topic of price comparisons for necessary products during this time of crisis, consider: 5¹/2 pounds of Preparation-H costs $500.72.

Count your blessings.

Changes by the Wagonload

Anybody who thinks kids aren't coddled these days should've been standing around when Saul Young showed off his shiny new red wagon.

Technically, this was Saul's wagon for just a few more hours. He had bought it as a birthday present for the two-year-old son of a friend. But during the interim, Saul wanted me and other *News Sentinel* colleagues to see how the state of toys had changed since our collective childhoods.

This little red wagon was an oo-by-gum-fish-ul Radio Flyer, the same kind you and I had as children. Well, sorta. Seems these new ones come with features and accessories that weren't available Back Then. A "no-pinch ball joint," for instance. According to information on the box, this "keeps fingers safe."

I got pinched often as a kid—screen doors, crawfish, and cracked toilet seats come immediately to mind—but I don't ever remember catching my pinkies in the ball joint of a wagon. Maybe I was overly cautious. Nonetheless, if this new design keeps blood blisters at bay, fine.

It also features "controlled turning radius" to prevent tipping.

Makes sense—although, again, I don't recall taking corners too tightly in my little red wagon and crashing. After the first wreck, I mean. Whether you're a forty-year-old trucker piloting an eighteen-wheeler loaded with scrap iron or a five-year-old tyke at the helm of a four-wheeled wagon filled with important dirt, rocks, and sticks, turning radius is one of those things you just naturally get a feel for.

On the new models, the "handle folds under for easy storage." Definitely a plus.

My wife and I happen to own a Radio Flyer red wagon. It came from my mother's condo after she died in 2003. Maw had used it to ferry garden supplies from her garage to her flowerbeds. Mary Ann uses Maw's wagon for similar botanical duties. She stores it in a corner of the boat shed near my bass boat.

This old warhorse doesn't have a fold-under handle. Instead, it stays cocked in the upright position, keeping it precisely at—how do I say this politely?—groin level. Whenever I attempt to sidestep in close quarters, one false move presents grave danger to certain items of domestic jewelry. I speak with experience.

But there are a couple of innovations that leave me speechless. These new wagons come with custom seats, seat belts, molded cup holders, and cooler pouches. There's so much add-on, in fact, I'm not sure if there's room for kids.

What's next, do you suppose? Air bags? Back-up beepers?

This is a child's wagon, for heaven's sake. It's supposed to haul toys or important dirt, rocks, and sticks, not be driven to the country club.

But there's one thing that never changes. Then or now, little red wagons require assembly. Pictures on the box showed which tools are needed for the job: wrench, screwdriver, and hammer. As any frustrated parent can attest, the wrench and screwdriver are necessary for attaching nuts and tightening screws.

The hammer?

That's for beating the hateful thing senseless when Bolt A refuses to line up with Hole B.

Adding Them Up

Unless you're a CEO, an accountant, or a corporate lawyer (preferably unindicted, but we won't be picky), you might not understand the complex details and highfalutin terminology associated with the scandals that have rocked the business world.

For weeks, the news has been full of stories describing such practices as "spring-loading," "off-balance-sheet-partnerships," "swapping network capacities," and other nuances.

In simple business terms, this means the people in charge boasted about the money that was coming in and stayed mum about the money that was going out. In simple Tennessee terms, it means they lied through their teeth.

But before you join the chorus screaming for flesh, stop and say a word of thanks. While it's true the fungaloids at Enron, Tyco, Arthur Andersen, Global

Crossing, Adelphia, and WorldCom made off with billions of dollars, at least they've given the rest of us an exciting new perspective on life.

They have showed us, oh-so-graphically, how to accentuate the positive and eliminate the negative.

Let's say you want to lose weight. In the old-fashioned, pre-scandal days, this meant counting calories and exercising. You had to add up all the calories going into your mouth and subtract the amount used during physical activity.

Sounded good on paper. But as any dieter knows, it was a depressing concept in practice. You had to jog something like 148,000 miles just to burn off a single ounce. And then if you so much as licked a doughnut, four pounds of fat immediately formed around your belly.

Not anymore. Thanks to innovative accounting methods, those unwanted pounds will drop faster than the NASDAQ. All you gotta do is count the calories burned (yeah! positive!) and ignore the ones taken in (boo! negative!).

I got on the Internet just now and found a calorie chart put together by Ohio State University. It says resting activity, like "reading, writing and watching TV," will use 80 to 100 calories per hour. Light activity, like "walking slowly or doing dishes," ups the loss from 110 to 160 calories per hour. Moderate activity ("walking fast, ping-pong, volleyball") runs it up to 170–240. Vigorous activity ("fast walking, bowling, skating") will use 250–350 per hour. And strenuous activity ("swimming, tennis, football, basketball, soccer") will trim 350 or more.

As any sharp-eyed accountant or lawyer has noticed already, the chart does not say you actually have to *participate* in the activity. It merely *lists* it.

Thus I recommend you ask your spouse to do the dishes (110 calories), walk slowly toward the TV (110 additional calories), and watch (110) football, basketball, and soccer (350 calories per). Do this for eight straight hours, and you've zapped an amazing 11,040 calories!

It gets better. Because we're eliminating the negative, we won't count the six beers and two bags of cheese curls ingested during this marathon exercise session.

> **Venable's Theory on Telephone Recordings: The more simple the name, the more eloquent the speaker. And vice versa.**
>
> If someone with a short, simple name calls you, he or she will speak in a virtual radio voice: "Hello, this is Bill Jones. That's Bill, like something you pay, Jones, J-o-n-e-s. Please call me at 5-5-5-1-2-1-2. Repeat, Bill Jones, at 5-5-5-1-2-1-2. Thank you."
>
> But what if the name is a bit confusing? All you'll get from the recording is a blur: "CallTheolonicusWhizenjammerhaggeninNatchitoches9975551212."
>
> Gar-ron-teed.
>
> And speaking of telephone numbers, my brother-in-law, Tony Deaton, has an innovative way to make sure you jot 'em down instead of trying to remember them in your head. For instance, if the number is 865-555-2222, he'll give it to you as "Eight billion, six hundred fifty-five million, five hundred fifty-two thousand, two hundred twenty-two."
>
> Yes, the boy desperately needs testing.

There's even more good news. According to nutritional experts, adults need roughly 2,400 calories per day just to sustain life. So, if we add those to what we've already burned, it comes to a whopping 13,400 calories consumed. At the rate of 3,500 calories per pound, that means we've ended the day with a net loss of 3.84 pounds.

Do this for seven short days, and you've dropped nearly twenty-seven pounds! I can hear 'em calling you "Slim" already!

That's just one application for modern accounting practices. Let's check out another one sure to be popular in Big Orange Country.

In 2001 the University of Tennessee played thirteen football games, including the Southeastern Conference championship and the Citrus Bowl. The team finished with a record of eleven wins, two losses.

Ah, but if we take the total points the Vols scored through the 2001 campaign (four hundred) and divide it by the number of games, this works out to an average of nearly thirty-one points per contest. Since we're accentuating the positive and eliminating the negative, this means the Vols shellacked each opponent, thirty-one to zero, through the season, winning the national championship by the most impressive margin in the history of college sports.

I've gotten so good at juggling numbers, I'm thinking about going into accounting full time. I hear there are a lot of openings at Arthur Andersen.

The Paper Trail

If you don't regularly shop for groceries you probably haven't noticed, but it takes a lot longer to go through a checkout line these days. You'd think that with computers and bar codes this chore would be easier than ever before. Nope. Just the opposite.

You remember the good ol' days, of course. Yes, that golden age of shopping when there was a clerk on every other aisle and price stickers were manually applied to every item in the store. When you reached the checkout, each price had to be manually entered into an old-timey cash register that crunched the numbers, rang a bell, and spit out the receipt. If the clerk had a problem reading the price on, say, a loaf of bread, he or she walked or called back to the bakery aisle for the correct information.

Doesn't work like that anymore. The process has been modernized, speeded up, made more efficient. Meaning it takes about twice as long.

First, the computerized cash register will invariably have a problem scanning one or more of the bar codes on your merchandise. The clerk will stand there, waving the item back and forth across the screen like a wand, waiting for a beep that never comes.

Having no success, the clerk will then attempt to punch in the numbers manually. Sometimes this works. Most times it doesn't. So the only thing to do is call back to the bakery aisle for a price check. That's OK in theory. But since the bakery aisle is now located in an adjacent county, a new millennium will pass before the correct information gets forwarded to the front.

Then things really slow down.

Remember that little receipt from the old-timey cash register? It has gone the way of the rotary-dial telephone. Cash registers don't issue short, terse receipts any more. Instead, they regurgitate writs that run the federal tax code a race for volume.

I hold in my hands two receipts from a local supermarket. The name of the joint isn't that important because everybody's wasting paper these days.

The first receipt measures 11 3/4 inches in length. It covers my recent purchase of two items—a twelve-pack of soft drinks and some plastic cups.

The rest of the space is taken up with cutesy notations indicating the check-out clerk's name, how delighted the store is to have me as a customer, how much I "saved" on this trip by using the store's "discount" card, and how much I have "saved" throughout the year with the same alleged "discount" card.

In point of fact, I have saved nothing. I have merely prevented the store from overcharging me if I don't carry its stupid card. Legal blackmail, as it were.

The second receipt is a whopper. It stretches 13 1/4 inches. I probably should rejoice, however, because even though it's longer than the first, it covers far more items: pears, carrots, two boxes of crackers, a box of tissues, and a bag of cookies.

Yes, there are the obligatory messages and greetings and "savings" (insert laugh here) calculations. Plus seven coupons for goods and services ranging from dental work to oil changes to hair products to Mexican fast food.

Does this mean I should expect a grocery store coupon the next time I go to the dentist, get my car lubed, have my hair cut or visit a Mexican restaurant? Just wondering.

Neither of these documents was published rapidly. Instead, the cash register had to cough and groan and say "ca-jung" and "ja-jing" incessantly until the paper slowly began to emerge. Indeed, the machine kept coughing and groaning and "ca-junging" and "ja-jinging" as the paper coiled from the contraption like a snake slowly exiting its den.

How can this process take so long? Are there itty-bitty monks down there in the bowels of the thing, scribbling with goose quill pens or turning the cranks on a Gutenberg press to produce it? Is this contraption hooked up to a pulp mill? Must it wait for paper to be manufactured for each transaction?

Grandpaw—who walked into Asa's General Store, asked for two cans of beans, and told Asa to put it on his bill—didn't realize how lucky he was.

DDDD

You'll be able to read this essay a lot faster than I wrote it. That's because I've been forced to type at the proverbial snail's pace.

Like most of the people in this business, I'm normally a pretty fast typist—even if I don't do it by the business school–approved "touch"method.

I'm a disciple of "refined" hunt-and-peck. This is hunt-and-peck on steroids. After nearly four decades of practice, my two index fingers can veritably dance across a keyboard with a Min%nemum off mIsteakks.

But today I'm on injured reserve. My right index finger is ailing from overuse. I'd file for workers' compensation, except they'd probably make me type out the form.

I'm a victim of DDDD—Dang Dreadful Delete Disorder.

There's a lot of it going around in offices and homes these days. In fact, wherever there's a computer, you'll find DDDD sufferers by the score.

Why? Because we spend much of every workday deleting those $#@% wormy e-mail messages out of our computers.

Aside from the technological aspect, there is nothing new about these attacks. They are the modern version of old-time vandalism. Instead of over-turning outhouses, rolling yards with toilet paper, or spray painting buildings with graffiti, today's hooligans do their dirty work by tickling the keys of a computer. Since these diseases spread rapidly via the Internet, the perpetrator(s) can infect multiplied millions of computers in a matter of hours.

It's been relatively easy the last little bit. I've only deleted around 100 of these computer-clogging electronic notes. One day last week, I started the morning with over 850, and my inventory grew continuously as the afternoon wore on.

I had to delete judiciously because several legitimate e-mails were hidden among the trash. Thus I couldn't wipe the entire slate clean in one motion.

One "delete" keystroke is no problem. Neither is one dozen. Or even fifty. But like water torture, this repetition eventually takes a toll. By the time you delete-delete-delete-delete-delete-delete-delete-delete, your index finger protests.

This mess is tied to the Welchia and Sobig worms that have been making rounds all over the world. They invaded the *News Sentinel*'s computers. Locally, systems at the University of Tennessee and Clayton Homes also were crippled.

Last go 'round, we were smitten by the I Love You virus. Unsuspecting users saw a sweet message on the screen, assumed it was from a spouse or close friend, and opened it. Whereupon their computer, instead of being smooched, instantly came down with a virulent strain of electronic flu.

I don't understand how these pests work. For that matter, I don't understand *anything* about my computer, except how to turn it on and off. I've been hopelessly lost on the Information Superhighway since they poured the first load of asphalt. All I know is that somewhere, a vandal designed these worms and then turned them loose on the public. As a result, digitized anthrax has been invading computers by the millions, filling their e-mail directories with truckloads of unwanted mail.

What's so scary is knowing these ailments will only get worse. It's just like the world of real medicine. As quickly as one virus is conquered, a new, more powerful hybrid emerges. We are advancing through an age of innocence that's no different than those quaint old days of passenger aviation, before metal detectors became de rigueur at airports.

And if you think having a locked-up screen is bad, wait till the hackers really kick up a stink. A Savannah, Georgia, computer company called TriSenx has just received a patent for technology that incorporates aromas with visuals. Seriously. It's the same theory as scratch-and-sniff advertisements in magazines.

This worries me on two fronts.

First, I suppose this means you could be reading an automobile story on the monitor and "new-car" scent wafts out of the tube, luring you to buy—just as the aroma of freshly baked doughnuts draws you into a pastry shop.

But the more frightening side of the picture is what will happen when hackers get hold of it. Can you imagine the varieties of maggot-gagging stenches they'll brew up? Might be almost as bad as it was in Granddad's day of overturned outhouses, proving conclusively that everything that goes around comes around. Or upside down, as the case may be.

Maybe I shouldn't complain too much about DDDD. Instead, I should look on the bright side.

With the Welchia and Sobig worms, I only got a few thousand bogus e-mail messages total. Some of my co-workers fared much worse. Sports editor John Adams received nearly thirteen thousand. His index finger might not recover until the Vanderbilt game.

What's more, I should be thankful that only my index finger is on the fritz and has slowed my ability to communicate in print. If this malady had hit my middle finger, I wouldn't be able to communicate at all.

Especially on the interstate.

Drying Out

The News Sentinel recently installed an automatic paper towel dispenser. Immediately I was showered by a wave of nostalgia.

Codger that I am, I've witnessed a lengthy evolution of hand dryers in public facilities. Among the earliest I recall were rolling devices that transferred a large orb of clean, cloth towels from Point A (pristine) to Point Z (gross). They had to be threaded. I know this for a fact because I spent one summer during college running a towel route for a Knoxville linen service.

Alas, my towel-threading skills never developed. My "delivery" end always came out wrinkled and tapered, meaning that by midway through the roll, the hateful machine jammed. I came to the sobering realization I wasn't cut out for honest work, so I went back to school and got a degree in journalism.

Next came electronic blowers, both push-button and automatic.

Neither was reliable, but at least the push-button models offered a creative outlet for journalists and other vandals. They came equipped with written instructions, as if the general public had barely graduated kindergarten. To wit:

1. Push button.
2. Rub hands gently under warm air.
3. Stops automatically.

Approximately ten minutes after being installed, each of these gizmos got defaced with a key or nail file. The instructions now read:

1. Push butt.
2. Rub hands under arm.
3. Stop auto.

And then an immortal line, a sentence known to every American by the age of twelve, was added: "Wipe Hands on Pants."

The push-buttons eventually gave way to automatics. These employed pictures instead of written instructions, the new assumption being that most Americans by now were flunking kindergarten. The sketches showed hands (yours presumably) rubbing below red, wavy lines (warm air presumably, but given our proximity to Oak Ridge's radiation, I never was certain).

Even though it was no longer possible to revise the instructions, it still remained necessary for someone to add "Wipe Hands on Pants."

On the paper towel front, I've seen the transition from "single" (insert laugh here; they either cough out twenty-five at a lick or else refuse to yield anything but damp shards) dispensers to ropes of tightly rolled papyrus snaking out for miles.

And now we have automatic paper towel doohickeys.

Theoretically, these things work by the principle of motion detection. I say theoretically because practical application is, of course, another matter. Already, I've watched some of my colleagues attempting to use the infernal beast. They stand in front of it, flailing their arms like a TV preacher whose contributions have fallen below projections, hoping for a sheet of paper to appear as if by a miracle.

Naturally, nothing happens. So they stomp off in disgust—which prompts the machine to go "rrrrr" and emit a fresh, crisp towel.

I wonder how long before someone writes "Wipe Hands on Pants" on it?

The Right Side Is Left

Perhaps it's safe for me to start driving again.

My knuckles are no longer white. I can approach oncoming cars and trucks without drowning in cold sweat. I no longer scream when pulling into traffic or changing lanes.

Just to be on the safe side, though, maybe I should restrict myself to public transportation for a few days. That way, I'll be certain my psyche is purged of backward thoughts.

All these precautions are necessary because I've just spent the better part of two weeks driving a rental car through Scotland.

Trust your Uncle Dipstick: Everything associated with the internal combustion engine Over There is reverse. *Everything.*

The steering wheel is mounted on the right side of the vehicle, not the left. Front-seat passengers enter from the left, not the right. The rearview mirror is tilted toward the right, not the left. Gears are shifted with the left hand, not the right. For all I know, the engine is mounted atop the roof, not underneath the hood—which, by the way, is called the "bonnet."

But the most sphincter-puckering aspect about motorized travel anywhere in the United Kingdom is the fact they drive—*aaaaiiieee!*—on the left side of the road.

This flip-flop is a shock to all visiting Americans, motorists and pedestrians alike. Simply walking across the street is a challenge because we're programmed to watch for oncoming traffic in right-side lanes.

No matter how much mental coaching we attempt, we still stop on the curb, look the "proper" way, assure ourselves the coast is clear—and then step, ker-splat, squarely into the path of a car. It's maddening.

To their credit, the Brits have painted the explicit instructions "Look Right" and "Look Left," respectively, in large block letters on the pavement at major intersections in London. This, I assume, holds the incidence of American ker-splats to tolerable levels.

Another marked difference Over There is the way they handle intersections. Mainly because there are very few "intersections" per se. Instead, they have doughnut "roundabouts."

If you miss your street, no sweat. You just keep circling till it reappears.

Initially, this is a very confusing system. But in practice, it's a far more efficient way of handling traffic than the Amurikan pattern of stop-and-go.

Ah, but they do have a form of stop-and-go, thanks to hundreds of miles of one-lane roads in the outback. Since the bulk of my driving occurred in rural areas of northern Scotland, I got plenty of practice at darting into well-marked "passing places" and waiting for oncoming cars to ease by, then resuming my travel.

Even though the entire experience was dyslexic, I've gotta admit the Scots were some of the most courteous drivers I've ever encountered. They were exceedingly tolerant of this bumbling, backward tourist, even when I committed obvious errors. Not once did I hear a horn honked in frustration.

Then again, I couldn't hear much of anything because I was screaming "Holy $#@%!" with every revolution of the tires.

Inside the Bubble

One of our business writers showed me a news release from a computer security company, touting its many services. The blurb droned on for two double-spaced pages, describing what a high-tech, cutting-edge outfit it is.

Or at least I think that was the intended message. It was hard to tell for certain.

You see, the news release was rife with computerized typos and glitches. Instead of English, it appeared to have been written in a combination of Russian, Chinese, Arabic, Norwegian, and Portuguese.

I wonder what their former chief of technology is doing for a living these days.

There's nothing new in what you're about to read. It is routine and predictable and occurs, at one time or another, on every mile of every highway in America.

It's the Bubble—the invisible space that magically forms around a law enforcement car as it rolls along the road.

Things are always tranquil within the Bubble. No matter if traffic is horn-honking, zip-zipping, and zig-zagging on every other square inch of pavement, life inside the Bubble remains courteous and law-abiding.

I encountered the Bubble on Interstate 40, eastbound into Knoxville, a few mornings ago. Or, technically, the Bubble encountered me.

I was tooling along in the middle lane, sipping a cup of coffee, switching radio stations to avoid commercial overload, scribbling a dozen mental notes to myself, and trying to safely keep pace in and out of one construction zone after another.

I glanced at my rearview mirror and—gulp!—there it was: a black and white with one of Knoxville's finest behind the wheel. Immediately, two thoughts flashed through my mind.

1. Where he'd come from?

2. How fast am I going?

The first question was irrelevant. It didn't matter how he—turned out to be a she, actually—wound up behind me. The far more pressing issue was my rate of forward progress.

This calls for double vision and a calm countenance. One eye stays glued to the road. The other nonchalantly inspects the speedometer while your brain screams, "Stay calm!" as the nanoseconds tick by.

Happily, my speedometer eye detected the red line hovering on the good side of fifty miles per hour. Whew.

Now for the next quandary. Stay the course with the confident air of ho-hum-all-is-right-with-the-world? Or yield my lane with the equally confident air of ho-hum-think-I'll-ease-over-because-I-feel-like-it?

The officer made the decision for me. She switched lanes and slowly overtook me on the left. I was now sealed inside the Bubble.

Not alone with the patrolwoman, of course. There were two or three other motorists immediately to our rear and to the side. All of us were pictures of driving excellence.

You don't stay inside the Bubble forever. Instead, you slowly evolve out—always to the rear.

Other vehicles began stacking up behind us. Some began tailgating. The more impatient ones started darting into one lane, then another, working their way toward the unseen impediment ahead. Then their brake lights would flash on, and I knew they'd broken into the Bubble themselves. At this point, they took over the mantle of driving excellence.

Slowly, methodically, the Bubble pressed into town. Near my exit, I saw the officer's blue lights flicker ahead. Apparently she'd pulled in behind a driver whose speedometer needle was on the bad side of fifty.

The officer was just emerging from the patrol car and walking toward her catch as we, former occupants of the Bubble, piously passed by.

Immediately, the Bubble vanished. But I knew after the ticket writing was finished and the cop pulled back into traffic, a new one was about to form.

Many Mixed Messages

The more I watch commercials on television, the more I'm convinced the end of civilization is near.

For instance: Among the 176,834 prescription medicine advertisements for "male performance," one shows a guy attempting to throw a football through the center of a tire swing. At the beginning, he has a frustrated look on his face.

Every time he lets fly, the football misses. His poor wife views the scene with an air of utter dejection.

But then—*shazam!*—he wolfs down some magic pills and his accuracy improves dramatically. He can hit the tire from any angle. His wife smiles approvingly.

Hel-looo! Hate to tell Mr. and Mrs. Loser, but if their problem with "male performance" revolves around a football and a tire swing, they need to revisit Biology 101. Unless, of course, they're into exceedingly kinky activities.

While mulling this conundrum, I flip channels and come across the newest commercial for a sport utility vehicle.

Oops. That's not wholly correct. The word "newest" in this context applies only to the vehicle model. The commercial itself has remained unchanged since four-wheel drive was invented.

Invariably, it shows the vehicle soaring across ravines, plowing through streams, churning clouds of dust on a backcountry road, or chugging up an eighty-nine-degree mountain at full bore. And just as invariably, a line across the bottom of the screen reads "Professional driver on closed course. Do not attempt."

So let me see if I've got this straight: I'm being encouraged to buy the latest Mongo Masher XJZ (a steal at only sixty-five thousand dollars, less my two-thousand-dollar rebate, plus eight thousand dollars for tax, title, registration, destination fee, docking fee, add-on fee, and FiFi fee) because it can soar across ravines, plow through streams, churn clouds of dust on backcountry roads, and chug up eighty-nine-degree mountains at full bore. Yet right there in front of me, the ad is telling me I can't use my Mongo Masher XJZ to soar across ravines, plow through streams, churn clouds of dust on backcountry roads, and chug up eighty-nine-degree mountains at full bore because I (1) am not a professional driver and (2) have no access to a closed course. Not to mention the fact that the EPA would throw me under the nearest jail.

But neither of those idiocies can match an ad I recently saw for toilet paper.

It showed two cute little girls attempting to clean mud off a puppy. One of the girls was using Brand X. The other was using an All-American, Church-going, Patriotic, Super-Clean brand.

Predictably, the Brand X girl (who had a look of dejection on her face and will no doubt grow up to marry a man who can't throw a football through a tire swing) failed miserably. The other girl deployed a single square of All-American, Churchgoing, Patriotic Super-Clean paper and rendered the puppy into a spit-shined model of canine perfection.

Hel-looo again! That isn't the preferred use for toilet paper, Brand X or other-wise. Those two girls need some serious potty retraining.

No Books to Hit

It's an autumn day far in the future, and some rickety-kneed BBG (baby boom grandfather) is being visited by his SNGs (snotty-nosed grandchildren).

"Give us ten dollars each and we'll listen to another boring story about when you were a kid," one of them says.

"Well, let's see," the old croak replies, extracting bills from his wallet, "how about when we didn't have TV or air conditioning?"

"Naaa. We've heard all that before. Also about how your family only had one car and the stores were closed on Sunday."

"Hmmm—then what about the first day of school, when the teacher passed out grocery bags for us to make covers for our new books?"

"Huh?" one of the little rug rats exclaims. "What's a grocery bag?"

Says another: "What's a book?"

"Hoo-boy," sighs the geezer, reaching back into his hip pocket. "This is going to be more expensive than I thought."

OK, so that's a corny, farfetched example. For all I know, futuristic urchins will demand twenty bucks, minimum, for suffering through tales of yore.

But if you think schoolbooks aren't headed for the antique mall, you haven't kept up with the latest education news. At Empire High School in Vail, Arizona, all students have been outfitted with laptop computers. No textbooks whatsoever.

The Associated Press recently filed a story about the project. It said students not only will study via computer, they'll also turn in their homework online.

The story said a built-in filter will keep kids from downloading porn and other contraband material. To deter cheating, there's software designed to catch plagiarism.

To which I insert my false teeth long enough to wheeze, "Horsepuckey!"

Please understand: I don't have a problem with the switch to computers. E-teaching is the wave of the future. Educators who still think reading can only be accomplished with printed words on sheets of paper bound between the covers of a textbook are as out of date as clodhopper shoes. (What's that? You say clodhopper shoes are back in style? Oops, my bad. Anyhow, you get my drift.)

But my point is, I have enough faith in kids to know that they can find a way to beat the system. Always have. Always will.

If we could dream up a lame excuse for missing homework, they can, too. No more of that "dog ate it" nonsense, of course. They'll have to shrug their shoulders and say, "A worm invaded my computer. The techies are working on it, but they say it'll take at least a couple more days before connectivity is restored."

If we could sneak a copy of *Playboy* into class and ogle it behind a propped-up edition of *History of Western Civilization,* they'll find a way to drool over

XXX-rated "Hottest Hollywood Honeys" when they should be studying the Magna Carta.

If we could turn a six-minute perusal of CliffsNotes into a ten-page paper on "War and Peace," they'll cut-and-paste their way through term reports, too.

But for the life of me, I can't imagine some pimply faced freshman screwing up his courage enough to ask the sweet young thang in the next aisle if he can help carry her mouse home from school.

The Un-right Reverend

"Bless you, my child."

"Go and sin no more."

"I now pronounce you husband and wife."

"The days are coming when there's going to be weepin' and wailin' and gnashin' of teeth—and them that ain't got no teeth, their gums are gonna have to take it!"

Oh, excuse me. I didn't mean to shout. Frankly, I didn't realize anyone was listening. I was just trying out various preacher voices and got a little carried away.

I'm still in the experimental stage at this point. I don't know whether to preach in one of those emotionless-drones-that-never-wavers-up-or-down-a-single-octave-and-could-make-a-bronze-statue-fall-into-a-deep-sleep or whether to HOLLER AND WAVE MY ARMS like some of them do on TV. I suppose I need to keep practicing till I find what works best.

Sign of the times: Don White was driving along Dutchtown Road when he saw a bicyclist approaching.

"A boy about twelve years old was on the bike," Don told me. "He was swerving in and out of my lane. I had to hit the brakes and really slow down."

Gosh. Was the kid sick, perhaps? Trying to outrun a swarm of wasps? Pursued by a pack of dogs? None of the above.

"He was talking on his cell phone," Don sighed.

Until a couple of days ago, I'd never given much thought about becoming a man of the cloth. It always seemed like such a dedicated, long-term commitment, replete with years of study and a burning desire to help people, not to mention a serious calling from above.

But then I walked into the office, clicked on my computer, and saw the light. All it takes is $29.95!

No schooling. No studying. No waiting. One swipe of your credit card ("swipe" being the operative word here, I'm sure) and you can officially be revved in forty-eight hours.

If you're hooked up to the Internet, you've probably seen this message, too. Ever since it first flickered across my screen, it's been repeated upward of a dozen times. Must be a veritable groundswell of religion out there.

Pedaling Slowly in the Fast Lane of Life

I printed out one of these appeals and hold it in my hands as we speak. It's from Denver Gomez. At least that's the name listed in the "from" space.

Brother Denver says once he makes me a preacher, I can perform weddings and funerals, forgive sins, or even start my own church.

That's not all. I'll also receive an eight-by-ten certificate "in color, with gold seal, professionally printed by an ink press," plus proof of my "minister certification."

But as tempting as Brother Denver's offer is, I'm gonna have to decline. The more I think about it, the more I realize I'm not cut out to be a preacher.

In the first place, I'm too much of a wimp. I get misty enough at weddings and funerals as it is. The last thing the wedding party—or the grieving family, as the case may be—needs is for Reverend Venable to be sobbing uncontrollably from the pulpit while the main event is standing—or stretched out—in front of him.

Don't think I'd be very effective in the sin-forgiving department, either. It calls for too much seriousness. If one of the flock started spilling his guts with stories of riotous and salacious living, I'd probably bust out laughing and blurt something totally insensitive like, "What?!? You mean the Widow Parsnip did that with you?!?! Oh, c'mon! Who you tryin' to impress? She's got higher standards than that."

But starting my own church would be the biggest disaster of all. I'd know waaaay too much juicy gossip on the preacher.

No Ice Would Be Nice

Dear Clay and Megan:

Let's make one thing clear right now, while I'm still of relatively sound mind. When I die, I don't want the two of you getting into a fight over whether or not to freeze my body.

As far as I know, I'm not on the Grim Reaper's immediate short list. In fact, I hope he doesn't come across my name for many years. But some day I'll wind up on his agenda of acquisitions, and when that time comes, I want to make sure he's not carrying a set of ice tongs, if you catch my drift.

You two have been the best kids a dad could ever hope to have. We had fun together when you were children, and we have fun together now that you're both adults. So all in all, I don't foresee any problems. Still, you never know.

Ted Williams, the great baseball player, didn't expect anything strange when the time came for his "final at-bat," as they say around the ol' clubhouse. But whoa-nellie! Look what's happened to him!

Not long after the poor man sucked his last breath, his son and daughter started tugging at the body. It's been worse than one of those reality game shows on TV.

His daughter says Pop wanted to be cremated and his ashes spread across his favorite fishing holes in the Florida Keys. But Junior allegedly snuck off with the old man's corpse and had him frozen in Arizona, hoping to preserve his DNA for future sale.

That ain't for me. The freezing part, I mean. If you're stupid enough to think anyone would buy the DNA of a sway-backed, beer-bellied, near-sighted typist, go ahead and try. You'd make a lot more money at a lemonade stand in January.

But this freezing business—cryonics, I think it's called—is out of the question. For a number of reasons.

First, you gotta figure the cryonics folks are nutty as pecan trees for setting up shop in Arizona, the hottest spot in America. They never heard of Minnesota or Alaska? Think what they'd save on electric bills!

Second, I'd be flat-out miserable the entire time.

I used to love cold weather. Couldn't get enough of it. Even though I still spend my winters sitting in duck blinds and deer stands, the cold affects me worse than ever. If my teeth chatter right now at twenty-five degrees above zero, just imagine what'll happen when they pull the temperature down to minus three-twenty. Brrr! Just thinking about it gives me the shivers.

Third is this matter of standing on my head for years at a time. From what I've read about cryonics, that's how they store a body. I've never liked doing anything upside down. Stiff as a fence post or not, nose goo will run backward and give me sinus fits something awful. Not to mention make me dizzy as a dope.

Which brings up the fourth reason I'm against getting frozen: acute overcrowding.

You know what the cryonicites, or cyronitians or whatever they're called, do to a body after they've turned it into an Eskimo Pie? They stick it into a vacuum chamber along with thirteen others, that's what. It's bad enough having your buns frozen off. But packed in there like strings of inverted Christmas tree icicles? Absolutely not!

The fifth, and surely the most compelling, reason I don't want to be frozen and later thawed is because I'll be hopelessly out of date.

This condition is bad enough right now. I'm barely sixty, yet when I look at the clothes everybody else is wearing and the music everybody else is listening to and the movies everybody else is watching and the books everybody else is reading, I might as well be 90. By the time I'm 190—or 290 or whatever age when they perfect the system—I'll be about as hip as Pleistocene man.

You kids want to involve ice with me when I die? Then prop me up next to a cooler full of beer. Have a few cold ones and remember all the good times we shared down through the years. Be sure to invite Mom, too.

Warmest regards,
Dear ol' Dad

Chapter 4

Cakes, Pies, and Super-sized Fries

Southerners eat.

I realize that's like saying birds fly and fish swim. But unless you've spent some time in Dixie, you can't appreciate the fervor with which we tamp down our vittles. Or the myriad occasions that call for feasting.

Upon hearing the news of the death of a friend, for instance, the first thing any southern woman of breeding will do is make a cake, bake a ham, or fry some chicken—maybe all three—and fetch it to the home of the dear-departed's family. This is a very practical sign of respect because she knows all manner of people soon will show up, and the last thing grieving relatives need to do is fix supper for everyone.

We eat when we're sad. We eat when we're happy. We eat when we're excited. We eat when we're bored. If we do happen to backslide and go on a diet, we then eat to celebrate the loss of five pounds, confident there is life beyond XXL. We even delight in making wagers on what we can eat and—forgive me, Robert E. Lee—much of the credit is due to a Yankee.

On September 26, 1820, in Salem, New Jersey, a daring man named Robert Gibbon Johnson ate an entire basket of allegedly toxic "love apples" and suffered no ill effects. According to the Salem County Historical Society, Johnson even predicted that these fruits, "rich in nutrition, a delight to the eye, a joy to the palate whether fried, baked, broiled or even eaten raw, will form the foundation of a great garden industry."

That, literally, was saying a mouthful, for those previously feared "love apples" were none other than tomatoes.

One summer at the Grainger County Tomato Festival, a gathering of tens of thousands to honor the region's most famous agricultural product, I made a survey of attendees to see if any of them had carried on Johnson's legacy.

Bite my tongue. These brave folks were *everywhere.*

Eighteen-year-old Matthew Cornett, for example, was forty dollars richer for his culinary experimentation. A few weeks earlier, some of the other farmhands where he was working had challenged him to eat a whole, raw jalapeno pepper. They put their money where his mouth was, and Matthew took 'em to the bank.

"Yeah, it was worth it," he said with a grin, "even though my mouth burned for four hours."

Becky Ericson of Bean Station understood the competition concept completely. She told me about a food dare she took years ago after a friend's father returned from a trip to India with packages of chocolate-covered grasshoppers and fried ants.

"I didn't throw up," she recalled. "In fact, they weren't bad. Kinda like Raisinettes, best I remember."

Did Becky win big money?

"No, but I earned the admiration of all the boys in my third-grade class."

Yet the all-time classic food dare I learned about came from tomato grower Lillard Stratton.

"My grandpaw had a store out on Highway 92," he said. "One day, this feller walked in and said he could drink twenty-four Co'Colas at one sittin'." That was back when they come in those little green, six-ounce bottles."

One word led to another, and the next thing you know the bet was on.

"The deal was, he could have 'em free if he drank all twenty-four," Lillard said. "But if he couldn't, he had to pay double."

And?

"Buddy, he drunk ever' one of 'em—hot, too! They weren't even iced-down! A little later, they found him sittin' up next to a fencepost. He was sicker'n a dog."

Nobody ever said winning was easy.

Speaking of weird eating propositions, I once proposed in print that southerners should eat to help save a regional food icon from ruin.

In early 2005, a company many southerners have instinctively called upon to help them out of an economic pinch found itself on the financial ropes. That, of course, was Krispy Kreme, the South's super supplier of sugary, sweet, succulent snacks.

Even if you don't follow day-to-day fraud, arrests of CEOs and other routine business news, you probably heard about Krispy Kreme's sad plight. Once an industry darling, this company had gone south faster than New Englanders in

Cakes, Pies, and Super-sized Fries

January. Krispy Kreme's shares fell to an all-time low. The work force was cut. And—oh, pity the fat cats!—the company jet was grounded.

Same song, ten thousandth verse. A small, solid, regional company suddenly gets discovered by the rest of the world. Before you can say "Dom Pérignon," the suits get drunk on power and fiction and wind up blowing millions of someone else's money. Company goes bust. Lots of little people, whose sweat created the fortune to begin with, are handed pink slips. And the suits find another lucrative venture to foul.

But this wasn't just another Enron. This was Krispy Kreme. Our Krispy Kreme. The Krispy Kreme that had helped churches, scout troops, baseball teams, cheerleaders, and civic clubs by the tens of thousands generate mountains of money for good works.

Well, OK. So the results also padded bellies and rotted teeth all across Dixie. Nobody's perfect. The point is, Krispy Kreme had been good to the South. Now it was time for the South to be good to Krispy Kreme.

I was not alone issuing this call to arms—or crullers, as the case may be. Oak Ridger Don Barkman also was quite concerned. "If the government can bail out Chrysler and if we can help tsunami victims, surely we can take a bite out of Krispy Kreme's financial dilemma," he told me.

Absolutely. These hard times demanded innovative thinking, and not by a team of Harvard-trained number crunchers holed up in a New York skyscraper. I meant by a batch of rotund good ol' boys munching their way through a bakery.

The way I figured, two new products could ease the pain. The first was a new doughnut, one created especially for these times.

Your basic glazed, jelly-filled, chocolate-covered, maple-topped, sprinkle-spritzed 'nuts had served admirably through the years. But the company needed a special recipe—a Kaloric Krispy Kreme Krisis Killer, as it were—that took selected ingredients from those all-time favorites and molded them into one grease-dripping, artery-clogging, waist-expanding orb specifically earmarked for debt reduction.

The other product I had in mind was not to be eaten. It was to be worn around the face and neck.

I'm talkin' perfume. Aftershave. Cologne. Smell-good.

You take the delightful aroma that wafts from a Krispy Kreme shop approximately twenty-three out of every twenty-four hours, seven days a week, then reduce it to a liquid, package it in bottles, put the bottles on the counter, and have the cash register primed and ready for action. "Eau de Doughnut" sure smelled like money to me.

OK, so maybe the doughnut perfume idea didn't work. But southerners did rally. And eat. Last time I checked, that delightful sign proclaiming the wonderful news—"Now Serving Hot Doughnuts"—still beams brightly across the face, and belly, of America.

By the way, what's for supper?

Cyber Cookies

Lori Wilson, a Knoxville Web developer, found a unique letter in her e-mail box a few days ago. It was a message from her niece, Sara Sipes, who lives in Norman, Oklahoma. Sara wanted to know if good ol' Aunt Lori was interested in buying some Girl Scout cookies.

"Sara sent the same message to all her aunts and uncles—here in Knoxville, as well as Cincinnati, Lexington, and Danville, Kentucky," Wilson said. "She did a good job. Her letter included a complete description for each type of cookie, how many were in each box, and the price. There was a major sympathetic appeal too—she told how many boxes she hoped to sell to earn her way to camp."

Naturally, it worked.

"I ordered ten boxes," said Wilson. "I'd never bought Girl Scout cookies from Sara before. I mean, she lives all the way out in Oklahoma! She's supposed to mail them to me."

I asked about postage.

"Hmmm. We never did discuss that," Wilson answered. "Maybe Sara will give me the family rate."

Cybercookies. I never thought I'd live to see the day.

It's one thing for gap-toothed Brownies to come door-to-door or hit you up at church, at the office, or at the grocery store, or in front of the local shopping mall. But to hawk their mint, vanilla cream, coconut, and chocolate-chip goodies cross-country by computer? Heaven—and Juliette Gordon Low—help us.

Shouldn't these little scoutettes be off somewhere tying knots, practicing first aid, or weaving baskets?

Then again, maybe enterprising young women like Sara are onto something bigger than merit badges and two free weeks at Camp Winnehohonakawampus. Maybe they have unlocked the key to guilt-free snacking, liberating countless millions of tubbos, Los Angeles to Manhattan, from the shackles of sweet tooth sin: virtual reality cookies.

Yum-yum. I can almost taste these nuggets right now.

It's a perfect plan. No more ruined diet plans. No more pigging out before meals, after meals and between meals. No more promising yourself to eat just one itty-bitty thin mint at bedtime and then polishing off the entire box.

Instead, all you gotta do is pour a glass of cold milk, sit down at your computer, punch a few keys (enter the all-important credit card number, of course), and then let your body be washed in virtual sensuous bliss. You can virtually watch as the ingredients come together to make the dough, virtually smell the cookies as they emerge from the oven, virtually unwrap the cellophane sleeve, virtually hold each delicate morsel in your hand, and virtually pop them, one by one, into your virtual mouth.

I'm so excited, I'm gonna run outside right now, rub two wires together, and build me a campfire.

Bachelor of Science in Beer

There is weeping, wailing, and gnashing of teeth at the University of Tennessee. And the football season hasn't even started.

What makes this grief so gut-wrenching is more important than athletics. More important than fraternity and sorority rush. More important than grabbing a barf burger at Smokey's. And much more important than (pardon my French) studying. So brace yourself.

The school has plummeted as a place to raise hell. The *Princeton Review* has ranked UT as the sixteenth party school in the nation.

As a once-proud alumnus of this venerable institution, I am sick with disgust. Just one year ago, Tennessee towered over all others in this regard. We were Numero Uno, and cheers could be heard from every bar on the Strip.

Arrrgh! How could we fall so precipitously? How could we tumble a full fifteen places down the chart in only twelve months? (Which, as any UT math major will tell you, is an average of seven places per month. No, wait. It's 8.543. Oops, I mean it's a 26 percent decline, compounded annually. Somebody help me out here: Do you divide the big number into the little number? Or is that the square root?)

In any event, how could today's crop of baggy-panted, backward-cap-wearing cretins permit this travesty to occur? And how could the faculty and staff sit still for it?

But at least I can drown my sorrows in drink. That's because PETA—People for the Ethical Treatment of Animals, not People Eating Tasty Animals—has set sights on UT for the renewal of its "Got Beer?" campaign.

Several of my buddies are still gagging and rinsing their mouths after feasting on a less-than-delicious country ham breakfast.

The lads had been in the woods all morning hunting for wild turkeys and returned to Ray Harper's camper trailer for R&R. Ray volunteered to fry up some slabs of meat. He dotted the skillet with a few drops of vegetable oil from a jar near the stove, browned the ham nicely, and laid it out on paper plates to drain. Folks gathered 'round for a banquet but lost their appetites after the first bite.

Oops. Turns out Ray hadn't used cooking oil, after all. Someone had brought along a jar of Pine-Sol to take the edge off the privy—and then made the crucial mistake of pouring the excess into a glass jar near the stove.

"Bill Hicks told me it was the first time he ever ate ham that tasted like soap," Ray said.

Oh well. At least it made the dishwashing a lot easier.

PETA originally launched this promotion back in the 1990s. It all came about after researchers at Harvard (or "Haaaavaard," as those snooty moneybags from Montana or Detroit or California or wherever Harvard is located pronounce their school's name) determined that moderate amounts of beer are better for the body than milk.

To the average college student, "moderate" consumption of beer means anything less than a keg. So I'm hoping those UT ingrates who let the party-school ranking drop out of sight will at least make us proud in this department.

It's amazing how much the average person can be enlightened by a campaign like this. Why, until now I never realized I was a vegetarian!

I thought belonging to PETA meant you had to swear off beef, pork, eggs, and cheese. And quit hunting and fishing and wearing leather. And join protest parades, screaming "Meat stinks!" And throw red paint on women wearing mink coats.

But then I discovered all you gotta do is drink beer instead of milk. Cool! Or as they'd say down on the agricultural campus, "Well, undulate my udder!"

There are many reasons why beer is better than milk. But the most important is refrigeration—or lack thereof.

Both of these liquids should be consumed cold. (The liquids, I mean; you can be whatever temperature you choose.) My preferred temperature is forty degrees Farrington, which, as I learned in UT chemistry class, is equivalent to minus-182 degrees Cassius.

But what happens if the power goes out and stays off for five or six days?

The beer does not go bad. It just sits there and gets warm. Then it goes back to being cold when the electric stimulators resume sending gamma rays through the wires leading into your house. But the prissy milk can't take the heat. It turns sour.

So if you're stupid enough to take a sip just as your buddy reaches the punch line of a raunchy joke, not only will milk come out your nose, you'll get a whiff of cat puke every time you inhale the rest of the day.

Naturally, some people have taken offense at PETA's efforts. They say it will encourage college students to drink even more beer. To which Bruce Friedrich, PETA's director of Vegan Outreach, replied, "No one's going to be pouring Sam Adams on their cereal."

Of course not. Natural Ice is better. A lot cheaper, too.

A Cup of Hot—Huh?

If coffee is so good for short-term memory, how come there's a cold cup of it sitting on my desk right now?

I poured that coffee five minutes ago. Or was it fifteen? I can't remember. In any event, I forgot to drink it.

That's why I question results of the latest coffee study. I say "latest" because coffee has to be the most analyzed, scrutinized food product since humanoids stood upright and learned to say, "Super-size me."

One of the scientists involved in the project, Dr. Florian Koppelstatter of Austria's Medical University of Innsbruck, told reporters, "We were able to show that caffeine modulates a higher brain function through its effects on distinct areas of the brain."

I have no idea what that mish-mash means, but when someone named Florian Koppelstatter speaks, you better believe I listen.

Maybe coffee proved its memory-enhancing qualities in Doc Koppelstatter's lab tests. But in your typical American office, the theory doesn't hold water—black, creamed, or otherwise. Consider this scenario: Herb has been sitting at his computer terminal for an hour. He decides to replenish his cup o'joe. En route to the coffee pot, he passes the mail room. Herb stops long enough to grab the envelopes protruding from his pigeonhole. One is a note from his old buddy, Bill.

Setting his other mail aside, Herb opens Bill's note and starts reading. He wanders back toward his desk, plops down, and fires an e-mail to Bill, pausing to field a couple of phone calls. One of the callers is a windbag. As the conversation drones on, Herb longs for the coffee he forgot when he ducked into the mail room. Blah-blah-blah-blah goes the caller.

Finally, Herb is able to say goodbye. He cuts a trail for the coffee pot. Which, naturally, is empty. So he digs into the supply drawer and fires the machine up. While it perks, he sashays to the restroom to recycle his previous cup.

Coming out of the john, Herb bumps into Betty, who reminds him to be sure to have the Findley report on the boss's desk by noon. Yikes, Herb thinks to himself; I had that stupid thing 95 percent finished the other day but got distracted. Back to his desk to complete the task. Then off to the coffee pot, which, of course, is empty again. He starts it back up and, not to be denied, waits until the dripping ceases.

Aaah! Good coffee.

Herb strolls to his desk and resumes working at his computer, sipping intermittently. He drains the cup and returns for a refill.

Yes, the pot is empty—you had to ask?—so while he waits for more to brew, he saunters into the mail room. On a table, there are the letters he had set aside to read Bill's note. So he won't forget the letters a second time, Herb walks directly to his desk and puts them down. As he turns back toward the coffee pot, his e-mail bell rings. Herb opens the file and discovers six new messages.

He sits down to read, forgetting all about the coffee pot—which is charring to an acrid, iridescent glow because he forgot to add water.

Trust your Uncle Maxwell House: Coffee may have many fine qualities, but perking up memories isn't one of them.

Correct Kitchens

If recent research into Americans' eating habits is correct, I should nibble my meals like a canary and be built along the lines of a no. 2 pencil—which I neither do nor am, proving these studies should be seasoned with a liberal shake of salt.

I refer specifically to a story aired a few days ago by television station WPBF in West Palm Beach, Florida. In the report, registered dietician Lisa Dorfman said the color of a person's kitchen could affect his or her attitudes about chow.

Blues or greens are best, Dorfman said. These are "cool, calming colors (which) will tend to diminish your appetite."

What's more, Dorfman advised the use of certain aromas, notably vanilla and mint, to curb hunger pangs.

In the same report, Marcie Gorman, president and CEO of Weight Watchers in Palm Beach County, recommended that eating quarters be well lit, not dim. The darker the environment, she noted, the more likely you are to tamp down excess vittles.

Finally, the experts advised diners to enjoy their meals with slow music in the background.

With all due respect to these dietary divas, baloney! At least in my case.

There are three walls in our kitchen—one on the west, east, and north. There's no south "wall" per se, since most of that area is the entrance.

Our west wall is covered with dark green wallpaper. The east wall is covered with a series of beige tiles, accented in the center by a large, clay, hand-pressed decorative tile featuring ferns. Ferns, for those who happen to be botanically challenged, are green.

The north, weight-bearing wall is composed of logs and chinking, a condition that comes with the territory when you live in a log house. (Unless the moss is particularly bad, however, the logs aren't green.)

The entire room is lit up like a photo studio, thanks to track lights, ceiling lights, and abundant windows.

So what happens in this "cool, calming" place?

I eat like a litter of Poland China piglets. I thought that was the purpose of mealtime.

Speaking as one who has taken his meals in every type of culinary environment from mess tents to country stores, greasy spoons to country clubs, I'm much more influenced by the color of my food than the color of my surroundings. Plop down a platter of green fried chicken or blue meatloaf in front of me and I promise to remain neither cool nor calm, no matter what the color of the walls. Instead, I will exit the premises quickly.

Not that I completely dismiss this research, you understand.

Cakes, Pies, and Super-sized Fries

I often listen to bluegrass music while eating, for instance. Unless it's a tune about lost love—hound or otherwise—bluegrass is usually upbeat and fast tempo. Naturally, all that foot tapping and finger snapping does tend to lead to faster chewing.

The more I think about it, there may be something to that business about the influence of vanilla and mint on the appetite, too. After ingesting a quart of vanilla ice cream, I have very little interest in eating, oh, much more than a pint of chocolate chip mint.

Bottled Nonsense

I've never understood modern society's addiction to bottled water.

If you're hiking or camping or living in an area where the local fare is polluted, fine. But for everyday consumption anywhere else? Makes no sense at all. Why anybody would pay outrageous prices for a product that flows from the faucet at a fraction of the cost is beyond me.

Back in the late '70s, when I worked winters for a duck-hunting club in southwest Louisiana, our well got contaminated by oil-field waste. We had to import every potable drop from that moment on. So trust me; I've drunk my share of the bottled stuff under extreme conditions.

Some folks insist bottled tastes better. I don't concur. With few exceptions, all water's the same to me.

Maybe my tongue isn't refined enough. Or maybe it's been permanently damaged by tobacco (before I took the pledge), alcohol, fast food, and Penrose sausages.

Health benefits? C'mon. This isn't 1836. Call me naïve, but I have to think municipal water-treatment systems approved by any state's health department are up to snuff. (Insert outrage from health zealots and bottled-water companies here.)

Instead, this craze is the lucrative fruit of an ingenious marketing campaign. Slurping cheaply at the fountain is out. Sipping expensively from a bottle is in. Case laughingly closed.

This is one area of financial disagreement in the Venable household.

My dear wife, normally a frugal, low-maintenance woman, loves bottled water. She purchases it by the case and takes a fresh jug to her office every day.

I keep a couple of old, much-reused soft drink bottles in the garage and refill them—from the tap—as I work in the yard. If this is our biggest difference of monetary opinion in nearly forty years of marriage, I consider us truly blessed.

But at least I'm not alone in my disdain. The Earth Policy Institute, an environmental think tank in Washington, recently uncorked a scathing report on the bottled-water fad.

According to the institute's findings, the United States is the world's leading consumer of this stuff. In 2004, Americans chugged twenty-six-billion liters, approximately one eight-ounce glass per person per day.

The institute charged that the energy and raw materials needed to produce mega-billions of disposable bottles require "more than one and one-half million barrels of oil annually, enough to fuel some one-hundred-thousand U.S. cars for a year." Adding insult to this grievous injury is the fact that 86 percent of these containers wind up as garbage or litter.

Still, I have feet of clay. Even though I may ridicule all the beautiful people hooked on this unmitigated nonsense, I wouldn't mind having a piece of the action.

Which is why, while speaking at the University of Tennessee's commencement exercises in December 2005, I told the truth, the whole truth, and nothing but the truth when I said to those graduates, "Back in 1969, if you'd told me people would some day fork over $1.89 for a bottle of water, I never would've stayed in journalism."

Calling All Turkeys

I have long accepted the fact that I'm a geek. I wear geeky clothes. I drive geeky vehicles. I listen to geeky music. I think geeky thoughts.

Even worse, I'm not a geek in the modern sense. Meaning I'm not a computer geek who pockets $175,000 annually to translate English into digitize and vice versa. I'm merely a geek of the run-of-the-mill, aging-baby-boomer, barely-scraping-by, pot-bellied variety.

That's why I get so irritated when people engage in mindless cell-phone chatter in the grocery store.

Point of order: I own a cell phone. I use it sparingly—just for making calls, never receiving them. I couldn't tell you my cell phone number if you put a cocked .38 to my head and gave me till the count of five to come up with it.

I happen to believe a telephone, cellular or otherwise, is a tool to be used for necessary conversation. And (even though this is the height of geekiness), the conversation should not be a recreational activity.

Let's say I'm walking through the dairy aisle when a guy whips out a cell phone, punches a num-

Thanks to singer Glen Campbell, I'll never again worry about weight gain.

Campbell, who was sentenced to ten nights in an Arizona jail after pleading guilty to drunken driving, contends he wasn't inebriated. Instead, he said in a recent interview, he had been "overserved" alcohol.

Perfect! Now I can quit complaining that my britches have mysteriously shrunk in the closet. Rather, I've been the innocent victim of overserving at the dinner table—and, by golly, somebody's going to pay for this heinous crime!

ber and says, "Suzy, it's Chuck. I'm confused. Did you ask for two quarts of sweet milk and one pint of buttermilk or two quarts of buttermilk and one pint of sweet milk?"

My initial reaction is to think to myself, This knucklehead needs to write things down before he leaves on his errand. But I always let the matter pass.

Or let's say I'm browsing through produce and a cell phone rings and a voice near the cantaloupes says, "Hello. Yes, I did get the Hootenville contract signed. Please tell Virginia I'll be arriving in about two hours with the necessary papers."

My reaction is to think to myself, This jerk should have called Virginia before he left the Hootenville negotiations. But I always let the matter pass.

However, let's say I'm standing in the checkout line and a cell phone rings and the jerk next to me answers and says, "Hey. Not doin' nothin', just standin' in line at Kroger. What are you doin? Standin' in line at Food City? Is it as boring as standin' in line at Kroger? It is? Boy, standin' in line at the grocery store sure is boring, ain't it?"

My reaction then is to think to myself, This person needs to be dragged outside and flogged with a belt, buckle-end first. And it usually takes every ounce of strength in my body to keep from acting on the impulse.

So maybe you will understand why I'm sitting here at my geeky desk, shaking my geeky head in dismay. It's because I hold in my geeky hands a news release from officials of the Butterball Turkey Talk-Line. This is the customer-service arm of a very large poultry producer—and if you can't guess which brand, you're even dumber than the bored idiot in my third example.

Frankly, I'm a bit miffed that turkeys get all the attention. In the name of culinary diversity, you'd think there would be a Beef Stew Hotline, a French Toast Hotline, a Cornbread Hotline and a Tossed Salad Hotline. Maybe the chefs who prepare those foods don't need help.

Anyhow, every year during the Thanksgiving and Christmas holidays, the turkey experts compile some of the more interesting telephone calls they have gotten regarding the proper care and cooking of a bird.

Some of these inquiries are frighteningly funny. For instance, one frantic caller discovered she had run out of room in her refrigerator and wanted to know if she could safely store the turkey in her car—for two days.

The woman was gently told it might be a better idea to knock on a few neighborhood doors and beg a bit of refrigerator space instead of running the risk of food poisoning.

Some of the requests come from consumers calling on the run. Literally. A Florida firefighter was in the process of thawing a thirty-pound bird for the firehouse feast when he got an emergency signal. En route to the scene, he called the talk line and asked how be could safely accelerate the thawing process when he returned to home base.

Just use cold water, he was told.

Some of the inquiries turn out to be tips. For example, one cook called to say she used raw carrots in place of a rack to keep her turkey off the bottom of the pan. It not only worked but also added flavor.

Then there was the bride who had a tiny oven and was worried that the bird would rise during cooking, like a loaf of bread, and be too large to remove when it was done. And the man who asked if a turkey would cook faster if he drove a railroad spike through it, like cooking potatoes on a nail in the grill. Not to mention the, uh, "charitable" woman who inquired about a turkey she had kept frozen for twenty-three years. Assuming it remained rock-hard for the entire time and hadn't been defrosted, she was told, it should be OK to eat—although the quality was not likely to be good.

"That's what we thought," she replied. "We'll just give it to the church."

But all of this gaiety was lost on me when I read one sobering statistic in the news release: "Call after call came from such locations as 'Aisle Thirteen,' 'Aisle Five,' and 'Frozen Foods Section.' In fact, more calls than ever originated on a cell phone from no place other than the shopper's local store, a breeding ground for turkey-related questions."

Amazing. If I were the Jolly Green Giant and realized that my sacred supermarket had just been turned into a cell phone chat room, I'd arrange a walkout—and I bet I could convince Betty Crocker, the Keebler elves, and Mr. Peanut to join me.

Grub That's to Dye for

Unlike a certain resident of the White House, I'm going to give you plenty of advance warning: This epistle is bugged. So bugged, in fact, my words are subject to scamper away or spread their wings and fly off the page. Perhaps you should keep a can of Raid handy.

I call your attention to a proposed rule change by the U.S. Food and Drug Administration. It involves an insect known as *Dactylopius coccus costa*.

That name probably doesn't ring a bell. But if you've ever eaten imitation lobster or crab, cocktail cherries, and certain flavors of ice cream, fruit drinks, yogurt, and candy, or anointed your body with lipstick, makeup base, eye shadow, eyeliner, or nail polish, you and Dactyl are friends of longstanding.

Dactylopius coccus costa is a native of Mexico and South America. For centuries, humans have been grinding the dead bodies of these critters and producing cochineal extract and carmine.

Hmm. Now that I mention it, "cochineal extract" and "carmine" aren't everyday words, either. But "red dye" is. Meaning—yes—the basic color ingredient for a host of food and cosmetic products once had six legs.

Again, let me stress there's nothing new here. The FDA is well aware of the process and for years has required manufacturers to include red dye on ingredient lists. This is usually accomplished with the words "color added" or "E120" on labels. But since the late 1990s, there's been a big push from consumer groups for a few more details.

Part of the reasoning stems from an apparent increase in food allergies, part from concerns by vegetarians and Jews wanting to remain kosher, part from folks squeamish at the thought of ingesting crushed bug shells. Thus the FDA is considering changes to reflect the source of dye. Whatever happens, however, don't look for the words "bug" or "insect" to appear on food lists. The FDA merely suggests the basic ingredients of "cochineal extract" and "carmine" be used.

This sterile approach has prompted an irritated retort from Michael F. Jacobson, executive director of the Center for Science in the Public Interest.

"Why not use a word that people can understand?" he told the Associated Press. "Sending people scurrying to the dictionary or to Google to figure out what 'carmine' and 'cochineal' means is just plain sneaky. Call those colorings what they are: insect-based."

I could argue either way.

On the one hand, if I'm going to eat buggy food, I want to know if the vermin arrived before, during or after the manufacturing process.

On the other hand, the hand that's holding an ice cream carton as we speak, as long as I'm wolfing down mouthfuls of—I'm quoting directly from the list of ingredients—"lecithin, mono and diglycerides, cellulose gum, guar gum, carrageenan," and other weird stuff, why worry if there's an occasional crispy critter in the mix?

Connoisseurs of 'Cue

The latest dietary news is so wonderful I may dedicate the next four months to constant chewing. I have just learned it's possible to eat barbecue with a clear conscience.

As anyone from the South will attest, there is something divine about attacking a platter full of pork that has been slow cooked in a thick fog of hickory smoke and liberally basted with a tasty, secret-recipe sauce.

It is of no concern whatsoever if half the county knows the secret ingredients of the sauce. Or if your secret sauce is exactly the same as my secret sauce. This is strictly a matter of confident pride. Sort of like how everybody in church, from the preacher to the deacons to the choir director, is on a first-name commercial basis with the local bootlegger. You just keep some things to yourself and don't worry about it.

In the last few years, however, barbecue has been tarred—not with a sauce ladle, but with the broad brush of criticism—by health experts. These heathens would have us believe barbecue is bad for our systems. Clogs the arteries, they claim. Damages the heart. Adds to the waistline. Raises cholesterol levels.

We barbecueaholics countered the best we could: If Gawd Hisself had not meant for us to dine in this manner, he would never have invented pigs. But now we have more ammunition to fight the anti-'cue heretics. We have scientific fact on our side.

First, I call your attention to a professional publication called the *Archives of Internal Medicine,* which recently reported that cholesterol levels naturally fluctuate during various seasons of the year.

Based on a study of more than five hundred individuals, researchers discovered cholesterol rises during the winter and drops during summer. And since summer is the official barbecue season, I contend this is proof the body makes natural allowances for prodigious porcine ingestion.

But it gets even better. We 'cue connoisseurs can now eat without shame because it's not our fault. According to a recent report by the Reuters news service, scientists believe the addiction to barbecue may be real. I quote directly: "A brain scan study of normal, hungry people showed their brains lit up when they saw and smelled their favorite foods in much the same way as the brains of cocaine addicts when they think about their next snort."

The findings went on to point out that stimulation was most significant in the "superior temporal, anterior insula and orbitofrontal cortices (of the brain). These areas are associated with addiction."

Among the favorite foods tested on subjects were fried chicken, cinnamon buns, brownies, chocolate cake, and—be still my trembling ticker—barbecue.

Thus since it is now socially, legally, and ethically acceptable to set personal responsibility aside in matters of addiction, I say to all those snooty anti-'cueniks, "I can't help myself. Please hush and pass the meat."

So eat up, America. And don't spill any secret-recipe sauce on your superior temporal, anterior insula, and orbitofrontal cortices.

Her Lightest Meal Ever

I've got to tell this story on Sarah White.

OK, so Sarah tells it on herself. The woman relishes a good laugh, even if the joke's on her.

It happened on Thanksgiving Day. All the in-laws and out-laws were coming over for dinner. As befits this holiday, Sarah prepared a royal feast: turkey, veggies, and desserts, replete with the fine china and silverware.

One of Sarah's specialties is mashed potatoes. Old-time, from-scratch "smashed 'taters," you understand. Not white paste out of a box.

Dinner was a resounding success. But later, when all the guests were sitting in the den, watching TV and patting tight bellies, Sarah discovered a problem. I'll let her tell you about it:

"My daughter was helping me clean up the table. There was a little bit of mashed potatoes left, so she started scraping it out. Suddenly she said, 'Hey, there's something bad wrong with this bowl.' I picked it up and saw what she was talking about. There was a hole in the bottom.

"I was thinking, Now, how'd that happen? when it dawned on me: I had served those potatoes in a light fixture!"

You mean one that attaches to the ceiling?

"Yep," she replied. "A big, clear, fancy, glass one.

"It's my husband's fault," Sarah chuckled. "He's cheap. He's always saving stuff because one of the kids might need it. Awhile back, we'd replaced the fixture in the kitchen. I ran the old one through the dishwasher, and he was supposed to take it upstairs. But somehow it wound up on the shelf."

It speaks highly of Sarah's potatoes to note they didn't leak out the aperture. However, she did observe, "It's just lucky I didn't grab that bowl for the peas!"

Why am I telling this tale now? Because it's the start of school in Knox County, and the woman who served that meal is none other than the director of the school nutrition program for the Tennessee Department of Education. In other words, the state's chief chef.

White and her minions face a daunting task. Every school day, cafeteria workers from Memphis to Mountain City prepare and serve 193,000 breakfasts and 573,000 lunches. Over the course of the year, that adds up to 105 million meals.

White, who lives in Lebanon, knows schools and children. She's a former teacher. She has four kids. She's been director of nutrition for thirteen years.

> Saw an interesting sign of the times in front of Messiah Lutheran Church: "Bread of Life, No Carbs."
> Which makes me wonder. What were the ingredients of those five loaves that fed the five thousand? Also, were the two fishes baked or breaded and deep-fried?

Even though classes are cranking up all around the state, she and her staff have been busy all summer conducting in-service programs. When I telephoned her office, she'd just come off a marathon round of training in Carthage, Cookeville, Memphis, and Dover. They cover the waterfront (or would "stovetop" be more appropriate?) in these sessions—nutrition, meal planning, health and safety, business, whatever.

But the overriding message she preaches definitely is food for thought: "Cafeteria workers are the only school employees who see every child every day. I try to remind them to smile and be happy and not act like they just ate a dill pickle."

Or potatoes out of a light fixture, as the case may be.

One for the Road

I have spent most of my adulthood drinking while driving. DWD, they call it. There's nothing I like better while tooling down a scenic highway than taking steady sips of my favorite elixir.

Coffee.

(What? Did you have something else in mind?)

Apparently I'm not alone. Based on a recent survey by a Michigan-based insurance company, lots of other folks enjoy their joe behind the wheel. Trouble is, some of them can't jiggle java and steer at the same time, and they're giving the rest of us a bad name.

The results of this nonscientific survey were announced a few days ago. It listed coffee at the forefront of the top ten most dangerous foods to ingest while driving. The others were hot soup, tacos, chili, juicy hamburgers, barbecued food, fried chicken, jelly and cream-filled doughnuts, soft drinks, and chocolate.

My immediate reaction was, "What other foods groups are there? Except for Cheetos, Twinkies, and Penrose sausages, doesn't this list cover all the vitamins, minerals, nutrients, and preservatives necessary for a healthy life?"

But I had to admit the researchers made a legitimate point. Indeed, there are inherent dangers associated with this form of DWD. Even though coffee doesn't impair a driver the same way alcohol does, its mere presence can lead to trouble if you aren't careful.

Over the years, I've developed several safe-sip tactics. In the name of public safety, allow me to share them with you.

First, never fill to the rim and never use a small-sized cup. If you commit either of these sins and roll over an object larger than a matchstick, you're bound to get a lapful of lava.

Second, have a handy-dandy cup holder within easy reach. Never let this sacred zone be occupied with anything besides a coffee cup. Motorists who fill their cup holders with cell phones, hair brushes, CD cases, wallets, and other items should have their licenses revoked for eighteen months.

Third, forget those so-called easy-sip plastic lids that come from fast-food joints—you know, the kind that have a perforated slot you're supposed to bend back before drinking. These things are instruments of the devil. They never work. At the very least, they dribble drops of coffee on your white shirt. At the very worst, they bust open in midsip, showering your face and neck with the most volatile case of prickly heat in the history of dermatology.

Finally, always keep a couple of large-sized empties in ready reserve. These are the actual drinking vessels.

Here's the procedure: Before you pull away from the drive-through, crack the lid on the coffee cup you just purchased, and pour a healthy dollop into one of the empties. Then re-cover the fresh cup and stick it in the cup holder. Slurp (forget Miss Manners) from the "empty." Refill as necessary at red lights and stop signs. Follow this procedure and you will enjoy low-risk DWD.

Yes, accidents can happen, even to those of us who practice safe sipping. I was the victim of one of these tragedies a couple of years ago, and I'm still not over the shock.

I was returning from an intensive session of field research in Sevier County (translation: bass fishing on Douglas Lake) and swung into a roadside deli for a quick bite. Ate my burger and drank my cola in the truck, still parked. I had ordered a cup of joe for the road. Just before pulling back into traffic, I cracked the lid as described above, decanted enough for a mile or two of safe sipping, and stuck the new cup back into the holder.

I hit the main road and was contentedly shifting gears when I touched the cup to my lips and took a long, deliberate slurp.

Aaaaak! Aarrrgh! Ptooie! The stuff was cold as a witch's heart.

Apparently the deli coffee pot had been switched off sometime earlier and nobody noticed. The sensation of that stale, frigid sheep dip hitting my lips nearly caused me to swerve abruptly into the ditch.

I momentarily flirted with the notion of filing a lawsuit for whiplash and emotional stress, but then thought, aw, what the heck—when you drink and drive as much as I do, you gotta be prepared for the unexpected.

Peanut Pleasures

It's a sign of the times in which we live. The children fly out of the nest, and Mom and Dad use their newfound freedom to go on a cruise or buy a sports car or take an extended vacation.

But when it happened to me, I did something a bit more pedestrian. I bought a jar of peanut butter.

Don't laugh. This was a bold step of childless independence on my part. The fact it took years to take that step shows how ingrained old habits can become.

A bit of background is necessary. Our son Clay is extremely allergic to peanuts and peanut products. We discovered this condition when he was a toddler. As anyone who suffers from a serious food allergy can attest, this is big-time stuff. Potentially fatal. Lord only knows the number of pedal-to-the-metal trips we took to hospital emergency rooms when Clay came in accidental contact with forbidden fruits.

We became ingredient readers long before it was the nutritionally cool thing to do. As a youngster, Clay probably got as much reading practice with food labels as he did with schoolbooks. And contrary to folklore, you don't "outgrow" a condition like this. Clay is just as allergic to peanuts today as he was in 1975. Thus we've never had peanut butter around our home.

I realize how blasphemous the previous sentence is. Peanut butter is the original all-American food. Folks of all ages, races, and national origins eat it. It crosses all societal and economic lines. It knows no regional bounds. Walk into any house—shanty to castle—in Anchorage, Miami, Los Angeles, Chicago, or Minneapolis, and I bet you'll find peanut butter on the shelf.

I was standing in the cafeteria line at Fort Sanders Regional Medical Center several evenings ago. One of the entrees was fried chicken wings. The diner in front of me inquired about the price.

"They're thirty cents apiece or $2.99 a dozen," the server replied.

The customer furrowed her brow as she mentally ran the numbers. Finally, she said, "Let me have ten."

Maybe the ol' gal wasn't very hungry. Maybe money was burning a hole in her pocket. Or maybe she was just dumber than a brick.

Duncan West had somewhat the same encounter at a fast-food joint.

"I ordered a pint of milk," he says. "The Jethro Bodine behind the counter looked at me and said, 'We only have half-pints.' He was serious."

Fine, West said. Just make it two half-pints.

"You could almost see the light go on in the empty cavern behind his eyes," West related. "He said, 'Oh, yeah, that would work.'"

Even though I was virtually raised on the stuff, I weaned myself immediately. For well over two decades, I didn't eat peanuts. Or peanut butter. Or peanut candy. Or peanut anything. Nor did anyone else in our tribe.

Now, fast-forward to the present. Both of our kids have graduated from college, gotten married, and are on their own. A few weeks ago, I was helping my wife buy groceries. I rounded the corner in one aisle and found myself standing in front of a peanut butter display.

At first, the significance was lost on me. Then suddenly, a ten-thousand-watt light bulb flickered in my brain. Hey! Peanut butter can be my friend once more!

Talk about a weird sensation. I felt like a soldier, lost in the wilderness behind enemy lines, who finally stumbles back into civilization and discovers the war's been over since way back when. In the words of my hero, Homer Simpson, "Whoo-hooo!"

I bought a jar of the crunchy style. It was always my favorite. On the trip home, I wanted to cradle it in my hands like a bottle of rare, expensive wine.

I removed the jar from the bag and placed it on a shelf in the kitchen. It looked oh-so-out of place.

Even as I closed the cabinet door, I was suddenly gripped with fear—like maybe it was going to leap out of hiding some time when Clay was visiting and lock him in a stranglehold.

I'm happy to report, however, that the armistice is growing stronger by the day. I'm on my second jar. Still crunchy. I'll get around to the smooth kind later.

This is like a second childhood. I slap big dollops with reckless abandon on crackers and bread. I have rediscovered the culinary joy of peanut butter and jelly sandwiches. Sometimes, my Y-chromosome instincts take over and I scrape out a big spoonful and shoot it down straight.

But so help me, I still feel guilty having peanut butter in the house. Any parent who ever watched a child struggle for breath knows what I'm talking about. I instinctively take my knife or spoon to the sink and clean it immediately. Can't help it. Once burned by something like this, you never forget.

And whenever Clay calls and says he's coming over, Mary Ann and I dash about the kitchen to make sure there's not so much as a smidgen on the counter or the edge of a plate.

We're worse than Baptists hiding likker from the preacher.

Yummy McSheep

Until I visited Scotland, I never thought much about sheep. My knowledge was pretty much limited to the notion that sheep are the main ingredient in sweaters, socks, nursery rhymes, insomnia relief, and bawdy jokes about love-starved rednecks.

But since touring the United Kingdom, my sheep consciousness has been greatly elevated.

I discovered there are more sheep than people in northern Scotland. Of course, that's not saying a lot because you can drive twenty-five miles in the Scottish highlands without encountering another human being—except for perhaps three dozen motorists who are traveling in the opposite direction on the one-lane road you're desperately trying to navigate.

Everywhere you look there are sheep. Sheep in pastures. Sheep on hillsides. Sheep on rock piles. Sheep at stream sides. Sheep in barn lots. Sheep on the left shoulder of the road. Sheep on the right shoulder of the road. Sheep in the middle of the road.

Scotland has sheep like Dixie has 'possums, but you don't see them flattened on the asphalt. This is either due to the legal fact that sheep have the right-of-way on Scottish thoroughfares or the practical fact that drivers realize there's a distinct damage differential between plowing over a two-hundred-pound ram versus a two-pound 'possum. Whatever the case, sheep don't worry much about cars.

They should, however, worry about roundup time.

You see, in addition to being raised for wool, sheep are the main course in a number of traditional Scottish dishes. Their flesh is consumed, in vast quantities, as steak, stew, soup, roasts, and meat pie.

But sheep-eating Scots don't stop there. These people are frugal by nature. They let absolutely nothing go to waste. That's why they also eat haggis and black pudding.

Haggis consists of chopped-up sheep guts, including the lungs, liver, and heart. This goo is mixed with oatmeal, spices, and suet. Then the whole mess is stuffed into a sheep's stomach and boiled for three hours. It is served with mashed turnips and potatoes.

The "black" in black pudding comes from sheep's blood. Lots of it. Plus oatmeal (clearly, these people have never heard of Quaker's maple and brown sugar), coarse wheat, suet, onion, and spices. It is eaten at breakfast, presumably under the belief that if you can keep it down, the rest of your day is a coast.

I sampled both. I survived. I credit this success to (1) an iron stomach, (2) copious intake of native elixirs, and (3) growing up southern around souse, chitlins, potted meat, and Spam.

The taste and texture of haggis reminded me of Thanksgiving dressing, albeit dark as chocolate. The taste and texture of black pudding reminded me of hell week during fraternity initiation.

But the experience did answer the question of why Scottish men wear kilts.

If you can tamp down a meal of haggis, black pudding, and a quart of Scotch whiskey, and show no ill effects, you can wear anything you dang well choose. Hey, ain't *nobody* gonna give you any lip.

Good Credit

Keep your low-carb diet, your low-fat diet, your grapefruit diet, your tofu diet.

I'm on the new "credits diet," and I'm so joyous I may eat a triple bacon cheeseburger to celebrate.

This diet works like those emission allowances that are all the rage in the energy business. Surely you've read about them.

The federal government doles out a certain number of credits to each utility company. Sorta like starting a game of Monopoly with a fistful of play money. But instead of advancing to Park Place or Boardwalk or some other fictive location, the utility actually gets to use these credits to buy its way out of pollution purgatory.

Let's say the Klean Aire Electrical Company runs an immaculate power plant with state-of-the-art equipment. As a result, its pollution emissions are rather low. At the same time, the Black Lung Electrical Company hasn't gotten with the program. It fouls the air with nasty cooties.

How can Black Lung get out of this mess? By going into debt for fancy new equipment? Of course not, you dolt! Black Lung simply buys emission credits from Klean Aire and keeps right on smogging away.

I was leery of emission credits when they were first announced. To me, these things make about as much sense as letting corporate crooks pay a fifty-thousand-dollar fine after they've bilked their employees and stockholders out of five hundred million dollars—oh, yes, and saying they're sorry and promising never to do it again, all the while lounging in their Caribbean villa, counting the pile that's left over. And then I realized—hey! that's *precisely* what corporate crooks get to do! So I figure if we can "credit" our way out of corporate corruption and air pollution, the same theory should apply to dieting.

Let's say you've just ordered an entrée off the low-fat, heart-healthy section of the menu. Excellent choice. That's a smart way to start trimming excess pounds.

But then the waiter asks, "Will you be having dessert today? Our special is a hot double-fudge macadamia nut brownie, topped with our special whipped cream."

Uh-oh. Big trouble. We're talking heart attack on a plate here.

Do you just say no and stick to your diet? Or do you indulge your taste buds and to heck with good health?

The correct answer is neither.

You whip out your cell phone and dial your buddy, Hank, who is built along the lines of a beanpole.

"You got a few diet credits for sale?" you ask.

"Certainly," he replies. "Even better, they're on special all week. Two for the price of one."

"Great, Hank. Put me down for fifteen-hundred calories and seventy fat grams. Just charge 'em to my account."

See how wonderful this new plan is? Can't you imagine the joy of stuffing your gut with sugary-sweet, high-calorie, fat-laden goodies and then erasing the evidence on credit? Don't you want to sign up immediately?

Me, too. This kind of innovative thinking has made America a true heavyweight in world affairs.

The S-Words

If you turned on your computer some morning and discovered your e-mail files littered with dozens of unsolicited ads for canned meat, would this be considered Spam spam? If so, would the resulting indigestion best be treated with Tums, Rolaids, or a sledgehammer through the screen?

OK, so those are lame attempts at humor. Forgive me. It's just that I've been thinking a lot lately about spamoid substances: both Spam (the Hormel meat with a capital *S*) and spam (lowercase *s*, the computerized crap that grows inside your monitor like mold in a petri dish.)

No matter what your dietary opinions on grease happen to be, uppercase Spam is definitely the lesser of two evils. While I can think of approximately 217,846 foods I prefer over it, this meaty mystery has rescued more than a few campfire meals for me.

Trust your Uncle Cholesterol: A predawn breakfast of fried eggs, fried 'taters, and fried Spam is just the sort of fuel a fellow needs before plunging into an icy trout stream.

It keeps you buoyant, for one thing. What's more, all those fat globules surging through your circulatory system will help plug any wounds inflicted by errant hooks, slippery rocks, angry wasps, and other outdoor hazards.

Jackie Langley sent me a marketing secret kept hidden for eons by sellers of tomatoes, beans, okra, potatoes, cucumbers, and other produce. It was revealed to Langley when she asked her grocer if his veggies were homegrown.

"All depends," the merchant replied, "on where home is."

That guy oughta forget food products. His true calling is politics.

Teasing about Spam has become a national pastime, but weep not for the folks at Hormel. They laugh all the way to the bank, thank you. Let comedians make jokes and nutritionists make faces; the fact remains that millions of cans of Spam find their way into shopping carts every year.

In fact, Spam festivals are popular all over the country. The big daddy is the three-day Waikiki Spam Jam, which draws thousands of fans to Honolulu. It features a variety of events, including a Spam-eating contest as well as the construction of the "world's longest Spam musubi"—a 132-foot block of rice topped with Spam and wrapped with seaweed.

On the local front, the Tennessee Valley Fair always sponsors some sort of Spam recipe contest. The competition occasionally is for kids, proving conclusively you're never too young to start clogging those arteries.

So much for good Spam. The rotten, evil, may-it-be-plagued-with-boils-and-locusts spam is the stuff that irritates Internet users universally.

The other day in Washington, the Federal Trade Commission opened hearings on how to regulate this miserable beast. Seems the ever-growing volume of insidious electronic junk mail has gotten so far out of hand, it is threatening to destroy all forms of mass marketing.

I wouldn't shed many tears if all unwanted, unsolicited swill vanished from by mailbox and my computer. But I know that's never going to happen. The best we can hope for is that regulators will find a way to separate legitimate mass mailers from the scoundrels and then give the no-good spammers the same treatment afforded a thick slice of Spam.

Five to six minutes on each side in a sizzling skillet would do for starters.

Chapter 5
Estrogen and Testosterone

Listen up, male friends. We better hope one of those so-called battles of the sexes never erupts in our midst. Because if it does, we're doomed. Compared with women, we're the proverbial ninety-eight-pound weakling.

You are welcome to disagree. But first, let me ask a couple of questions.

But how many Bubba Joes, Billy Rays, and Tom Bobs are ready to endure "monthly problems" until age fifty? And how many are willing to carry an ever-growing baby inside their guts for nine months, putting up with the accompanying legs cramps, nausea, incontinence, lack of energy, hemorrhoids, mood swings, and backaches—and then deliver Junior out a certain orifice? I rest my case, thank you.

Let me state, unequivocally and for the record, that I am a strong supporter of *all* peoples' rights—male, female, and those who haven't quite made up their minds about the matter. There oughta be equal pay for equal work, equal laws, equal regulations, equal access, and equal opportunities, straight down the line.

That being said, there are some humorous, albeit significant, differences between the he's and the she's, which I occasionally convey in my columns. For instance, I recall reading several reports about the bedroom practices of men versus women. Bedroom practices of the sleeping variety, I hasten to point out.

In a 1997 survey, people said they were spending more time than ever in the bedroom. But they still weren't getting enough sleep. The study didn't delve into great detail about certain assumed activities conducted behind closed doors. Instead, it was geared toward finding out what else goes on.

In a word, everything.

The study was based on interviews with one thousand men and women. It was conducted by a New Jersey group called Bruskin-Goldring Research on behalf of the Company Store, a Wisconsin firm that specializes in bedroom furnishings. People were asked, "Other than for sleeping and engaging in romantic acts of extreme friendship, what do you use your bedroom for?"

Looking over the replies, I realized I was totally out of touch with humanity, male or female.

Eleven percent said this is where they eat. Eat entire meals, mind you.

I can understand nibbling a snack while flat on your back watching Monday night football or Jay Leno (by the way, 46 percent listed TV viewing as a favorite bedroom pastime). But for the life of me, I can't imagine attacking roast beef, mashed potatoes, green beans, and a salad.

While you're chewing on that one—Hey! Be careful with that gravy! Those are good sheets!—consider that 10 percent picked the bedroom as their favorite place to entertain guests.

Huh? For a teenage slumber party, perhaps. But surely not for a typical social gathering with three or four other couples. Unless, of course, you throw some really kinky parties.

Other nontraditional activities listed by respondents included playing musical instruments, hosting weekly poker games, operating a model train, running a tax preparation service, and—let me stress I am not making any of this up—playing table tennis and conducting séances.

You think it's aggravating when your spouse keeps you awake by clicking the TV remote? Imagine trying to sleep while Ping-Pong balls are bouncing about and ghosts are floating through the walls.

There was another statistic I didn't understand. It was the one about getting dressed. Only 75 percent of respondents said they put on their clothes in the bedroom—leaving me to assume the other 25 percent performed this necessary chore in the kitchen, dining room, den, hall closet, or garage.

How much cumulative time are we talking about in the bedroom, in addition to sleeping? About one entire month per year. However, since respondents reported only an average of seven hours of snoozeburg per night, most said they felt sleep-deprived.

All I can say is, this is their parents' fault. Years earlier, if they had spanked more butts instead of sending naughty children to their bedrooms, none of this would have happened.

In 1998, the same company released even more bedroom statistics—this time involving whether people sleep on their right side, left side, stomach, or back.

It turned out that 30 percent of men and 36 percent of women snooze on the right, while 21 percent of men and 30 percent of women prefer the left. What's more, 24 percent of men sleep on their back, compared to 13 percent of women, while 14 percent of men sleep on their stomach, as opposed to 13 percent of women.

That was perplexing enough in and of itself. But there was yet another category of answers. Six percent of the men and 2 percent of the women said they sleep in "other" positions.

What "other" positions, pray tell? On their heads? Standing up? Hanging by their knees in the broom closet?

Oddly enough, I had never wondered about what position I sleep in—until then. I've spent roughly one-third of my life in the sack, and not once have I slipped into the percale thinking, Hmmm, right or left, stomach or back? It's always a rather spontaneous activity. I just close my peepers and start snoring.

Now I'm not sure.

If I happen to flop over on my right side, am I doing so because it feels comfortable? Or because that's what the majority of men do? Am I expressing my own individuality, or am I merely following the crowd?

And while I was mulling those possibilities, the scare factor really kicked in. That's because of yet another bedroom survey conducted by S. C. Johnson and Son Inc., of Racine, Wisconsin.

These people put normal bedroom lint and dust under a microscope and discovered it contains up to thirteen thousand mites per ounce! I quote directly from the company's report: "One of the most common indoor allergens is produced by the house dust mite, a microscopic creature that feeds on shed human skin. No matter how clean a home is, dust mites are there."

Gross. While I'm lying there between the sheets, wondering whether to turn to the right or left, bazillions of teeny-tiny cooties are chewing away below me and my spouse. Not conducive to snoozing, any way you cut it.

I'm sure these high-brow bedroom researchers mean well, and I'm certain there are valid uses for their information. But there's got to be a better place than Wisconsin for it.

Indeed, I can think of two right off the bat. When it comes to swarms of annoying vermin, male and female, who flip-flop, in bed or otherwise, Washington and Hollywood simply can't be beat.

Lathering Up

I'll be danged. Seems I've been exercising rigorously, on a daily basis, for more than forty years and never knew it.

OK, so maybe these haven't been strictly "daily" calisthenics, as in precisely every twenty-four hours. Because of the nature of the program, I don't participate every single, solitary day. Sometimes I even skip entire weekends. Nonetheless, I've been associated with this regimen of physical fitness since JFK was president.

It's called shaving.

I made this startling discovery not long ago while reading a news story about skin care products for men. That's a phenomenon in and of itself.

I'm a product of the soap-and-water generation. It's a common trait among us baby boomers of the male persuasion. Like our World War II–era fathers, we are not into gels, creams, moisturizers, rejuvenators, and other frou-frou unguents. Frankly, I've never spent a lot of time worrying about the intimate care of my skin—other than applying a Band-Aid or getting stitched, depending on the severity of a cut.

Features editor Susan Alexander passed along a press release touting the hot new "over-belt" look for men. Seems a pot gut is now considered classy in fashion circles other than sumo wrestling.

"Some of our sexiest male celebrities are sporting a beer belly," it said.

Nice to know I'm a trendsetter.

Well, maybe in winter. During cold weather, I do indulge in an occasional squirt of hand lotion because my hands are continually exposed to duck decoy strings and frozen fishing line.

But when I saw the headline "Men's Skin Has Its Own Special Needs," my curiosity was piqued. Once I started reading, I was hooked.

The piece began by discussing "exfoliation."

I've always been intrigued by that word. It seems naughty, exotic, like some sort of venial sin usually addressed in fire-breathing sermons.

I can just imagine a gym teacher from the '50s talking to young boys about the dangers of self-exfoliation and warning them they might go blind.

Or maybe overhearing whispers around the office coffee pot: "Did you get the word about Bob and Regina? They supposedly snuck off to Gatlinburg last weekend and spent the whole time exfoliating."

But I kept reading and discovered, to my shock, that I exfoliate myownself every time I shave!

The story quoted a dermatologist, Dr. David Orentreich, who is affiliated with Mount Sinai Hospital in New York. He said this daily routine tends to make men's facial skin smoother than women's as they age. Then I came across the part about shaving and physical exercise.

Estrogen and Testosterone

According to the doc, the act of whisker scraping—with its obligatory neck-stretching and chin-jutting and corner-of-mouth twitching—gives a man's facial muscles a regular workout. Couple that with the benefits of daily exfoliation, and it's easy to see why a man's skin tends to weather better than a woman's over time.

You better believe I logged this important information in my aging noggin. I intend to quote it in great detail the next time my wife suggests I start exercising.

"I'll have you know I'm working out extensively on the Gillette plan," I'll tell her. "It's the latest rage among health experts."

She might be so impressed, she'll suggest we sneak off somewhere and exfoliate.

Men Are All Wet

A reader named Brenda Heiskell telephoned recently with a burning question.

"Why do men spit all the time?" she wanted to know. "They spit everywhere—in parking lots, at the drive-thru, on the street. *Everywhere!*"

Naturally, my immediate response was, "And your point is?" That's because, as a guy, I understand this phenomenon completely.

But then I thought, Hold the rush to judgment, fellow. As a person of the female persuasion, Brenda wouldn't have a clue about this situation any more than men would have a personal understanding of certain functions every twenty-eight days. You need to explain.

And so I will.

Brenda, the reason men spit is best summed up in three simple words: Because we can.

This is not an acquired talent. It automatically comes with the gender. Male babies emerge from the womb knowing how to spit. They spend the rest of their lives putting this knowledge into practice. Individuals may have to perfect certain skills as they age, but from a he-infant's first drool to a he-geezer's last dramatic *pa-too-ie,* men flat-out own the expectoration market.

I'm no biologist, but I think this has something to do with muscular development of male mouths and lips. It's one of the basic physiological differences between Us and Them. Besides some notable exceptions farther to the south, I mean.

Whatever the case, men are able to make a smooth, fluid, almost athletic exercise out of spitting.

Sadly, it just doesn't work that way for women. If a woman is forced to spit—like maybe a bug flies in her mouth while she's jogging or she's in the dentist's chair and has to get rid of a mouthful of polishing gel—the poor thing acts and sounds like she's choking on a fish bone.

'Tis such a pity, too. Women don't know what they're missing by not being able to orally irrigate the premises.

Spitting is *soooo* relaxing. It relieves *soooo* much tension. It's *soooo* addictive.

As a former tobacco chewer, I speak with great authority in this matter.

I smoked for a decade, then took up chewing to help wean myself of cigarettes. Chewed leaf tobacco by the virtual handful, nearly every waking hour, until all those mouth, gum, and throat cancer ads finally sunk in and I bid adieu to the Evil Weed for keeps.

Which do you think was harder to abandon—smoking after ten years or chewing after three?

Wasn't even close. Still isn't.

I haven't put cigarettes to my lips since 1979. I have long since quit thinking about them. Indeed, cigarette smoke irritates my eyes and nose. I can't stand to be around it. Conversely, I haven't chewed since 1982—and every time I'm downwind of a freshly opened pack of Beechnut, I nearly go into the DTs.

Addictions notwithstanding, spitting is fun for men. It is gender-based recreation. Doesn't matter if it is fueled with 'bakker juice or ol'-time saliva.

Men spit when they're at ease; they spit when they're on edge.

They spit when they're happy; they spit when they're sad.

They spit in July when the sun is shining; they spit in February when snow is piling up in drifts.

The way we figure it, if God hadn't wanted men to spit, he wouldn't have given us the ability to clear our throats in public.

Soap and Water

You know the world is at relative peace when the most riveting news from opposite sides of the globe involves bathroom hygiene.

A few days ago, the American Society for Microbiology reported that millions of people don't wash their hands after visiting the john. That revelation came on the heels of a decree by the Singapore government, announcing fines for miscreants who don't flush after using public restroom facilities.

The microbiology project involved more than six thousand men and women in five U.S. cities. Researchers hung out in public restrooms, acting like they were combing their hair, while unwitting subjects did their business. Then the researchers—who surely have perfectly coiffed locks by now—wrote down whether or not a subsequent hand washing occurred.

According to this report, New Yorkers led the ranks of the unwashed. Chicagoans were among the cleanest.

The researchers also said the lowest rate of washing occurred among men (no mention of women) at an Atlanta Braves baseball game. Only 46 percent took time for soap and water before heading back to the stands.

Inconclusive finding, I say. Much more study is needed.

Was this Beer Night at the Braves games, perhaps? Was it a close game? And at what point during the event was data gathered? Inquiring minds want to know these things.

You pump any baseball fan, Braves or otherwise, full of suds and send him duck-walking toward the porcelain midway through the ninth inning of a tie game, and I'll guarantee the chances of a thorough scrubbing are remote indeed.

Inquiring minds also want to know more about the crackdown in Singapore, where nonflushers can be fined $106 on first offense and up to $700 for repeat arrests.

Fines? In Singapore? I thought the favored mode of punishment for a misdemeanor in Singapore was a cane across the back and butt. Seems to me this would be the perfect time and place for it.

Then again, this could be self-defeating. If I walked into a public john and saw some sinister-looking cop standing there, idly tapping his palm with a whipping cane while waiting on customers, I'd probably become involuntarily moist before I even touched the stall door, let alone the flush handle.

No matter what the method of punishment, though, Singapore's approach will likely get more attention from the masses than the potty law enacted a few years ago by the Tennessee General Assembly.

Surely you remember. It's the law requiring us to Wash Our Hands! for good health after performing Numbers One and/or Two. The exclamation mark is a critical part of this regulation. It must be included—and it must be at least six inches tall. That's the official law of the land.

Of course, based on Tennesseans' typical reaction to ridiculous legislation—not to mention the unsavory condition of most public restrooms—I can only assume a lot of folks have told politicians Where to Shove! this law.

Something related to Where the Sun Don't Shine! if I'm not mistaken.

A Very Hairy Study

My wife does most of the grocery shopping around our house. Typically, my contribution to this effort is limited to rummaging through the sacks when she returns and loudly complaining that she didn't buy enough high-fat, high-priced, high-calorie junk food.

But ever since I saw the results of a survey on shopping habits, I'm going to start paying a lot closer attention to the items Mary Ann brings home. Particularly shampoo.

I've never thought much about the brand, or volume, of shampoo my wife purchases. Perhaps I oughta prowl around under the bathroom sink where she keeps these things stored. No telling what sort of exotic secrets might be revealed.

The survey I'm talking about was conducted among seven hundred women from various parts of the country. It was taken by the Integer Group, a Colorado company specializing in marketing and promotions. It posed a bunch of hypothetical questions, most of which I filed in the ho-hum category.

But one of them immediately caught my eye. It wanted to know in what section of a grocery store women felt the most sensual. (We pause for a moment so crude, cheap, sophomoric, and socially unacceptable comments, including mine, can be aired in private. During this respite, you are encouraged to throw an old *Animal House* video into the VCR and fast forward to zucchini's finest hour—that hilariously hormonal scene where Otter runs into Dean Wormer's wife in the produce department.)

So where is this grocery erogenous zone? This sizzling section of a supermarket where women veritably wilt in the throes of passion? This aisle that should be banned from public view lest minors be tainted and Baptists be embarrassed by bumping into each other?

The shampoo department, that's where. It was the number one response in Integer's report.

Shampoo ranked at 14 percent, followed (11 percent) by the candy counter. A distant third (7 percent) was fruits and veggies—leading me to think *Animal House* may have helped shape both the sexual and dietary tones of an entire generation.

Perhaps this revelation shouldn't be too startling to anyone who has seen one of those scintillating Herbal Essence commercials on TV. But old habits tend to die hard. Oafish men still mired in the "candy's dandy–likker's quicker" mindset should at least be thinking along the lines of "Pantene's mean" or "Prell's swell."

In case you're wondering, the least-sensual area of the grocery store for women was the cash register. Only two-tenths of 1 percent of respondents listed it.

For obvious reasons, the survey didn't quiz men about supermarket sensuality. Speaking as a veteran person of the male persuasion, I'm here to tell you that men experience sensual thoughts thousands of times a day, in the grocery store or otherwise. But roughly 99 percent of these thoughts involve nakedness, real or imagined. We could just as easily have a sensual thought at the Piggly Wiggly as we could at Wal-Mart, Home Depot, or a traffic light down the street.

There was one more question in this survey that highlighted yet another stark difference between men and women. It posed this weird situation: If you couldn't have one million dollars, what would you take instead?

A plurality of women (15 percent) said they would settle for a week on an island with actor Brad Pitt. Obviously, these women had just purchased several cases of Herbal Essence shampoo.

In second place, 9 percent said they would be OK with a helmet worn by the late Dale Earnhardt. That's certainly understandable, given NASCAR's broad appeal across gender lines.

In third, 5 percent said they would accept a week-long tour with the rock group 'N Sync.

But while reading down the list of replies, I immediately realized why men hadn't been included. It's because they would've given a much more simple, direct answer.

If a researcher asked any man what he would take instead of one million dollars, the response would be instantaneous and voluminous: "Two million dollars."

Skirting the Issue

Currently showing at the Metropolitan Institute of Art is an exhibit called "Bravehearts: Men in Skirts." As the name implies, it features the latest in dress wear for men—with the emphasis on "dress."

In press reports from New York, associate curator Andrew Bolton insists this show is not a masculinity-versus-femininity sort of thing.

I agree totally. If a man wants to wrap a skirt around his loins, more power to him. Men have been wearing skirts for centuries, and in many cultures they still do. While visiting Scotland, I saw quite a number of men wearing kilts—men who looked like they could start, actively participate in, and finish a fight in any Cocke County beer joint.

But I don't plan on joining their ranks because I'm convinced pants are a much more practical, comfortable option than skirts.

Have I tried both? No. I don't need to. All I have to do is look around at the she-people and realize how many of them are wearing pants these days.

Women aren't dumb. They know from years of experience that britches make more sense than any other type of lower-body garment. That's especially true in winter.

Pants are warmer. They keep drafts at bay. They don't get caught in car doors. Thanks to the wonders of elastic, they are more forgiving of bulbous guts. And if you want to cross your legs while seated, you don't have to worry about exposing the epicenter to curious onlookers.

Women had to suffer through years of discrimination before they could wear pants freely. When my wife and I were undergraduates at the University of Tennessee in the mid-1960s—technically, she was my girlfriend at the time—there was an honest-to-gosh temperature dress code for women. Mary Ann, a certified she-person, remembers it was seventeen degrees.

No joke. Seventeen and below, female students could wear pants to class. Above that magic mark, skirts were required.

Like a lot of silly social rules Back Then, this was blindly accepted as rote. It has long since been abandoned.

"Who decided when and where it was officially seventeen degrees?" I asked her the other day. "What if, say, you lived in Kodak and your thermometer registered sixteen, so you put on pants, but by the time you drove into Knoxville, a thermometer on the Strip was showing nineteen? Did you have to go home and change?"

Mary Ann couldn't remember for sure. However, she did note that I was always eager to assist anytime a change of clothes was in order.

Yeah, I sorta remember it that way myself.

Yesterday's Old Man

I finally joined millions of TV viewers and tuned into the new hit program *Queer Eye for the Straight Guy.* Unlike the masses, though, I won't have to worry about setting aside a block of time to watch this show in the future.

Oh, it's entertaining enough. There were some funny lines and interesting scenes in the episode I caught last week. I certainly understand the attraction. But throughout the program, the same questions kept rolling through my head: Why change? What's wrong with being happy the way you are right now?

Queer Eye is not necessarily about sexual orientation. Instead, it's a show about fashion, style, dining, and other matters of alleged fine living. The show's gay hosts—the Fab Five, as they call themselves—undertake to "remake" a straight guy. They shine him up and suit him out, buffing the rough spots and reshaping him into Today's New Man.

Fine—if you want to be Today's New Man.

But surely I'm not the only straight guy out there who is perfectly content in his role as Yesterday's Old Man.

The latest e-mail circulating through my office described the differences in how women and men approach romance.

The essentials needed by women ran over three pages and included such key elements as "Console, cuddle, nuzzle, smooch, minister to, forgive, support, humor, placate, spoil, embrace, linger, dazzle, pamper, serenade, charm, and enchant."

Men's requirements were summed up in three words: "Show up naked."

Those of us of the YOM persuasion don't need someone to tell us how to dress. We can wrap an entire wardrobe around plain blue jeans and khakis, golf shirts and button-downs, blue blazers, loafers, and sneakers, and feel comfortably equipped for 98 percent of sartorial demands. Quite frankly, we don't worry that the clothes on our backs were starting to fade from fashion around the time Bushy the Elder was campaigning for the White House.

And speaking of backs, bushy or otherwise, we don't worry about that, either. We restrict body hair removal to our faces. And we follow the procedure with a splash of Old Spice, not some frou-frou designer unguent.

When it comes to cuisine, we YOMs favor just about anything that's naught haute. We can eat healthily or foolishly as the situation dictates. We enjoy the taste of broccoli just as much as beef, and we are not hesitant to cook using basic ingredients. We ascribe to the "ain't-no-bad-beer" theory but also have a distinct fondness for iced tea, buttermilk, and cola.

In matters of interior design, four key words apply: function, comfort, leather, wood. Enough said.

Please understand. This is not a question of dirt and crude versus clean and civil. There are certain "rights" and "wrongs" that come with the YOM territory, and every brethren understands the perimeters. Membership in this fraternity does not preclude a working knowledge of soap, shampoo, toothpaste, and deodorant. YOMs are able to pick up after themselves. They use "ma'am" and "sir" with regularity. But at the same time, they can uncork a coarse joke, unsheathe a visceral noise, or deliver a good cussing if and when necessary.

The young straight guy on the program I watched is not likely to evolve into a YOM. In point of fact, he was a pure-T slob. He lived amid squalor. The Fab Five completely transformed his apartment, threshold to patio.

Doesn't matter. I predict he will backslide quickly. You can dress a hog in a tuxedo, but he still wants to roll in the mud.

The Cutting Edge

While rummaging through some old editions of the *News Sentinel,* I discovered two errors I made on Thursday, September 4, 2003.

That day, I was writing—or ranting, as the case may be—about shaving. I was angry because razor companies were locked in a race to see who could make follicle-felling history by stacking the most blades into one unit.

"Schick has just unveiled a razor with four blades," I wrote. "This, presumably, is in response to Gillette's three-bladed monster (the Mach3). Any day now, I suspect Bic will come out with a five-bladed jumbo." My goofs were contained in the last sentence—and if you've been following whisker news, you know what I mean.

Bic didn't come out with the next mega-bladed razor. Gillette did.

I was wrong about the number of cutting edges, too. Gillette's newest razor doesn't contain five blades. It has six.

The company's Fusion razor apparently contains enough metal to set off an airport alarm from three miles away. The first five blades are stacked, one atop another, on one side of the device. This is for attacking stubble across the vast, open prairie of the face and neck. A smaller, sixth blade is affixed on the back of the pivoting head. It's designed for trimming around ears and under the nose.

After being oh-so-wrong before, I'm hesitant to predict what's next.

Eight blades? A dozen? The Schick Centurion, perhaps, with a full one hundred blades piled high?

If this nuttiness continues, the business end of your average safety razor will soon take on the size, shape, and weight of a cinder block. No more holding the handle between two fingers, either. The shaving experience is going to be more like working out with extra-large barbells.

In addition to expanding the dimensions of razors, the blade race is going to change the size and shape of bathrooms and luggage. No more "shaving shelf" in your average American medicine cabinet. Indeed, the entire cabinet will be rezoned for razor storage—meaning that aspirin, aftershave, toothbrush, toothpaste, dental floss, and other former residents will have to find new digs.

And you can forget about the discreet "shaving kit" that used to be tucked into the corner of any suitcase. These new razors will be luggage in and of themselves. Maybe they'll even come equipped with wheels and a trailer hitch for easy towing behind your car, truck, or SUV.

But far be it from me to complain. "Bigger is better" is the motto of American business. Only a godless, unpatriotic leftist with terrorist leanings would refuse to belly up to the sales counter and join this commercial evolution.

What's more, I suspect this is only the beginning of change. In the not-too-distant future, we'll probably be buying shaving cream in fifty-five-gallon drums.

I'm headed to my banker right now to start the loan application process.

Backyard Biology

My wife called me to the kitchen window the other day. She pointed toward some trees leading into the woods out back.

"Isn't that cute!" Mary Ann exclaimed.

"What?" I replied. "A bunch of oak trees? Cute?"

She rolled her eyes. "No, the chipmunk."

I looked again. Sure enough, there stood a chipmunk on its back legs, surveying the scene. Content no danger was near, it dropped to the ground and continued feeding on leftover seeds and acorns. It stood again, cheek pouches full. Then it scampered into a crevice at the base of one of the oaks—its hideout, I suppose.

"Those are precious little animals," Mary Ann said.

"Wrong," I answered. "They're lucky little animals with a good public relations manager."

Mary Ann gave me one of her patented looks. "What on earth are you talking about?"

"Chipmunks are lucky to have fuzzy tails and little stripes down their backs. Otherwise, they'd be called mice. People don't say 'ooh' and 'aah' when they see mice. They scream and set a mouse trap or put out poison. People don't buy expensive wildlife prints of mice, either. With the exception of Mickey and Minnie, people don't spend any money at all on mice, except to kill them."

I was on my soap box by now. Mary Ann was wishing she'd never brought the subject up.

"If you stop to think about it, the world is full of inconsistencies like that. Take carp. They're a fish, just like bass or trout. But carp don't have a fancy PR consultant like bass and trout do.

"Right now, Sevier County is proudly unveiling the spanking-new Bass Pro Shop. It's a huge investment by the Bass Pro Shop people, one that will ultimately bring millions of dollars in sales tax revenues to Sevier County. But you couldn't find a community in the United States that wants a store like Carp Pro Shop."

I paused to take a breath. Mary Ann took the opportunity to duck out of the room.

"Just look at our yard," I hollered as she vacated. "What do you see in places? Chickweed, that's what—the curse of homeowners everywhere.

"Chickweed is green, just like fescue. It covers bare spots faster than fescue. With some good spin doctoring, chickweed could be the crown jewel of the lawn. But no. Fools like me spend tons of money to kill chickweed, then we turn right around and spend tons more money for seed, fertilizer, and water trying to grow fescue. It doesn't make any sense."

I heard the door to the breezeway close quietly and saw Mary Ann walk into the back yard, shaking her head and throwing her hands in the air. She tends to react that way when I launch into a philosophical discussion.

"Think about the food we eat," I philosophized, aloud and alone. "As long as human beings are going to eat meat, there's no reason why it can't come from horses. Can't be any worse for us than beef or pork.

"Farmers raise cows and pigs for slaughter, and most people never think twice about it. But if a farmer raised horses for the meat market, it would create a world of stink. TV crews would show up at the place. So would angry picketers carrying signs. The poor farmer would probably be forced to move."

I looked out the window again. Mary Ann was standing in the shade of a stately oak tree—hmmm, have you ever heard anyone describe a dorky mimosa tree as "stately"?—watching the cute little chipmunk, which had reemerged and was feeding again. She seemed to be enjoying herself immensely.

I picked up the newspaper. The first story that caught my eye was about a bunch of wanna-be politicians running for Congress. And I couldn't help but think that all of them are doing their best to convince voters they're a chipmunk-bass-trout-fescue-horse-oak candidate, while everyone else in the race is mouse-carp-chickweed-cow-pig-mimosa material.

"It's a crazy world," I said to myself.

Had she been there, Mary Ann surely would've agreed.

Crown Prince of Aggravated Stupidity

Once again, my title as Crown Prince of Aggravated Stupidity (Home Repairs Division) is safe.

I was worried for a while. It's been at least five months since I committed one of my trademark blunders with pliers, hammer, paintbrush, or screwdriver. I was afraid some bumbling upstart might attempt to pry the title from my grasp.

But after the events of last week? Not a chance. I'm good for another long reign.

Of course, it would be tough to top the stunt I pulled several years ago, the one that vaulted me to be the championship in the first place. This occurred the day I was trying to mount a heavy wall fixture in our downstairs bathroom.

Knowing it would be too weighty for dry wall, I decided to drill a hole and install one of those molly bolts, or whatever they're called, to carry the load.

I was plowing away with an electric drill when the bit struck something. Hmmm, I thought; must've hit a nail. I'll just drill through it. So I soused down harder.

Fortunately, my drill bit was duller than a four-hour lecture. Whatever I'd struck simply would not yield.

Hmmm, I thought for a second time; the only thing on the other side of this wall is a closet. What could be in there that's so stubborn?

I put down the drill, walked to the adjacent room, opened the closet door, and dang near fainted. What I'd been attempting to bore through turned out to be the switch box supplying electricity for that side of the house. Had my drill bit been sharp enough, I would've shorted out half the valley and vaporized myself, all in 0.0002 second.

Last week's idiocy wasn't as potentially fatal—unless you factor in the effects of elevated blood pressure. I was simply attempting to find the end of a drain-pipe I'd buried in the back yard several years ago.

Yes, of course, I originally knew where it was. Had even marked it with a ring of rocks. But we had some earthwork done last spring and the rocks got covered. No sweat. I knew roughly where the pipe was hiding. What I didn't know was how far off "roughly" can be.

First, I probed with a length of rebar. Nothing.

Feeling the need for heavier artillery, I switched to a shovel. Nothing.

Then a mattock. Still nothing.

My wife, who enjoys challenges like this, cheerfully suggested I dig shallower, deeper, and in different directions. I did, not so cheerfully teaching her new versions of old words in the process.

Eventually, I excavated a trench eleven feet long, six inches wide, and eighteen inches deep. Rest assured the lengths I just quoted are accurate; I measured them to see. Still no pipe.

I stomped away from the trench and, in frustration, sunk the mattock deeply into the lawn.

Thunk!

Turns out I'd been oh-so-close at the very start. But not finding the pipe initially, I had, I swear, dug that %@$@ trench in the wrong &*$# direction!

The end of the pipe has now been cleaned out and marked for the future. I accomplished this by driving a piece of rebar into the ground, leaving *juuust* enough exposed so I can discover it later with my lawnmower.

When you're the Crown Prince of Aggravated Stupidity (Home Repairs Division), nothing is left to chance.

Eternal Thermostat Wars

You're a college student from Ohio. The only thing you want for Christmas is a trip to Florida during spring break. Your folks cough up the cash, and all you can think about during January and February is the glorious time you're going to have in the fun and sun. The magic moment finally arrives. You pile into a beat-up car with five friends, burn up the interstates to Panama City, and then freeze your collective buns off as a record-breaking cold wave blankets the Southeast.

Or let's say you're an investments broker from the Big Apple who tires of the rat race and sells everything you own to buy a fruit farm in south Georgia.

This is your first year in business, and you're already counting the profits. That is, until the thermometer goes south, taking your entire budding crop with it in one icy swoop.

Or perhaps you're a ski resort operator about to shut down for the year. Thinking you can milk a few extra weeks out of the season, you sink a bundle into an extended schedule—only to see the mercury soar into the eighties.

No matter where you turn in the South, the weather interrupts many plans. Nearly every winter and summer, we set new records for lows, highs, precipitation, and drought—and then break 'em all over again the next time around. The National Weather Service might just as well throw its books away.

How come? Turn to the Weather Channel or listen to a meteorologist and you'll hear ten thousand stupid theories. The jet stream races south, forcing an arctic high into an abnormal trough, which is then offset by a massive surge of tropical breezes racing up from the Gulf of Mexico, blah-blah-doppler-radar-blah-blah-El Niño-blah-blah-tornadic-activity-blah-blah-blah.

Nonsense. I happen to have the real skinny on this insanity: It's because Old Man Winter and Mother Nature keep fighting over the thermostat. Has to be. That's the only explanation possible for such screwed-up conditions.

Just ask any husband or wife. They know all too well about the constant bickering, and subsequent adjusting, that takes place over temperature control.

I don't know who starts these wars. Nobody does. But I do know things rock along just peachy until either Mother Nature decides it's too cold ("It's freezing in this place!") or Old Man Winter figures it's too hot ("For cryin' out loud, woman, the sweat's rolling off me like a waterfall!"). One of them sneaks into the living room and adjusts the thermostat, and we mortals have hell to pay.

One day, the mercury bottoms out at seven below. As our blood coagulates into red Jello, it hits eighty-one. Steam forms in our arteries, just in time to see it fall back to twelve above. On and on this battle rages, killing flowers and infuriating humans by the jillions.

With all the politicians we have in Washington, you'd think someone would draft legislation requiring Mother Nature and Old Man Winter to stay on opposite sides of the room and keep their cotton-pickin' mitts off the danged thermostat!

Whoever engineers a bill like this into law gets my vote for president.

Estrogen and Testosterone

Happy Motoring

I'm either the most unobservant driver in the history of the internal combustion engine or else the women of East Tennessee are totally out of step with their sisters around the country.

Why? Because, in a lifetime of traveling up and down the highways of this region, I have never seen a woman engaged in sex while she's driving.

I came across this realization while perusing the results of a national survey—about hair, of all things. The survey was conducted for Salon Selectives, a brand of women's shampoo and conditioner. One thousand women, ages eighteen through twenty-eight, were interviewed about their hair care habits. Many of their answers were quite surprising.

For instance, 65 percent said they often brushed and combed their hair while behind the wheel.

Talk about a surprise! Only 65 percent? Based on my observations, I would think at least 99 percent of women—and a good 75 percent of men—wait till they're barreling down the interstate before they start coiffing their locks. I don't know what these people do in front of the bathroom mirror before they leave home. Probably hold their hands in front of themselves, like they're gripping a steering wheel, and practice shifting gears. Maybe they even make "vaaarooom" sounds for realism.

Another surprise was that 72 percent said they talk on a cell phone while driving.

You mean to tell me that on any given day on any given roadway, only 28 percent of women—and an equal number of men—are *not* yakking away while they swerve from one lane to another? Highly doubtful.

Indeed, the only believable statistic I saw was the revelation that 92 percent of these women said they eat while motoring. That sounds about right—and also explains why God invented the drive-through window. Or was that Ronald McDonald? Maybe Dave Thomas? I forget.

But the statistic that caused my eyeballs to bug out was the one about having sex. According to this study, which I am not making up, 38 percent of these women said that's what they do while driving.

Unfortunately, the researchers did not elaborate. Which is a real shame because all manner of questions immediately popped into my head. Such as:

Were any of these participants—the sexors or the sexees—professional contortionists?

To quote a certain Mister Former President, did any of them want to know what the definition of "having sex" is?

Does this explain why women have become such huge fans of NASCAR?

Is a winding road more conducive than a straightaway for this type of activity?

When engaged in the Deed while flying down the highway, is it considered "safe sex" as long as you're wearing a seat belt?

When shopping for a car for this purpose, is it permissible to take it for a test spin?

Do you get better mileage before, during, or after?

All of those are important queries that could benefit from a thorough, uh, "fleshing out" session. But the most obvious question that flashed through my mind when I read that 38 percent of women engage in sex while driving was: *Where the hell were they when I was a teenager?*

One Mrs. Is Quite Sufficient

Right off the top of my head, I can think of two excellent reasons why it's better to be Sam Venable than Warren Jeffs.

First, there's not a one-hundred-thousand-dollar reward for my arrest. Recently the FBI elevated Jeffs to its Ten Most Wanted Fugitives list, doubling the bounty from fifty Gs.

Jeffs is wanted on numerous charges related to his leadership of the Fundamentalist Church of Jesus Christ of Latter-day Saints. This is a different group than the mainstream Mormon church, which renounced polygamy more than a century ago.

The second, and far more important, reason is because I don't have fifty wives. That's a rough estimate of the number of Mrs. Warren Jeffses in the Utah-Arizona region. Nobody knows for certain because Jeffs's sect is exceedingly close-mouthed. In addition, the guy has been on the lam for years. For all I know, he could have sixty or seventy wives by now. Maybe even more.

Holy hair curlers!

I've had the same wife since April 2, 1969. It's been a delightful experience. I recommend it highly and hope the arrangement continues for decades.

But even if I could clone my dear bride, I wouldn't want fifty versions of her. Let alone fifty completely different women. One wife is precisely the right amount. And even without discussing the matter with Mary Ann, I'm certain she would share the same opinion about having more than one Sam Venable in her midst.

I'm pretty good at remembering statistics—birthday, wedding anniversary, holidays—vital to matrimonial harmony. At least I am with a single set of dates. But multiply that by fifty, and there aren't enough scratch pads, notebooks, Palm

Estrogen and Testosterone

Pilots, and BlackBerries under the sun to keep track. It'd be easier to memorize a single day's listing of the New York Stock Exchange.

That's the least of it.

Consider the fact we've all got idiosyncrasies. You know, quirks that take a bit of getting used to if people expect to live under the same roof in peace.

Our relationship is no exception. And in the spirit of full disclosure, let me stress that the dozens of quirks Mary Ann has had to overcome far exceed the handful thrown my way.

But strictly, ahem, for discussion purposes, Mary Ann is a neatnik. I, on the contrary, am a junknik. I've never seen a pile of papers or clothing than couldn't be improved with the addition of seven new layers.

Seen on the back of a white sports car whizzing along Interstate 40 in west Knoxville: "Happiness Is Being Single" on the left bumper sticker and "I (Heart) My Wife" on the right bumper sticker.

This guy is either a divorce lawyer, a marital counselor, or a high-ranking employee of the federal government.

Over the years, I've trained myself to be a caring husband, sensitive to my spouse's needs. These days, I'm content to max out my junk piles with a mere six additional layers.

But can you imagine the terror of trying to strike this same happy medium with fifty separate wives?

Junk aside, what about household duties? Favorite foods? Vacation sites? Cars, clothes, and a thousand other areas of potential discord? And don't even think about PMS times fifty.

Trust your Uncle Ring Finger: One is a wonderful number.

Seeing Red

I take great exception to a study I recently saw in the professional journal *Annals of Family Medicine*. This study concerned anger in men. Specifically, how it can result in bodily harm to the "angeree."

Researchers interviewed injured men and asked them to describe their emotions leading up to the time of their accident. They found that men who were angry had up to a 50 percent greater chance of being hurt than those of the calm-collected ilk.

Stands to reason. As mommas preach to their sons, a hothead rarely makes cool decisions.

But based on my personal experience, it's not anger before the fact that leads to my injuries. Instead, it's post-injury anger. I'm always mad at myself for being such a bumbling numbskull that I got hurt in the first place.

The Case of the Sheathless Hatchet serves to illustrate.

This is a famous chapter of medical lunacy in the Venable tribe. I still carry a scar on my right ring finger as proof. And it all came about because I was attempting to be safe.

A friend's wife had given him a hatchet one Christmas. It was the sharpest hatchet in the history of tools. But, alas, it didn't come with a sheath.

No problem. I had another friend who was skilled at leatherwork. I made arrangements with Hatchet Buddy and Leather Buddy and agreed to be the go-between. On the appointed day, I was leaving my house, hatchet in hand. I was holding it oh-so-safely, blade pointed outward.

But just as I stepped out the garage door, I dropped some papers I was carrying in the other hand. Instinctively, I reached down to grab them—and dang near took off a finger.

Note the words "dang near." They're important.

You see, by some miracle, I didn't run a finger across the blade. Not even a nick.

"You fool!" I scolded myself. "You know better than that! You could've sliced off your hand reaching out that way! Don't *ever* do that while carrying a sharp object!"

"You're right," I replied to myself. "I won't do it again."

You know what happened next, of course.

Yes, I redropped those same papers about four seconds later. Yes, I instinctively reached out to grab them. Yes, I cut myself to the bone.

Arrrgh! Words cannot describe the hostility.

I stormed back into the house, blood cascading down my arm.

Mary Ann screamed, "What happened?" But all I could do was stand there and curse about what a blithering, lame-brained, idiotic cretin I was.

Then I looked at her, blinked once or twice and, as calmly as I'm sitting here right now, said, "Aw, hell; now I'm gonna faint." And wilted to my knees.

Apparently the sudden rage, combined with hemorrhaging from the laceration, dropped my blood pressure abruptly. Fortunately, I was OK in a few moments—and then it was off to get the hateful gash repaired.

I can't speak for other men and other situations. But for my money, the time for white-hot anger is after a stupid accident, not before.

Plus, it gives your family something to tease you about twenty-five years later.

Fast Moves

As an All-American, itch-scratching person of the male persuasion, I enjoy watching machinery work.

Part of being a guy is having natural curiosity about mechanical functions. Women, as a rule, don't share this trait.

If Jane and John are walking past a construction site and there's a large, noisy excavator, backhoe, bulldozer, or rock crusher in operation, each of their reactions are predictable.

Jane will scrunch up her face and say, "Gosh, that's loud."

John won't hear Jane's complaint—for two reasons.

First, the equipment is, in fact, painfully loud, but John's ears have long since been damaged by country music, shotgun fire, and other components of Y-chromosome living. Second, he's too busy thinking to himself, Cool!

Even if his butt has never settled behind the controls of a D-9 Cat, John enjoys watching the action. He will stand there, mind blissfully locked in neutral, as mountains of dirt are shoved around and boulders are pounded into pebbles.

It's for this reason that I'm quite impressed by the newly upgraded Cray XT3 supercomputer at Oak Ridge National Laboratory.

"High speed" doesn't do justice to this computer. It can perform fifty-four teraflops. In layman's terms, that's fifty-four trillion (with a *t*) mathematical calculations per second.

I have no need whatsoever for a gizmo like the Cray XT3. Never will. Not even in a trillion years. Inside my desk drawer is a Casio SL-300Ve pocket calculator, which I purchased from Walgreens a few years ago for $3.98. All I ever ask it to do is add, subtract, multiply, and divide. Nonetheless, this digitized whiz-bang has more functions than my feeble mind can comprehend.

I have no need for one of those monster wood-chipping devices, either. You know, the kind utility companies use for clearing power line rights-of-way. But it's still fun to watch workers fling tree limbs into one end and see clouds of fiber fly out the other.

In the same vein, the guy in me would love to watch the Cray XT3 run through its paces, even on a minuscule level. I'd like to take a year's worth of credit card receipts, pay stubs, canceled checks, and other papers, chuck everything into Cray's maw, and have my completed IRS 1040 tax form spit out the other end before I could blink.

This would give me more time for listening to country music, firing my shotgun, and watching heavy equipment at construction sites.

Briefly Bewildered

The blond-haired woman was driving her husband's car and noticed it was low on fuel. So she wheeled into a nearby gas station–deli, pulled alongside the closest pump, and stopped.

However, when she stepped out and reached for the pump handle—oops— she remembered the fuel tank cap on her husband's car is on the opposite side of hers. Meaning she was parked on the wrong side of the pump for easy fuel dispensing.

No big deal. We all have our routines interrupted by momentary confusion.

The blond-haired woman set the pump handle onto the pavement, climbed back into her husband's car, and drove around to the exact opposite side of the car. Meaning that when she stepped out and reached for the pump handle— oops II—the fuel tank cap was still on the wrong side.

The blond-haired woman then pulled straight forward, changed gears, and backed straight up. Meaning that when she stepped out of the car and reached for the pump handle—yes, she had set it on the pavement again during the repositioning process—the fuel tank cap was *still* on the wrong side of the car. Oops III.

Anyone else would have grown frustrated by now. Anyone else would have said heck with it and driven off, or else dragged the gas hose all the way around to the opposite side of the car. But this blond-haired woman is not anyone else. She becomes a woman on a mission at times like this. It had become a matter of principle.

Before she set the pump handle down on the pavement once more—there wasn't a lot of traffic at the gas station–deli; thus she had time for serious debate and repositioning—the blond-haired woman took the time to carefully think her way through the process. She decided to pull out, hook a wide circle in the parking lot, and reenter on the appropriate side.

Voilà! When she stepped out of the car this time, the fuel tank cap and the pump handle were perfectly aligned.

Just as she began dispensing gasoline, the blond-haired woman glanced toward the deli side of the station. At the window sat two male diners.

Obviously, they had been watching the entire affair, for they were still as statues, mouths agape, as if they couldn't believe the spectacle unfolding twenty feet before their eyes. One held a fork frozen halfway to his mouth.

The blond-haired woman reacted accordingly. She gave them a broad smile and a hearty double-thumbs up. Everyone erupted in laughter.

Before you fire off an angry letter calling me a sexist pig and berating me for poking blond-joke fun at an innocent person who made a common mental

Estrogen and Testosterone

error, please be advised that the only reason I know about this little scene is because the blond-haired woman told it on herself.

She's the same blond-haired woman who inherited her dad's ability to see the humor in nearly every situation, even when—*especially when!*—the joke's on her. In fact, she couldn't wait to telephone her dad and spill her tee-heeing, hoo-haaing guts about being such a bonehead.

Trust her dad as he types these words: With this blond-haired angel, it's happy Father's Day all year long.

Chapter 6

Reasons for Seasons All Year Long

Newspaper columnists dearly love holidays. *Any* holidays—from New Year's Day to the following Christmas, plus all the birthdays, anniversaries, routine celebrations, and special occasions in between.

Why? Because each one of these observations gives us a cheap column. Which likely explains why we keep a dog-eared copy of *Chases's Calendar of Events* at ready reach. You never know when a National Tap Dance Day, National No Talk Day, Hand Tools Safety Week, International Pickle Week, Book Blitz Month, or other unique celebration might pop up and need mentioning.

We're a lot like politicians in this regard. I've yet to discover the office holder who's not quick with the pen when it comes to signing fancily worded documents, dripping with paragraph after paragraph of "whereas" and "wherefore" and "Thus I hereby proclaim (insert your favorite official holiday here)." Once I actually kept a tabulation of all this public-relations paperwork and discovered a typical year contains more than twelve months, fifty-two weeks, and 365 days.

A *whole* lot more.

The governor proclaimed 40 "official" months, 130 "official" weeks, and 83 "official" days in Tennessee—including such gems as National Soup Month, Citizens Saving Bank and Trust Company Day, Baton Twirling Week, Stop and Smell the Flowers Day, Metric Week, and Pets Are Wonderful Month.

During the same period, Knoxville's mayor proclaimed 20 "official" months, 77 "official" weeks, and 148 "official" days. Such as Gourd Seed Day, Stamp

Collecting Month, Friends of the British Isles Day (lotta Brits in Knoxville, you know), Bike Month, Medical Laboratory Week, and Operating Room Nurses Day.

Once the ink starts flowing, it's difficult to stop. The mayor had signed Cathedral Quartet Gospel Singing Day not once, but six times in June. Two months later, he issued three separate proclamations for Firefighters Appreciation Week. Maybe the city had a contract with the Paper Mate pen company.

Can't say that I blame these dedicated public servants. They're simply doing a job. They issue reams of "official" proclamations for voters. Columnists write "official" holiday articles for readers. Same difference.

No matter how many times a certain holiday has been written about, there's always some new twist, some different angle to explore. Why, you could fill a book with them! I know this for an iron-clad fact because I authored such a volume in 1991. *One Size Fits All and Other Holiday Myths* contains one hundred essays spanning the four seasons, starting with Groundhog Day on February 2 and concluding with Martin Luther King Jr. Day the following January.

One of my favorite holiday writing tricks is to spoof and satirize. As you will see in some of the entries in this chapter, I love to subject traditional celebrations to the official writs, procedures, and regulations which—for better or for worse—have become part and parcel of American life.

In October 2004, I accidentally stumbled on a heretofore untapped vein of Halloween lore. It was all because our metro desk was being bombarded with telephone calls from anxious parents wanting to know when their kiddies were supposed to go trick-or-treating.

Huh? Even in these idiotic times, how hard can that be to figure out? Children are supposed to go trick-or-treating on October 31—like they have for eons.

"But October 31 falls on Sunday," the parents continued to protest. "Doesn't that mean they should celebrate on Saturday night?"

It wasn't just here in the Bible-belted Southland, either. Across the nation, several cities—Quincy, Washington, among them—officially moved Halloween to Saturday that year.

My reaction? At first, I screamed something like, "Arrrggh! Get a life, people! There aren't any rules about something as mundane as this! Worry about something that matters! Sheesh! Sunday Halloweens were no big deal when I was growing up! Why should they be a problem now?"

And you know what? I was wrong. I made this startling discovery while cranking through microfilmed editions of October newspapers during my childhood. In my day, Sunday Halloweens never occurred. Not once. Ever. I'm serious.

If you don't believe me, grab a perpetual calendar and see for yourself. That's what I did, and it took me weeks to polish off the last crumbs of humble pie.

I was born in 1947. During my childhood, the only years October 31 fell on Sunday were 1948 and 1954. Clearly, 1948 was out of the question for candy grubbing, as I was still wearing diapers. I have no recollection of Halloween '54, but at age seven I'm sure I was judged too young to be turned loose for house-to-house shakedowns. Remember, Halloween back then was a virtual afterthought on the holiday calendar. It was nothing like the mega-million-dollar, glitzy-costumed festival Americans celebrate today.

Because of the way leap years figured into the plan, it wasn't until October 31, 1965, that a Sunday Halloween rolled around again. I was a student at the University of Tennessee by then, and can assure you the only treats and costumes I was interested in were (1) female and (2) skimpy.

So what was my recommendation about when to unleash trick-or-treating rug rats on the neighborhood? I told readers to let 'em go whenever they dang-well pleased—Saturday night or Sunday night or both. It didn't matter either way. Just as long as they split the goodies with Mom and Dad, of course.

Do the talented people who come up with hilarious lines for greeting cards make their own cards for family and friends instead of buying them at the store?

Also, do you suppose they hang out in card shops three or four weeks ahead of every holiday, browsing through the competition and muttering angrily under their breath, "Dammit! Why didn't I think of a catchy verse like that?"

Another interesting tidbit of holiday research occurred one year shortly before Independence Day festivities kicked off. Admittedly, this wasn't a wholly original thought with me. A reader had called to complain that the U.S. flag she had just purchased for her Fourth of July barbecue was made in China. Her tip started me on a search of Knoxville businesses that ultimately proved Uncle Sam's import empire was alive and well and manning the cash register.

My first stop was Walgreens. Just inside the store I found a holiday display featuring sheets of U.S. flag stickers ($1.99), a flag necklace ($4.99), a flag wall hanging painted on slate ($5.99), and a plaque proclaiming "God Bless America" ($5.99).

Down the highway at Dollar General, a sign on the front door said the store would be open July Fourth for my shopping convenience. Inside was another assortment of patriotic merchandise. I was especially taken by the flag pin featuring red, white, and blue "jewels." A bargain for a buck, for sure.

At Kroger, I found a vast array of those car window flags that have been so popular since our national day of infamy, September 11, 2001. They were only $3.99 each.

I then swung by Dollar Tree and struck the mother lode. Holy holidays! I could all but hear a drum-and-fife corps playing in the background. The first thing that caught my eye was the nineteen-foot flag banner with the words "Show Your Support" on the package. There were single flags, too, including a plastic version powered by batteries.

Also, I found iron-on stickers featuring a heart-shaped design with "USA" in the center. Plus a four-pack of car flags, along with instructions to "Show Your Colors."

What if shoppers were buying these items as presents? No problem. Among the Dollar Tree's array of fancy gift bags was one featuring a pair of teddy bears holding red, white, and blue geegaws. The capitalized word FREEDOM was printed along the bottom. I'm not certain of the connection between stuffed animals and liberty, but it's the thought that counts.

Across the highway at the Bi-Lo grocery store, I found more car flags. One in particular, proclaiming "Proud to Be American" on the label, came complete with suction cups. What's more, the store was offering a three-by-five-foot U.S. flag for $7.99. Or $6.99 with the store's bonus card.

It was here that I also discovered some rather unusual July Fourth merchandise. This was the "Protectors of Freedom" airplane set, presented by the Heritage Mint Collection. These wooden, hand-painted replicas, mostly of World War II–era aircraft, were billed as a "salute to American flying heroes." Prices ranged from $12.99 ($9.99 with card) to $24.99 ($19.99 with card).

All in all, here was a diverse assortment of red-blooded, chest-swelling finery, perfect for celebrating this All-American holiday. Yet despite their variety, they had one stark thing in common.

Not a single one of them was made in the U.S.A.

Mostly, they came from China. A close second was Taiwan. Mexico was represented here and there, too, as was Canada.

There is nothing illegal about importing and selling American icons. Indeed, this is capitalism in action. But it did strike me as odd that the very items designed to tug at the heart were not produced in the heartland.

Reckon the Founding Fathers would be offended? Or would they be lining up to buy a piece of the action?

Don't let me spoil your fun, I advised readers. Have a happy Fourth. Eat a hot dog, light a firecracker, say the Pledge of Allegiance, and check your portfolio. In the meantime, let's all sing along:

> *It's a sad ol' flag, it's an imported flag.*
> *On some far distant shore it was made.*
> *It's an emblem of, what once was loved,*

'Fore we sold our souls to world trade.
Every heart keeps track of accounts in the black.
Too bad if some jobs were not saved.
Let's pay the CEO even more,
And don't let that stock price sag!

One Year to Live

We're not a full week into the new year, and already an important seasonal icon has disappeared faster than wilted Christmas trees and hastily made resolutions.

Where, pray tell, is Baby New Year?

You know who I'm talking about—that cute little dimple-faced tyke, clad in diapers and draped with a banner, who made his grand entry to the tune of "Auld Lang Syne." For twenty-four hours, this fellow was everywhere. I noticed in the comic pages a couple of days ago that four separate panels were devoted to his arrival. But ever since, he's been missing.

This comes as no surprise, of course. Baby New Year goes AWOL every January, shortly after being introduced. He never shows back up until twelve months later. By then, he isn't a baby. He's grumpy, bent-backed Old Man Year, complete with a long white beard, a scythe, and one foot squarely in the grave.

I want to know what happens to the guy between January 2 and December 30.

Anybody who makes the transition from infancy to codgerdom in 365 days (or 366 in the case of leap years) surely knows how to cram two tons' worth of experiences into four cubic inches of space. Yet he never shares this secret with us. Nor does he give us a glimpse of his physical changes along the way.

Nobody even knows where he goes. Maybe to some remote Caribbean beach. Maybe to a hideaway lodge in Alaska. Maybe he's part of the federal witness protection program. Whatever the case, the boy, quickly growing into manhood, spends the rest of the year engaged in riotous living, gorging on rich foods, drinking the bar dry, staying up 'til all hours, and carousing with women of low moral character. How else do you explain his haggard condition on December 31?

What do you suppose he looks like around, say, January 25 or February 18? Reckon he's been potty-trained by then? Into the Terrible Twos? Or has he already advanced to kindergarten?

And what's the score by, say, March 10 or April 13? Will he have hit puberty? Face broken out in zits? Voice cracking? A patch of peach fuzz on his chin?

This is pure speculation on my part, but I figure the guy has to be in high school or college by May 24, at the least. You'd think we could at least see a photo of him at the prom.

By the beginning of summer, he probably has embarked upon a career. Does he sell insurance? Drive a truck? Drill holes in teeth? Preach sermons? Exterminate termites? Lay brick? Own a restaurant?

Chances are he's also gotten married by now—to whom I haven't the foggiest notion.

Hmm. Which brings up another point: How come Baby New Year is always male? Isn't the sex ratio between boy babies and girl babies roughly fifty-fifty? If so, why don't girls ever get selected for this honor?

In any case, do we hear so much as a peep from him? Get an update on job changes? Hear about a new car? Receive a snapshot of the wife and youngins on summer vacation?

Nope. Not one word. Nor do we have an inkling about what's going on in his life as his children leave the nest and he and the missus chart a path toward retirement.

He may get a gold wristwatch, but we get nothing. Our only reminder that he ever existed comes at the end of December, when he shuffles in, bag-eyed and stoop-shouldered, and hands the reins over to the newest Baby New Year.

Weep not for the kid, however. Even though he has only fifty-two weeks to kick up his heels, his job's a breeze compared to animals with a similar life expectancy.

No, I'm not talking about professional football coaches. I'm talking about 'possums. According to *The World Almanac*, your average 'possum lives the exact amount of time as Baby New Year. During those twelve months, the poor 'possum has to grub around in garbage cans for leftover food, get chased by dogs over hill and dale, and outmaneuver pickup trucks on country roads.

I'm quite content with my lot in life. I have no desire to change. Neither the 'possum's job nor Baby New Year's job interests me in the slightest.

But if forced to choose between the two, I'd put on that diaper and let the good times roll for as long as they could.

A Valentine's Day Dilemma

Let me see if I've got this straight. There's this Cupid character who makes his living by drawing a bow and hurling an arrow through peoples' hearts, right? And that causes them to fall madly in love with each other instead of flopping around like headless chickens and bleeding to death, right?

Fine. I'm not one to argue with tradition. But what if Cupid flinches just as he releases the arrow, causing it to pierce, say, the shin, elbow, foot, or arm instead of the heart? Would the misfire then manifest itself in some form of fetish?

Also, why hasn't an aggressive district attorney taken the guy aside and explained the legal consequences of assault with a deadly weapon?

Then again, why don't sporting goods retailers take advantage of the occasion by running specials on compound bows, crossbows, arrows, quivers, and other archery equipment?

Oh, and has anyone checked with the Tennessee Wildlife Resources Agency to see if an archery license is required for this type of activity? Is there a daily or seasonal bag limit? Since license fees vary by state of residence, what if Cupid draws his bow in Tennessee but doinks a target in Alabama, Georgia, or Mississippi? Should the highest or lowest fee apply?

Frankly, those are the least of my worries right now. The more pressing issue is what to get my wife for Valentine's. No doubt a lot of other men are in the same boat. We're not in the complete panic stage yet because V-Day doesn't arrive for another seventy-two hours. There's plenty of time to ponder.

One thing's for certain, though. On this Valentine's Day, or others in the future, I'm not going to give Mary Ann diamonds of the personal variety.

Exceedingly personal diamonds, I reiterate. The type of diamonds that come from the heart of the giver. Also the giver's liver. Plus his lungs, bones, teeth, arms, legs, and stomach.

If the previous paragraph causes you to scratch your head—hmm, the head's also an important part of this equation, now that I think about it—you obviously haven't heard about a Chicago company called LifeGem.

What these folks do is turn human remains into diamonds.

I'm serious. Cross my heart and hope to—oops, poor choice of phraseology. Suffice to say I'm not making this up. The company already has produced diamonds from animal remains and one cadaver. It expects fifty orders per year.

Based on what I have read, the process more or less picks up where cremation leaves off. You take Uncle Ferd and roast him at scorching temperatures, then squeeze him under tremendous weight and—voilà!—Uncle Ferd becomes a sparkling diamond.

A company spokesman explained the process as "kind of a natural progression," since humans and diamonds are mostly carbon to begin with. All that's required to change one form to the other is heat and pressure.

For how much dough? Depends on what size diamond you intend to become. A quarter-carat runs $1,995. Three-quarters of a carat will cost you—or your heirs—around $9,995.

To the best of my knowledge, my name's not on Saint Peter's list for immediate admissions. Whenever that time comes, however, I have no intention to wind up as a fancy bauble on my wife's night stand or dresser. For several reasons.

First, there's the heat. I break out in a sweat whenever the mercury pushes above eighty degrees. Can you image how I'd react at six thousand? Lord, have mercy! There's not enough iced tea in this state to cool me off.

Second, there's the pressure required. The story didn't elaborate, but if my memories from high school chemistry class aren't extraordinarily foggy, we're talking mega tons per square inch. Ouch. And to think I break out in hives on a crowded elevator. About the time I'd turn around and yell something witty like, "Hey! Your armpit's in my face!" it would suddenly dawn on me that my armpit *is* my face.

Besides, this process requires at least a month inside a giant press. I can't hold my breath that long.

The cost is another limiting factor. No way a man of my earthly XL dimensions is going to be whittled down to a quarter-carat. The Hope diamond is more like it. Or maybe something along the lines of a beach ball. Perhaps even a watermelon, if I happen to croak when I'm in super-tubbo mode.

However I turned out, this surely would blow my meager life insurance payout to smithereens. I suspect Mary Ann will have more pressing financial matters than whether or not she can bail me out of hock.

Then there's this business of having to be cut into shape. Truly scary. You see, I'm the world's biggest klutz around sharp instruments as it is. I have a lifetime of scars to prove it. No doubt this trait from Sam Venable, human, would carry over to Sam Venable, diamond.

Meaning that the first time a jeweler tried to cut or polish me, I'd bust into a jillion pieces. Instead of a rare, gorgeous gemstone, I'd wind up as a mundane industrial drill bit. Not my idea of a peachy way to spend eternity.

Thanks, but no thanks. If Mary Ann gets diamonds after I've been carted off to the bone yard, she's going to have to do it the old-fashioned way.

By marrying up.

Painfully Powerful Puckering

Note to travelers who may visit Saint Paul, Minnesota, or the South Pacific's Trobriand Islands the next few days: Avoid kissing at all costs.

Yes, I know Valentine's Day is nigh. I know you're thinking thoughts of love, if not outright lust. I know you feel inclined to pucker up. Fine. Abundant kissing is permissible, even expected, this time of year. (Then again, nothin' says lovin' like cooties by the dozen. Given the flu epidemic, you might want to opt for nothing more intimate than a sincere handshake, followed by mutual hand washing with plenty of hot water and antiseptic soap.)

But if you do insist on lip locking, steer clear of the two locations I mentioned earlier. Especially if you're not into extreme pain.

I bring you this warning after perusing some neckin' news that has left me drenched with sweat. Cold, fearful sweat.

Last year in Saint Paul, for instance, police charged a forty-three-year-old woman with assault after she planted the world's most horrendous French kiss on the mouth of her forty-seven-year-old boyfriend. One thing led to another and, in the height (or depth, as the case may be) of this oral ecstasy, she wound up biting off—*aaaiiieee!*—an inch and a half of the guy's tongue.

It gets worse.

I quote directly from a dispatch filed by the *Minneapolis–Saint Paul Star Tribune:* "After talking with the couple, officers returned to her home to look for the tongue, but they couldn't find it. Police said the woman might have swallowed it."

Is this what the song "Love Hurts" is all about? If so, count me out.

But if you think the Minnesota situation is bad, check out the physics of South Pacific smooching. According to Michael Christian, author of *The Art of Kissing,* participants in the Trobriand Islands are quite aggressive.

"The custom begins with gentle hugging and kissing," he writes, "progresses on to biting each other's lips until bleeding commences *(aaaaiiieee! II)* and concludes with biting off the eyelash tips."

Here are a few other kissing tidbits, courtesy of Christian's manual: The Japanese have always been extremely shy about kissing; public puckering is taboo. The longest kiss in movie history (three minutes, five seconds) was between Jane Wyman and Regis Tommey in the film *You're in the Army Now.* Most people incorrectly assume the term "French kiss" originated in France. Actually, it was coined by the English in the 1920s as a slur on French culture.

Did you ever stop to think that dashing through the snow in a one-horse open sleigh, going o'er the fields and laughing all the way, ha-ha-ha, would be an excellent way to catch hypothermia, plow through a barbed-wire fence, be charged with trespassing, and get patted down for drugs?

The French call it "tongue kiss" or "soul kissing." In Belgium, you are expected to bestow three kisses on anyone ten years your senior.

How did I learned about Michael Christian's "kissology" book? Through a news release from a toothpaste company, that's how. Far be it from me to stoop so low as to shill for these corporate giants by revealing the brand name. But if you want to get *close up* with the partner of your choice on Valentine's Day, be my guest.

Just keep your tongue-lopping, lip-gnashing, eyelash-trimming mouth away from mine.

Bunch of Blarney

Memo to: Saint Patrick.

From: Hiram Horsehinney, director, U.S. Department of Meaningless, Erratic, Dumb Details and Lunatic Excesses (MEDDLE).

Dear Saint Patrick:

We here at MEDDLE have received your application for a special holiday on March 17. Unfortunately, we must deny this request for the following reasons:

- It celebrates the unauthorized removal of snakes from Ireland. This is in direct violation of all environmental regulations, here and abroad. Snakes, venomous or otherwise, are a valuable part of an ecosystem. To remove them for any reason would be an environmental travesty. In fact, we are assigning agents from the Office of Endangered Species to look at this request for possible prosecution.

- This holiday would honor the residents and descendants from a single country. Namely, Ireland. This is in direct violation of the government's intent to promote cultural diversity. We here at MEDDLE do not think one nationality should receive preference over another. In fact, we are assigning agents from the Office of Civil Rights to look at this request for possible prosecution.

- The majority of people who would take part in these festivities are Catholic. This is in violation of the government's adherence to the principle of separation between church and state. In fact, we are assigning agents from the Office of Equal Opportunity to investigate this request for possible prosecution.

- This holiday, as proposed, would encourage the consumption of massive amounts of alcoholic beverages with resultant brawling, in violation of the government's stance against substance abuse and civil unrest. In fact, we are assigning agents from the Bureau of Alcohol, Tobacco and Firearms and the FBI to study this request for possible prosecution.

- This celebration, as outlined, would contribute to the misuse and over-application of green paint on sidewalks and streets throughout America. Not only would this demonstrate an unfair preference against other colors in the spectrum, but it would result in water pollution from run-off in cities where temporary pigments are used. In fact, we are assigning agents from the Environmental Protection Agency for possible prosecution.

In conclusion, even though MEDDLE cannot approve your request for a so-called Saint Patrick's Day, we do appreciate your interest and thank you for filling out 4,376 pages of permit applications.

Which brings up one more point.

The official permit process calls for the use of only 4,375 sheets of paper. Thus we have no recourse but to assign representatives in charge of the Reduction in Paperwork Act to study your request for possible prosecution.

Thank you for letting us here at MEDDLE be of service.

A Half-baked Idea

In honor of the vernal equinox, I seriously considered doing everything fifty-fifty for twenty-four hours.

As any science teacher will tell you, the vernal equinox is the one day every spring when the sun sits directly above the equator. Day and night are equal everywhere on the planet. Thus I proposed to coordinate all my activities on a half-and-half basis so as not to upset Mother Earth's delicate balance.

At first, the concept seemed oh-so-simple. I was going to clock myself in the shower and spend the same amount of time washing as drying. Then I was going to shave my whiskers and brush my teeth with alternate hands. Being right-handed, I figured facial safety could best be accomplished with strictly right-hand razoring. My choppers could tolerate left-hand brushing, as awkward as it might feel.

Beyond that, though, the experiment fell to pieces. The more I delved into the details, the more I realized how frustrating it would be.

Consider clothing. Should I wear pants but no shirt or a shirt but no pants? Or was I supposed to get out the scissors, cut both articles of clothing down the middle, wear a complete outfit on one side, and be buck naked on the other? Any way I sliced it, the results weren't going to be pretty.

Fifty-fifty food was another guaranteed failure in the making.

I could've eaten half of my usual breakfast and followed up with a lunch and a half. But then supper would have thrown a monkey wrench into the entire equation. It was a situation of too much math, too little munching.

Well, yes, I could have taken all meals on a normal schedule, provided I shoveled the loads to my mouth, in rotating fashion, with right-hand fork, left-hand spoon, right-hand spoon, left-hand fork. I wasn't overly worried about stabbing myself in the jaw with a left-hand fork, but the whole process sounded too much like one of those weird West Coast diets.

On the bright side, driving to and from the office wouldn't have presented much of a problem. For more than three decades, I've been coming into town on Interstate 40–East and going out on the parallel Interstate 40–West. That's about as fifty-fifty as you can cut anything of an automotive nature.

But what if I encountered a traffic snarl somewhere along the line? Silly me. *Of course* I would have encountered a traffic snarl! This is Knoxville, for Pete's sake. So how could I make certain my delays, eastbound and westbound, would be of the exact duration? If I happened to be off by even a few minutes either way, it would've thrown my finely tuned vernal equinox timetable completely out of kilter.

But then I hit the coup de grace: Work.

This was uncharted territory, for sure. A veritable wilderness. How could I possibly spend 50 percent of an entire day working when I've never hit more than a 10 percent lick at the top of my vocational game?

Far better to put this ill-advised scheme back on the shelf and not think about it again until the autumnal equinox. If then.

Poor Peter Cottontail

Easter morning at the Holiday Diner. The place is all but deserted. Just Gladys, the waitress, is at the counter. The door swings open. In stumbles Peter Cottontail.

"Wha'smatter, Pete?" asks Gladys, reaching for a cup and the coffee pot. "You look beat. Have a rough night?"

"The worst," Peter replies. "They get harder each year." He notices the coffee headed his way.

"No joe for me, Gladys. The last thing I need in my body right now is caffeine. I just want a quick drink, then I'm headed home to crash."

"What about a nice warm cup of hot chocolate?" the waitress says. "That oughta relax—"

"NO!" Peter blurts. "No hot chocolate! In fact, I want *nothing* made out of chocolate right now!"

"OK, how 'bout a shot of carrot juice?"

"Now you're talkin.' I'll take it on the rocks."

Gladys pours a tall glass of liquid carrot and sets it on the counter. Peter downs it in a swallow.

"Hit me again," he says. "And throw in some radishes. I need strength."

Gladys brings a second drink. This time, she sits down next to Peter and looks directly into the eyes of her old friend.

"The Easter bunny business is really gettin' to you, isn't it? You gettin' too old for the job?"

"I don't think so," Peter answers. "I still enjoy hoppin' down the bunny trail every Easter day. It's just that things—"

"It's the lawsuit, right?"

"Naaa," says Peter, wiping carrot juice from his whiskers. "The American Dental Association filed that thing just for the public relations value. They know

Reasons for Seasons All Year Long

I'll beat 'em. I got enough lawyers to drill those dentists into the ground. It'll serve them right for tampering with the time-honored tradition of filling children with sugary sweets on Easter morning."

"Is it, uh, the ears?" she probed, tentatively.

Gladys knew this was a sensitive subject with Peter. For years, it had been a seasonal joke around the Holiday Diner. Everybody teased him about biting the ears off chocolate bunnies.

"Naaa, not that either," Peter answered with a shrug of his shoulders. "After awhile, you just have to resign yourself to the fact that bunny ears are an easy target. Leno, Letterman, the Hallmark card folks—everybody takes a dig this time of year. I've gotten used to it."

"Well, what's the trouble then?" Gladys pondered aloud. "You and I have always been close, Pete. Tell me straight, pal. Why so blue?"

"It's the inequity of the work load between me and ol' fatso," he replied, gesturing across the Holiday Diner to a picture of Santa Claus.

"Talk about a guy who's got it made! Sure, he has a grueling schedule on Christmas Eve, but look at the support staff he has at his disposal. First, he's got all those elves to crank out the toys. And he's got eight reindeer to pull the sleigh.

"What have I got? Nothin'! It's just me. I'm the one who has to order all those thousands of tons of candy. I'm the one who has to go hippity-hoppity down the bunny trail. I'm the one who has to fill all those baskets. And then I've got to limp back home to an empty nest. Claus has a wife waiting for him with his slippers and his pipe and—"

The Holiday Diner door swung open just then. In strolled handsome, trim Tom Turkey.

"I'm starving!" he announced with a loud gobble. "Feels like I haven't eaten in a week. Give me one of everything on the menu, Gladys. For some reason, everybody keeps tellin' me to gain weight. They say I need to be good and plump by Thanksgiving Day. I don't know what all the excitement is about. I'm just gonna keep on eating like there's no tomorrow!"

A contented smile crossed Peter Cottontail's face. There was a noticeable spring in his step as he rose from the counter. He paid his bill and gave Gladys a peck on the cheek.

"Maybe life ain't so bad after all," he spoke as he reached for the doorknob. "See you this time next year, kiddo."

"Be sure to duck when you go through the door," Gladys teased. "You know how easily your ears break off."

Quite an Education

I'm entering a few numbers into the calculator. Feel free to watch. The figures I'm working with are dollar amounts. There's nothing official about them. But they're probably in the ballpark of "average."

I'm trying to find out how much it costs to go to a high school prom these days.

Again, I stress this is little more than a partially aimed shot in the dark. I only made spot inquiries to businesses. Prices, high and low, ran all over the map. Even on a meager budget, any high schooler who isn't worried about useless status symbols and fancy designer names can have a grand ol' time at the ball. Conversely, if a student has been saving for months—or, more likely, daddy is loaded—the sky's the limit. With that in mind, let's see what's available.

There's the prom dress, of course. From what I gathered talking to shops, this is a one-time garment for most girls. After the prom, they either sell it or send it to the attic for nostalgia purposes. At any standard department store, expect to plunk down $160–$200.

If you go to a more stylish outlet, the tab rises. At Bella Boutique, the average price range was $275–$300. At Classy Lady, the average quote I got was $160, but by the time you figured in shoes, jewelry, nails and hair, the total edged upward of $450–$600.

The guys get off easier as far as clothes are concerned. Mitchell's Formalwear said your basic tuxedo rents for $50, plus another $10 for shoes. Ah, but there are added costs for the lads.

Dinner, for instance—and we ain't talkin' the drive-through with Ronald McDonald. The consensus I got was $60–$75. "It stays pretty low," one proprietor confided, "because they can't order wine."

Then toss in a prom ticket, $25 on average.

Plus a prom picture. Jeffrey Photo says $15–$18 is the norm.

Plus prom flowers. Petree's Florist said to allow about $15 for the corsage, another $5 for the boutonniere.

And if you really want to take your date out in style, there's always the limousine. South Fork Limos quoted me an average rate of $60–$65 per hour, with a five-hour minimum.

Outside of the prom itself, there's the class ring, plus invitations. Balfour sells rings from $79.95 all the way to $600, but said $200 is a happy medium. As for invitations, Balfour says you can get 'em as cheaply as 60 cents apiece (in increments of five) or order the "basic" kit of invitations, return labels, cards, memory book, tassel, and school stickers for $95.

OK, let's hit the "total" button. *Chinka-chinka-chinka-ziiing!* (Sorry. I have an old, noisy calculator.)

Looks like an "average" girl's investment will run around eight hundred smackers. For the boys, you're looking at about five hundred, plus another three C-notes if a limo is included.

Pretty steep fun, if you ask me—especially now that the Fabulous Nineties are history and we're reeling from a recession. Jobs are scarce these days. Layoffs are common. Times are tough.

Oops. Did I say "tough"? Bite my tongue. As bleak as things are today, we're on a cakewalk compared to 1934, the heart of the Great Depression.

I picked 1934 because that's the year of the Knoxville High School *Blue and White* newspaper I hold as we speak. Bill Harr sent it to me. This was the graduating class of his sister-in-law, Elaine West Ballard. Inside there's a piece about the high price of graduating. I quote:

"Eight dollars for a class ring; a dollar and a half for cards; two dollars for invitations; a dollar for the senior banquet; a dollar for a senior picture in the *Blue and White;* twenty-five cents for admission to the senior class play—such is a partial list of the expenses which accompany a student in graduation from KHS."

I know all the kids who are looking forward to this year's prom are tired of hearing their parents moan about the outrageous cost of today's festivities. I know they roll their eyes. I know they can recite when-I-was-in-high-school sermons verbatim.

But let me tell you something, kiddos: Your mom and dad are right on this one. So are your grandparents.

Going to the Dogs

On the Fourth of July, if you consider yourself a red-blooded, flag-waving, tax-paying, Ten Commandment–displaying Amurikan, by golly, go out there and do something really patriotic.

Eat a hot dog.

Hot dogs and the Fourth of July go together like politics and campaign contributions. Since July is National Hot Dog Month, you owe it to your fellow citizens—not to mention your bulbous belly—to ingest your rightful share of the two billion pounds of these babies the National Hot Dog and Sausage Council says we shove down our throats every year.

I am not making up the part about National Hot Dog Month. Or the National Hot Dog and Sausage Council, either. Only in this great, cholesterolic nation can an entire month and an industry association be dedicated to tube steaks.

The reason I know so much about hot dogs—aside from the fact they are part of the four basic food groups, along with doughnuts, beer, and potato chips—is because the National Hot Dog and Sausage Council sent out a bunch of press kits. Frankly, I'd be a lot happier if they'd sent me a couple of slaw dawgs, but why complain?

The kit included volumes of information about hot dogs. Some boring. Some interesting.

In the boring category were pages of text detailing the nutritional aspects of hot dogs, sales charts, demographics, history of hot dogs, blah-blah-who-cares-blah-blah-so-what-blah-blah-pass-the-mustard-please-blah-blah.

Ah, but in the interesting category were etiquette guidelines for proper consumption of this sacred sustenance. As a public service, allow me to highlight a few of the more important entries.

According to the experts, DO:

Apply condiments in this order—mustard, chili, relish, onions, sauerkraut, shredded cheese, salt, pepper. Serve on plain, sesame-seed, or poppy-seed buns, never sun-dried tomato buns or basil buns. Use paper plates or everyday dishes, never fancy china. Lick condiments from your fingertips. Use toothpicks to serve cocktail-sized hot doggettes, never a cocktail fork.

Conversely, the diplomats of dogdom insist that you DON'T:

> *How come Halloween candy corn never has suggestive messages stamped on it like Valentine candy hearts? And how come they don't make Valentine hearts out of candy corn ingredients? Maybe then they wouldn't taste like toothpaste.*

Put toppings between the dog and the bun. Use a cloth napkin; always choose paper. Take more than five bites to finish a standard-sized dawg; seven are acceptable on a foot-longer. Leave bits of bun on your plate. Defile a dog with fresh herbs. Bring wine to a hot dog dinner; instead, choose beer, soft drinks, lemonade, or iced tea. Send a thank-you note. "It would not," cautions the council, "be in keeping with the unpretentious nature of hot dogs."

OK, you got all that? Fine. Let us please bow our heads for a moment of thanks for the grease we are about to receive: Good food! Good meat! Hot dog! Let's eat!

Amen, brothers and sisters.

A Respite from Respites

What this country needs is a vacation-vacation. In other words, a session of R&R to help us overcome the R&R we just experienced.

Nostalgia and slick TV commercials notwithstanding, vacations aren't always what they're cracked up to be. Often you come home and go back to work more worn out than you were before the trip began.

But don't take my word for it. In a recent Gallup survey of one thousand American adults, more than half (54 percent) said they returned from their vacation feeling tired. Twenty percent pegged their condition as "very tired" and even "exhausted."

Dr. Roger Cadieux, a professor of psychiatry at Penn State University's College of Medicine and an expert on sleep problems, analyzed the survey results. In a report by the Scripps Howard News Service, he said, "You'd expect that vacation would dramatically reduce the number of people reporting tiredness, but instead there was an increase. Clearly, vacations are fraught with obstacles to sleep and relaxation."

I *(yawn)* concur.

My family—maws, in-laws, outlaws, girlfriends, and anyone else who shows up in the caravan—stays a week every summer at Ocean Isle Beach in North Carolina. There's usually around a dozen in the drove. Some years more, some years less. We rent as large a house as needed to keep everyone under the same roof and spend the entire time imitating tourists.

At any given moment, one or more will be engaged in fishing, swimming, beach walking, sun bathing, riding the waves on boogey boards, shopping, cooking in the kitchen, grilling meat or frying fish outside, mixing adult beverages, making ice cream, working puzzles, reading, playing board games, or watching videos.

Somehow, we also find time to eat and sleep a lot—usually in that order.

But no matter how many logs I saw at night or how often I study the back of my eyelids during the day, I invariably drag home feeling like I just ran the Boston Marathon. In snowshoes.

Maybe it's because our gang is collectively starting to age, but I've also noticed that we suffer more vacation ailments than we did a decade ago.

There were eleven of us this year, and during seven scant days various members of our tribe managed to log a case of restaurant food poisoning (we aren't going back to that joint *ever* again), a gall bladder flare-up, a case of sun poisoning (despite repeated layers of sun block) that required medical treatment, a bathroom fall (no broken bones, thankfully), a sinus attack, plus the usual strains and aches from trying to cram thirty-six hours into every day. And to think we actually pay for this pleasure and drive five hundred miles each way to enjoy it.

My most spectacular contribution to sick bay was a wrenched back.

Someone please tell me: How in the name of Eli Lilly can a man who regularly traverses the ridgelands of southern Appalachia take off walking down a beach that's flat as a pool table and throw his back out so bad it hurt to breathe?

I suffered for two days like I'd been bending over and hauling field stones dawn till dark. My pain likely would have continued for the remainder of the week had I not wisely treated it with massive doses of Vitamin B—the foamy, amber, liquid variety that comes in twelve-packs.

Then, after the trip's over, what's left is a Matterhorn of dirty clothes with sand in every pocket and fold, a car layered in salty grime, rusty fishing tackle, a week's worth of unread newspapers and unopened mail, thirty-one (by actual count) phone recordings and 148 (again, by actual count) e-mail messages.

Since vacations exact such an irksome physical, mental, financial, and vocational toll, the sensible thing would be to not go next year, right?

What? Are you nuts? Why, I wouldn't miss family week at the beach for anything! It's way yonder too much fun!

But I would, however, propose that the nation's employers, out of the kindness of their corporate hearts, give us poor workers a vacation-vacation. That way, we could hit the ground running on the first day back, bright of eye, bushy of tail, and eager to resume chipping away at the mountain.

If largesse was good enough for the big dogs at Enron and WorldCom, it's still good enough for us.

Take This Job and Shove It

Mac Cissna is the only person I've ever known who got fired from a job he didn't have, and every time Labor Day rolls around I feel obliged to tell his story.

Cissna owns a battery company in Knoxville. He sells and services heavy-duty stuff—four-hundred-pounders up to three tons. Definitely not D cells for a flashlight.

One day Cissna drove to Johnson City to install one of these batteries in a pallet jack at a large manufacturing plant. The job was going to take several hours, so a worker inside the plant was assigned to assist.

"Everything was going fine," he told me. "We had the job about half finished when the fellow left. I didn't know if he was going on break or to lunch or what. He just said, 'I'll be back' and took off. There wasn't much I could do by myself, so I folded my arms and leaned up against some equipment and waited."

Five minutes became ten.

"I looked up, and here came this young management guy with a lady in tow," Cissna said. "He looked at me, and I looked at him, and they walked on. I didn't think much about it."

Fifteen or so minutes had passed by now. Still no sign of Cissna's helper. But the suit passed through again.

Cissna recalls: "He stopped and stared at me and walked off. I figured he was going to find me some more help.

"He came back in a few minutes. Just walked right up and said, 'You come with me.' I thought, OK, now I'm about to get some help. We walked on through the plant, past the cafeteria, on up toward the front. We wound up at the personnel office. We went inside, and he told the woman behind the desk, 'We're firing this guy. We don't need his kind working here. I've walked past him twice, and all he does is lean on equipment.'"

Cissna was about to bust a gut to keep from laughing. He would've set the record straight had the big cheese not acted like such an impetuous jerk. Instead, he decided to play along.

"The woman asked for my social security number, and I gave it to her—my real number. As she was typing it into her computer, I said, 'I've still got ten vacation days left, and you shorted me twenty bucks on my last check.'

"She kept trying to enter my social security number, but it wouldn't go. Finally, she turned to me and said, 'I can't find you in the system. What department do you work in?'

"I told her, 'Ma'am, I don't work here at all. I'm just tryin' to change a battery.'

"That little banty rooster got red as a beet," Cissna laughed. "The woman with him looked over at him like, 'You're an idiot.'

"I explained what I was doing there, and that made him even madder. He tried to get me to tell who'd been helping, but I wouldn't. I knew he was in a mood to fire somebody."

Eventually, Cissna returned to the pallet jack, rounded up some help on his own, and finished the job. Mr. Big Britches was nowhere in sight.

"I've been back to that plant a couple of times since then, and I've never seen him again," Cissna said. "I reckon somebody up there wised up and fired him."

Or more likely, named him CEO.

> *Now that the Yuletide shopping season begins the day after Halloween instead of the day after Thanksgiving, shouldn't the "Twelve Days of Christmas" be expanded to twenty-four?*

Not a Guy Thing

Whenever Christmas rolls around, fear and trembling run rampant among men.

This angst has nothing to do with the impending arrival of out-of-town guests, ingestion of old family recipes that should have been purged generations earlier, or decorating chores involving knots of twinkling lights last unbraided during the Eisenhower administration.

It has everything to do with wrapping presents.

Shopping is bad enough for those of us of the Y-chromosome persuasion. We never know what to buy, nor are we particularly adept at taking subtle hints. (For Pete's sake, what wife, daughter, or sister wouldn't want to find a new shotgun, chain saw, or cordless drill under the tree?) Try as we might, we rarely wind up with the appropriate item. It's one of the curses of being a guy.

But regardless of how carelessly we acquire gifts, that's merely step one on the road to failure. Step two is making them presentable. "Presentable" in estrogen circles, that is.

As far as men are concerned, presentable covers a vast territory meaning "more or less in working condition."

It's a matter of practicality. When one man asks another to "toss me that nine-sixteenths wrench, willya?" that's precisely what he means. Pitch it over here, and I'll catch it and use it. He does not intend for the wrench to be offered on a platter like pheasant under glass.

Men take the same no-nonsense approach for gift wrap. Frankly, we see no need for it. If shrink-wrap was good enough for the manufacturer, it's good enough for us.

Nonetheless, sentimentality does overtake us in late December, and we foolishly attempt to sheathe the goods with gaily colored paper and bows.

Invariably, all we do is make a mess.

I remember once, as a boy, going with my mother to a department store and watching one of the sales clerks gift wrap a present.

(Historical note for anyone under forty: Stores provided this service, either free or at minimal cost, back then. They also hired enough staff to help you carefully select your purchases and check them out in a timely manner. Think about that the next time you're standing behind seventeen people in the three checkout lanes—out of twenty-five—that are actually open.)

With sheets of floral paper and streamers of ribbon, she transformed a simple box into a work of art.

Note I said "she." Men cannot complete this task with any degree of skill.

Perhaps there's a difference in the muscular structure of male and female hands. Men's fingers may be deft enough to perform heart bypass surgery or lay a line of bricks straight as a laser beam or carve intricate designs into walnut, but we cannot fold the edges of wrapping paper neatly, tape the ends discreetly, and anoint the creation with an ornate bow.

Instead, what we wind up with looks like it was assembled by committees working in Iowa, Texas, Oregon, and Virginia and communicating by Morse code.

This explains why, on the eighth day, God created the gift bag.

And he saw that it was good.

Getting the Bugs Out of Shopping

A catalog featuring new and unusual Christmas tree ornaments arrived at the Venable house a couple of days ago.

"Unusual" is a key word in this discussion, for right there among the snow-flakes and angels and miniwreaths and Santas was a full line of—I am not joking—spiders. There was a legend alongside the ad.

"A long time ago in Germany, a mother was busily cleaning for Christmas," the story began. "The spiders fled upstairs to the attic to escape the broom. When the house became quiet, the spiders slowly crept downstairs for a peek. Oh, what a beautiful tree!"

The story went on to describe how the spiders raced from limb to limb, spin-ning webs. When Santa arrived that night, he saw how happy the spiders were at their handiwork, but he knew the woman of the house would be on the warpath about the mess. So Santa used his magical powers to turn the dusty, gray cob-webs into gold and silver.

"The tree sparkled and shimmered and was even more beautiful than ever before," the legend concluded. "That's why we have tinsel in our tree, and every tree should have a spider in its branches."

I've heard of commercial reaches, but this one charts new ground. I doubt even Martha Stewart would think of it. And if Martha Stewart *did* want spiders on her tree, she'd build her own traps, catch her own spiders, freeze-dry them in a dehydrator she made from an old coffee can, color them with leftover mascara, and attach them to ornament holders using a special glue rendered from horse hooves she'd found in the garage.

I realize manufacturers think they have to keep broadening Christmas shop-ping horizons. Just imagine what sort of sorry world this would be if consumers didn't have something new to buy every year.

But I can only marvel at what's next on the innovative ornament list. Rattle-snakes, perchance? Dust mites? Boll weevils?

Don't laugh. When Christmas dollars are at stake, no option is too outland-ish. Some December night, a group of carolers might show up at your door singing traditional holiday tunes like:

> *Crusty, the cockroach, was a jolly, happy bug.*
> *She had squiggly legs, and she laid her eggs,*
> *Underneath your bathroom rug. . . .*

I hope Santa leaves a can of Raid in my stocking.

Nothin' to Sing About

I ran into my old pal Arlo Dewberry the other day. He looked terrible.

"What's with the sad face?" I asked. "Cheer up. It's the Christmas season."

"That's the problem," he replied. "My neighborhood association elected me chairman of the annual Christmas carol party. It's turned into a nightmare."

"Oh, for Pete's sake, Arlo. Christmas caroling is a wonderful tradition. Everybody gets together on a clear, cold night in December. You stroll around the subdivision singing songs, then relax over hot chocolate and cookies."

Arlo eyed me suspiciously. "What planet you been livin' on?" he snapped.

"Huh?"

"This is a new age, fellow. Haven't you ever heard of diversity? Sensitivity? Inclusiveness? Making sure nobody gets offended by one tune or another?"

"Meaning?"

"Meaning every time I suggest a carol, somebody finds a reason to oppose it," he said. "I've run through seventeen songbooks for naught."

"What's wrong with some of the old standards like 'God Rest Ye Merry Gentlemen' and 'We Three Kings'?"

"There's no mention of women," he answered. "All the feminists in the neighborhood are upset."

"Then throw in 'Bring a Torch, Jeanette, Isabella' to include them."

"Can't. The fire marshal rejected that one. Says torches are unsafe."

"Hmmmm. Well, what about 'The Holly and the Ivy'? Now there's a beautiful number."

"Not when both plants are on the endangered species list. Same goes for that ditty about roasting chestnuts. The fire marshal nixed that one, too. No open fires."

"Then just go for something totally frivolous. Who could possibly be offended by 'All I Want for Christmas Is My Two Front Teeth'?"

"The dentists," he sighed.

"Any chance for 'Rudolph the Red-Nosed Reindeer'?"

"Not if PETA has anything to say about it. They're prepared to file a restraining order."

"This is ridiculous, Arlo!" I exclaimed.

"My sentiments exactly," he said dejectedly. "I've been running into dead ends at every turn."

"Well, there's got to be something. I've always been partial to 'Do You Hear What I Hear?'"

"The feds have had a fit over that one. They say it violates the Patriot Act. In fact, the FBI is sending agents to town next week to find out exactly what everybody heard and when they heard it."

"'White Christmas,' perhaps? 'Blue Christmas'?"

"We're supposed to be a colorblind society."

"'Good King Wenceslas'?"

"Promotes monarchy."

"'The First Noel'?"

"Too competitive. What about the second and third noels? Aren't they allowed to have a role?"

"Then try something totally festive, like 'Jingle Bells' or 'Silver Bells.'"

"Forget it. We've got a neighborhood noise code."

"Boy, this is serious, Arlo," I said. "You really do have a problem, don't you?"

"You better believe it," he replied. "I'm sick of the whole caroling idea. In fact, the first guy who suggests 'Why Can't Every Day Be Like Christmas?' gets a punch in the nose."

Chapter 7

That's Where I Come From

You gotta love a place that has built an international reputation for producing firewater as well as fire and brimstone. Two of Tennessee's most famous products—whiskey from Jack Daniel and George Dickel distilleries and Bibles from Thomas Nelson Publishers—are available in marketplaces around the world.

The locals don't worry one whit about this paradox. Instead, we consider it proud testimony to the fierce independence of a land and a people unfazed by preconceived notions of "typical."

This concept comes, literally, with the territory. Stretching 482 miles from west to east, and 182 feet above sea level in the Mississippi River bottomlands to 6,643 feet along the spine of the Great Smoky Mountains, Tennessee is a case study in contradictions.

This amalgam is evident anywhere you look. It flows from the northwest, where Reelfoot Lake was created in two years by an act of nature, to the southeast, where TVA's "Great Lakes of the South" were created in four decades by an act of Congress.

Here is southern country for sure, steeped in southern pride and southern manner. More Civil War battles were fought on Tennessee soil than any Confederate state except Virginia.

Ah, but even when these bloody lines were being drawn, Tennessee didn't fit the mold. Torn by rebel sympathies to the west and union allegiances to the east, this was the last state to secede and the first readmitted.

Don't blame this quirk on native inability to make decisions, however. It's simply because Tennessee is blessed with too many options on too many fronts.

What other state chooses a veritable Noah's Ark for its "official" animals?

Only Tennessee has a state bird (mockingbird), not to be confused with a state game bird (bobwhite quail). Plus a state sport fish (smallmouth bass) and state commercial fish (channel catfish), as well as state insects (firefly and ladybug), state agricultural insect (honey bee), state butterfly (zebra swallowtail), state wild animal (raccoon), state amphibian (Tennessee cave salamander), state reptile (eastern box turtle), and state horse (Tennessee walking horse).

You want more crazy contradictions and comparisons? Then chew on this: We celebrate food like nobody else.

As native son Jeff Bradley noted in his definitive *Tennessee Handbook,* our meals tend to revolve around such delicacies as fried chicken, fried catfish, ribs, country ham, hushpuppies (deep-fried, of course), lard-rich biscuits served with butter and preserves, okra (did I mentioned fried?), as well as pinto beans, green beans, and collard greens simmered for hours alongside a chunk of seasoned pork (translation: magnum sodium). Plus a couple of fried pies for dessert.

Then we start thinking about what's on tap for tomorrow.

In East Tennessee alone, you can sink a celebratory tooth at the Cosby Ramp Festival, the Dayton Strawberry Festival, the Erwin-Unicoi County Apple Festival, the Grainger County Tomato Festival, and the South Pittsburg Cornbread Festival, plus enough fall homecomings and craft fairs in every borough to corner the market on funnel cakes and barbecue.

These might explain why the state's Office of Health Statistics has labeled 25 percent of Tennesseans as obese—and yet the U.S. Department of Agriculture estimates 11 percent go to bed hungry every night.

Still game for contrasts? Consider this gem of an East Tennessee factoid: Dayton is home of the 1925 Scopes trial, which resulted in a forty-year ban on

John Orr, back in his native Knoxville after a thirty-two-year career with the FBI, recalls his brief link with a musical legend. It occurred in the fall of 1962, the start of his senior year at West High School. Mrs. Jessie Hooper, his English teacher, was handing out textbooks.

As was the practice in those days, Orr opened the cover of his book and started to scribble his name at the bottom of the long list of previous owners.

"I was pleased to note that the top name on the list was Phil Everly (younger of the two Everly Brothers, who by that time had left Knoxville and were topping the charts in Nashville.) "In my usual loudmouthed manner, I announced my discovery to the class.

"Mrs. Hooper said, 'Let me see that.' I handed it to her, and she promptly gave me another book. I guess that one was formally retired. Maybe it made it into her celebrity book collection. I have no idea whatever happened to the book. Today, it's probably fodder for eBay."

That's Where I Come From

the teaching of evolution. But two counties away in the atomic city of Oak Ridge, studies in genetic research have been making scientific headlines for more than half a century.

You're looking for something "typically Tennessee" in nature? Sorry. There ain't no such animal. Which is one of the many reasons why I love this land so dearly.

Well, yes, now that you mention it, we *do* have a rather bizarre side—especially when we get into our cups. A few summers ago, I wrote a column describing the Blount County Cheese Caper and the Hawkins County Beer Run. I never could decide which one of these shenanigans was better or which spoke more highly of East Tennessee culture. See for yourself.

In Blount County, the cops arrested a man after he allegedly celebrated his twenty-third birthday in a most unusual fashion. According to police reports, he was naked, covered with nacho cheese, and (duh!) "had a strong odor of alcohol" about him.

They made the arrest after someone scaled an eight-foot fence at the John Sevier School swimming pool, broke into the snack bar, smeared cheese and taco chips all over the place, and, in the process, managed to make up for a lack of clothing by covering his torso in the latest nacho fashions.

Not surprisingly, alcohol also played a role in the other situation. It occurred in Rogersville—not to be confused with Mayberry.

Seems a quartet of inmates at the Hawkins County Jail found an unlocked door at their high-security facility. Discovering this unusual condition, the four did what most inmates would do. They hoofed.

But not for long.

They simply walked to a local store, purchased some beer, and brought it back to share with their fellow prisoners.

When the first load of suds was depleted, they went to another store for more. Then they returned, and a good time was had by all—at least until someone in charge finally figured out what was going on and locked the jailhouse door.

As I specified at the time, far be it from me to assess guilt or innocence in either case. That was a job for the legal system. The defendants had their charges read in open court and examined by impartial judges and juries. Punishment was meted according to long-established principles. After laughter died down in the courtroom, of course.

Regardless of legal complexities, however, I was certain of one thing. It was a lead pipe cinch, a truism on which I'd bet the farm. If there's not a chart-busting country music song buried in these antics, there ain't a guitar in Nashville.

Lest you get the wrong impression about our citizens, please know that Tennesseans—particularly those of the eastern persuasion—are among the friendliest you'll find anytime, anywhere.

Marti Davis, a reporter in the *News Sentinel*'s community news department and a 1983 transplant from Saint Louis, was at a party recently and got to trading "moving–to–East Tennessee" stories with some of her friends. She passed along a few of the gems to me.

"Dorothy Folz Gray and her husband, Dan, had just moved here and heard a grocer say, 'Y'all come back.' They actually turned around and walked back to see what he wanted!

"Nancy Young, from New York City, was alarmed when she didn't get a receipt at the dry cleaners. She said, 'I figured I'd never get those clothes back again.' She did, of course."

Marti's personal contribution to the tale-swapping stemmed from an episode at the former White Store in Bearden.

"I bought seventy dollars worth of groceries, then found out I didn't have a check left to pay with, or enough cash," she said. "The bag boy (the manager, I later found out) had never seen me before in his life. He said, 'That's OK, little lady. Come back and pay us tomorrow.'

"He proceeded to load the groceries into the trunk of my car (with Missouri plates) while I was still trying to pick my jaw up off the floor. Needless to say, I went back to pay the next morning and shopped nowhere else until the White Store sold out."

Marti's been here long enough that she qualifies to poke fun at other immigrants. She was telling me that once, while standing in a food line during the Tennessee Fall Homecoming at the Museum of Appalachia in Norris, she overheard one Yankee ask another if "'beans and greens' meant baked beans and salad. The whole line waiting for lunch was in stitches over that."

I trust they interpreted for the Yanquis—and then held a foot-warshin' to welcome these furriners into our midst.

A Pop Quiz

In honor of the start of Knox County schools, I'm delighted to present the all-new edition of cognitive testing, East Tennessee style:

ALGEBRA

1. Steve leaves home at 7:26 A.M. and walks .3 mile to the bus stop, with an average stride of 2 feet, 7 inches, into a wind of 6 mph. Bill leaves home at 7:32 A.M. and walks .2 mile to the bus stop with an average stride of 2 feet, 5 inches, with a 5.75 mph wind at his back.

Determine the number of Code Red Mountain Dews and blueberry Pop Tarts each had to consume during breakfast to supply the calories needed to fuel his respective journey.

2. The back window on the second floor of the school library is 26.7 feet off the ground. The principal's new convertible is parked 6 feet, 3 inches from building. The bottom limb of a Bradford pear growing 10 feet, 4 inches from the right front fender of the car covers 28 percent of the surface area of the vehicle.

Calculate the saliva pressure (in pounds per square inch), plus angle of arc, required to propel the juice from a half-pinch of Skoal toward a direct hit on a point triangulated by the antenna, steering wheel, and left rear stereo speaker.

3. Madelyn, Stephanie, Caitlin, Heather, and Brittany each go to different stores to buy a dress for the big dance. Each has a budget of $350, but the actual amount spent decreases by 7.3 percent per student, respectively, starting with Stephanie.

Determine the odds that each will show up at the dance wearing exactly the same outfit. Extra credit: What is the diameter of the gonzo zit that will erupt on Brittany's nose the morning of the dance?

4. The school's groundskeeper applies 10-10-10 fertilizer at a rate of .002 ounce per square yard across the surface of the football field, both end zones, plus a border 15 feet wide on either side of the field between the 20-yard lines. Each stem of grass produced by this effort grows at an average rate of .039 inch per day during the first month of the season.

How deep a crater will be formed when the goalposts come crashing down after the home team is shellacked, forty-two to zero, by the homecoming patsy?

> My wife conducts computer software courses for the University of Tennessee these days, but early in her career she taught math at several East Tennessee public schools.
>
> Even though this happened more than thirty years ago, she and I still laugh about the time a seventh-grader at Bonny Kate Elementary turned the tables and "learnt" her a math lesson.
>
> "Miz Venable," he said, "always 'member that naught plus naught equals naught."
>
> As Mary Ann has remarked on several occasions since, it's hard to argue with that principle.

BIOLOGY

1. Draw a simple diagram of a fish, indicating spiny dorsal fin, soft dorsal fin, lateral line, caudal fin, anal fin, pelvic fin, pectoral fin, gill opening, and gill cover, plus proper insertion point of knife blade (including angle of cut) to produce two boneless fillets for frying.

2. Describe two basic differences between mammals and reptiles—without using the term "hooters."

3. Explain the role of fungi, parasites, algae, mold, and mildew in the American political process. It is not necessary to name names.

4. At what point during the process of human-cell division does the head cheerleader telephone the captain of the basketball team and say, "Honey, I think we've got a problem"?

5. In fifty words or less, explain why humans, who take in oxygen and give off carbon dioxide, need a swish of Scope every morning, while trees, which take in carbon dioxide and give off oxygen, can live hundreds of years and never stink up the joint.

ENGLISH

1. Multiple choice: The word "ranch" means (a) a large farm, (b) a tool used to work on truck engines, (c) an injury suffered by twisting the knee or elbow, (d) what you do to your hair after applying shampoo, (e) all of the above.

2. True or false: The preposition is a word you should never end a sentence with.

3. Multiple choice: When writing a letter, composing a theme, or typing an e-mail, how many exclamation points should be used at the end of a sentence to indicate emotions like anger or surprise: (a) seven, (b) thirteen, (c) four hundred, (d) as many as needed to fill out the line.

4. Why are limericks rarely worth reading unless they contain the words "Rangoon" or "Nantucket"?

5. True or false: The spell checker is a knew devise witch has removed hour knead for the diction airy bee cause it can illuminate awl miss steaks.

6. The letters *a, e, i, o* and *u* are vowels. Nouns and verbs must agree. John Steinbeck wrote *The Grapes of Wrath* and other works of—aw, who cares? If you can, like, score four touchdowns, you know, per game throughout the season, uh, what difference does any of this $#@% test junk make, anyhow?

Baring It All

Down through the years, *News Sentinel* columnists have enjoyed a proud tradition of writing about people who got caught with their pants down.

The late Bert Vincent started this trend when he told the story of a Knoxville man who went to a downtown movie theater on a particularly warm night. The man was "rather portly," as people politely said in those days. These days, he would be described as a "lard ass."

In any event, the guy was uncomfortable and the theater was dark. So he decided to loosen his clothing—including his belt and zipper. About midway through the main attraction, a woman sitting way down his row decided to visit the powder room. As he stood to let her pass, the man suddenly recalled his condition. Hurriedly, he zipped up.

But not hurriedly enough. The woman's dress got tangled in his zipper and the two strangers found themselves hopelessly entwined. They had to walk together in lockstep to the lobby, where, red-faced, they quickly parted company.

A story by the late Carson Brewer—hmmm, I'm starting to notice a disturbing pattern involving deceased columnists—described the plight of a vacationing couple who were driving their camper into the tourist-packed Great Smoky Mountains National Park.

Correction. The wife was driving. Her husband was in the back. Asleep. In the nude.

The woman made a jackrabbit start from an intersection, simultaneously throwing (a) the camper door open and (b) her husband out of the camper. In the midst of mountain traffic and wearing nothing but a look of panic, he sprinted down the road until his wife finally noticed him in her sideview mirror.

Now, it's my turn.

The story you are about to read was given to me as truth. The people who told it swear and double-swear it happened a few days ago. It involves a local couple out for a night on the town. On the way, the

> *Either I need speech lessons or Ma Bell needs to brush up on her southern Appalachian dialect.*
>
> *A few days ago, I dialed an automated directory to obtain the phone number of a man in Roane County. I gave the name, city and state. Second later, the machine recited the name and produced a number. But the city and state were off a wee bit.*
>
> *I still can't understand how my pronunciation of "Kingston, Tennessee" was interpreted by the machine as "Dallas, Texas."*

wife realized she had a run in her pantyhose. Her husband pulled into one of those twenty-four hour gas station–deli-food shop–convenience stores found on virtually every corner in American so she could buy another pair.

While she was inside, he decided to top off the gas tank of his automobile, a white Lincoln Town Car. Just as he finished the job, another car pulled up for gas. It was another white Lincoln Town Car. As a courtesy to the second driver, the husband moved his auto to the perimeter of the store and went into a side door to pay for his gasoline.

You know where there is going, don't you? Yep. You're exactly right.

As he entered through the side door, his wife exited through the front door with her purchase. Without so much as a glance, she hopped into the white Lincoln Town Car at the pump and began wiggling out of her old pantyhose. That's when the startled driver announced, "Lady, I think you've got the wrong car."

She nearly moistened herself.

No, those four words aren't the exact ones she quoted to me. If I'm not mistaken, the term "(rhymes-with-hissed) in my britches" was used to describe the awkward situation. But you get the picture.

Pantyhose around her ankles, she leaped from the car and duck-walked toward her own vehicle, where hubby had been frantically waving his arms for several seconds.

If you have any friends who drive a white Lincoln Town Car, ask 'em about it.

Behaving Like a Real Native

Welcome to our fair city, Mr. and Mrs. Newcomer. It's a great place to call home. We're glad you're here.

How do I know you're not a native of this region, or at least a transplant with many years of K-town time under your belt? Because there's talk of snow in the air and you're reading instead of doing something far more important.

No offense. I love readers. Without them I'd have to find honest work to make a living. But there will be time for reading in an hour or so, after you've taken steps to ensure the survival of you and your family.

You need to be out buying groceries.

Not just any groceries, either. You need emergency supplies to weather the snow—eggs, bread, beer, and toilet paper. Only then will you qualify as a bona fide Knoxvillian.

It doesn't count if you buy eggs, bread, beer, and toilet paper on a regular basis. We're talking about emergency shopping, stocking up for a sure-nuff crisis. You must dash out and buy these items each and every time the word "snow" creeps into the local weather forecast.

Oh, and by "dash out," I mean you must complete this task madly, as if something truly horrible—like a nuclear holocaust or Steve Spurrier being hired by the Tennessee Titans—were about to occur.

I don't care how you used to prepare for emergencies in Chicago or Buffalo or Milwaukee or Minneapolis or wherever you came from. You don't live there any more. You live in Knoxville, where things are done differently.

This is not theory. This is undisputed scientific fact. It's because the emotions and physiology of *Homo sapiens* in and around Knoxville bear little in common with those of persons living to the north.

From the emotional standpoint, snow evokes a primal fear absent from any other facet of human existence. Native Knoxvillians will fight, tooth and eyeball, over the slightest grievance or injustice, real or imagined. But we turn to jelly at the thought of You Know What.

An irrational fear? Not on your life.

Any Tennessee historian will tell you snow has wiped out entire civilizations of morons who didn't prepare. Like Osama bin Laden, snow exists for a single purpose: to kill us. If you think I'm lying, consider that the temperature of a snowflake is no more than 32 degrees and the temperature of a human being is 98.6. No way these two can be compatible.

In order to protect our bodies from this insidious onslaught, we must stock up on the essentials for life. That's where the physiological differences between Knoxvillians and other folks come into play.

You see, whenever snow is discussed—I'm talking everything from random flurries to a full-blown blizzard—it changes the internal organs in our bodies, creating a life-or-death demand for certain foodstuffs.

Eggs, for instance. Even if we normally limit our egg consumption to one or two per week, our bodies demand that we buy five dozen every time snow rears its frostbitten head.

Same with bread. Five to six loaves per threat is a bare minimum. No fancy stuff, either. None of this sun-dried-tomato-with-basil bagel nonsense. It must be plain, sliced, enriched-flour, loaded-with-preservatives white bread. (Call it "light" bread, and you'll truly be among the anointed.)

Ditto beer. Even if you took the pledge in '83 and haven't sipped so much as a teaspoon full since, it is mandatory to buy a minimum of one six-pack. A full case is preferred.

Naturally, this massive influx of eggs, bread, and suds creates havoc in the digestive system. That's why you'll need twenty rolls of toilet paper per winter storm forecast.

If you doubt my words, go to your favorite supermarket at the next mention of the s-word. See how many shopping carts are loaded to the point of axle collapse. See how barren the egg, bread, beer, and toilet paper aisles are.

This will be just as true at 3 A.M. as it is at 3 P.M., any day of the week. When we are gearing up for a two-inch avalanche, we will not be deterred. I urge you to do likewise.

Be advised.

Be prepared.

Be a Knoxvillian.

Gifts from the Heartland

Christmas is a time of giving. You give money to a store, the store gives you a gift, you give the gift to someone else, they give it to a rummage sale. So let us find something Tennessee can give to a region in need.

I got to thinking about this opportunity after learning how the kind people of Alaska shared their wealth with underprivileged Puerto Ricans.

No, not lumber or salmon. It was something a bit less exotic for Alaskans.

Snow. Sixty-five thousand pounds of it.

The white stuff was plowed off an Anchorage parking lot and dispatched to San Juan. There, it will be dumped onto the floor of a refrigerated warehouse so tropical children can build snowmen. I am not making this up. The effort was organized by an export company specializing in carnival celebrations.

"Craziest thing I've ever done," said one of the workers assigned to the task.

That was my initial reaction, too. Then the trash-to-treasure reality of the situation hit me upside the head. The Alaskans gave away something they didn't need to a group of people who wanted it. Such a deal.

Tennessee needs to get in on this action. That way, we can dispose of rubbish that's piling up around here—I mean, we can donate our abundant resources to a deserving sister state.

Orange barrels, for instance.

The average Tennessee interstate highway contains approximately 5,385,254 orange barrels per mile. Roughly two dozen of these are used to outline actual construction zones. The others are deployed well ahead of the construction zone to funnel traffic into one lane. Or occasionally as weight-lifting devices for highway workers who have tired of waving flags, running heavy equipment, or rotating the "slow" and "stop" signs.

Surely there is a state with a dearth of interstates that would be tickled pink, or orange as the case may be, to have some of our excess.

Nevada comes immediately to mind. Nevada's land mass is a whopping 109,806 square miles, compared to our piddling 41,220. Yet except for Interstate 80 through the top of the state and a tiny piece of Interstate 15 through Las Vegas, it is completely devoid of an opportunity to stick orange barrels in the paths of motorists. I say we load up a few semis' worth and head 'em west.

Nevadans needn't give us anything in return. The best they could offer is drought, something we have plenty of ourselves. In fact, I propose we bag up about three or four weeks of our drought and ship it to a deserving area. Like Olympia, Washington.

I've got a logger friend who used to work along the upper Pacific Coast. He tells me it's so rainy out there that slicker suits and rubber boots are as common as ball caps and blue jeans around here—and that's for the people who work indoors. The ones who stay outside all day grow moss down their backs.

Think how appreciative they'd be for a dry-as-toast Tennessee drought! And think how happy we'd be to get shed of it!

The spirit of giving is veritably overflowing in me now. I just thought of a gesture of goodwill the entire Tennessee Valley region can undertake.

We can give the fragrant waters of the Tennessee River to a less-fortunate state—Maine, perhaps—that's up to its eyebrows in lakes, rivers, and streams with no aroma whatsoever.

Think how much these poor people are missing. Why, I bet they've never seen so much as a clot of foam or pieces of particulate matter drifting along in the current. It's up to us to give them relief.

Instead of hogging 652 miles of effluent, runoff, diesel fuel, PCBs, mercury, farm waste, and industrial bilge for ourselves, let's jug it up and share it with those desperate people in the Northland.

If they want to ship down a few thousand pounds of fresh lobsters as a gesture of appreciation, fine. But just knowing we have shared our bounty is thanks enough.

Researching Research

What do southern white men think when they read about an experiment that supposedly measures their "honor and integrity?"

They think the people who conduct hokey experiments ought to find a real job. At least that's the opinion of the southern white man who is typing this essay.

The experiment was conducted at the University of Michigan under the direction of psychologist Richard Nisbett. Here's how it worked:

Male students were asked to fill out a questionnaire, then take it to a table at the end of a narrow hallway. En route to the table, though, their path was blocked by another guy working at a file cabinet.

(A southern white male question: What kind of moron would put a file cabinet in a narrow hallway in the first place?)

The file cabinet person closed the drawer and let the student pass. On the return trip, however, the file guy acted mad about having to close his drawer again. He slammed it shut, bumped the student with his shoulder, and called him "an insulting, scatological name."

(Another southern white male question: Did it rhyme with "elbow"?)

When the student completed the trip, his saliva was checked to see if there was an increase in testosterone.

(Yet another southern white male question: Wow, is *that* where testosterone comes from?)

The results? Southerners showed a 12 percent increase in testosterone. Northerners showed none. And that, according to the learned Yankee scientists, proves southern white men are quicker to react to save their "honor and integrity" than northern white men.

Horse hockey. This test proves nothing of the kind. It merely proves some guys are complete jerks, no matter where they're from.

This experiment wasn't even necessary in the first place. The researchers acknowledged as much. They noted that southern white men are not accustomed to public displays of impolite behavior like the hallway scene, "whereas it may be part of everyday rudeness in the north."

Do tell.

Those learned Yankee scientists want to know what provokes *all* males—southern, northern, eastern, western, white, black, and everything in between?

It's wasting good time and money trying to prove the obvious.

Seven Springs

Despite what your calendar says, it's never spring—as in singular—in East Tennessee.

Unlike other parts of the country, we never have "a" spring season. We have springs—as in plural. Seven of them. East Tennessee's spring is far too complex to be wasted on one solitary burst.

It's OK if other parts of the land want to rush through their spring, completing the transition from winter to summer in one showy display. We'd rather take it slowly, deliberately. That way, if we get homesick for snow or anxious for drought, no problem; we can throw those into the mixture as well.

The stages of spring in East Tennessee may vary a few days from year to year, but across the board this cycle follows a distinct, logical pattern.

It starts sometime in February with Hint of What's to Come Spring. This ranges anywhere from February 1 to February 28—or February 29 during leap years.

When March arrives, we get down to brass tacks about spring. Or brass monkeys, as the case may be. Dying Gasp of Winter Spring arrives in early March, giving way to August Heat Wave Spring in mid-March, which precedes Return of Ice Age Spring in late March.

Then comes April, a most unusual month.

There are only two springs in April, Sleigh Bells Spring and Suntan Lotion Spring, but they frequently arrive and depart within twenty-four hours of each other. As any East Tennessee native will tell you, it is possible during these springs to shovel six inches of snow off your driveway while wearing shorts or attend the gala opening of the Dogwood Arts Festival wrapped in woolens.

Bob DeShane was driving into Knoxville on Interstate 40 and noticed one of the Tennessee Department of Transportation's flashing new signs announcing the 511 phone service for road conditions.

Said DeShane, "It seems silly to me to spend money on signs encouraging motorists to use their cell phones. I suspect one day we'll see a sign that says, 'Wreck Ahead Caused by Driver Dialing 511.'"

And speaking of roadway sights, I caught a great bumper sticker in Monroe County. It proclaimed, "I'm Filthy, Stinking Rich" in bold letters.

The second line, in much smaller type, read, "Two out of three ain't bad."

Ah, yes. Dogwoods. That brings up yet another quirky form of East Tennessee weather.

Once we have finally achieved Honest to Gosh Spring—mid- to late May, but that's not guaranteed—it's time for Dogwood Winter, Blackberry Winter, and Whippoorwill Winter.

(Occasionally, we also have Ha-Ha Fooled You Spring in April. It can take one of four forms: extremely hot, extremely cold, extremely wet, or extremely dry. But since you're just learning the basics, I shouldn't confuse the issue with minutia. Forget I mentioned it.)

It was Return of Ice Age Spring that zapped your shrubs and trees a few nights ago and painted the blossoms brown. At least I think it was.

Some would argue this was Dying Gasp of Winter Spring. They could be right.

Then again, it could have been a combination of Dying Gasp of Winter Spring and Return of Ice Age Spring because this wasn't a regionwide freeze.

But what do I know? I've only lived here since I was born. I still need to do a lot of research.

"Shall We Gather with a Dinner"

Only in Knoxville would a funeral procession—hearse, mourners, the dear-departed and all—put official duties on hold long enough to hit the drive-through at a fast-food joint.

And only in Knoxville would such a pit stop not raise eyebrows.

"We did block a couple of people coming out of the restaurant," said Charles Baldwin, "but they didn't seem to be too disturbed."

Baldwin is a veteran of funerals—fast-food or otherwise. He's a retired Army chaplain and Lutheran pastor who lives in High Point, North Carolina. But in this particular instance, the ceremony had a personal connection. He was attending final services for his father, Clifton Baldwin, a longtime railroad worker.

When Baldwin the Elder passed away, Baldwin the Younger and other family and friends gathered in Knoxville for the funeral. As is customary in these situations, the pastor of the local church, First Lutheran, asked everyone if they'd like to share a meal afterward.

Thanks for the kind gesture, family members said, but the burial was going to take place in Tazewell, so they really needed to get up the road. A full-blown meal wasn't necessary.

Not a problem. The pastor arranged for fried chicken dinners to be purchased from a nearby KFC outlet.

Oops. Due to a mix-up, the meals didn't make it to the church.

Not a problem II. Since KFC was on the way to the cemetery, why not just swing by and pick up the food en route?

Oops II. When the cortege arrived, the meals weren't ready.

Not a problem III. Everybody simply waited—with headlights on and funeral home flags attached to their vehicles.

"I must admit this was a first for me," Baldwin said with a chuckle. "The people at Stevens Mortuary told me they'd never taken a funeral procession into the drive-through, either."

After chicken dinners had been distributed to every car in the procession, the entire caravan resumed its journey out of Knoxville and toward Claiborne County.

Which brings up another first.

"It was the first time I'd ever driven to an interment while eating fried chicken, slaw, biscuits and mashed potatoes," Baldwin said.

The humor and irony weren't lost on the mourners.

"My dad would have loved it," said Baldwin. "He would really have gotten a kick out of the thought of us stopping in the middle of his funeral services to get fast food."

But the choice of meat definitely would've been an issue.

"He never was a big fan of fried chicken, or chicken of any kind for that matter," said Baldwin. "He was a cook in his early years and once had been required to fry up some chickens that were 'beyond their freshness date.' He never liked poultry after that. In fact, at Thanksgiving every year, he always insisted on having ham."

Oh well. Like the Good Book says, whether a meal involves loaves and fishes, fowls of the air, beasts of the field, or any other type of victual, it's the brotherly love that counts.

(Oh, and if you don't mind, hold the steering wheel for me just a second. I gotta pour more ketchup on my fries.)

Smile for the Camera

I was busily dodging tourists in Gatlinburg not long ago when the solution to the economic woes in Great Smoky Mountains National Park reached out and smacked me so hard, I'm surprised it wasn't heard in Knoxville.

The answer is so obvious it should have dawned on civic leaders, politicians, park service officials, and tour directors long ago. But you know how the saying goes out there in the crowded Smokies: Sometimes, you can't see the forest for the knees.

In any event, time's wasting. If someone will put my plan into action, the money will pile up faster than cars in Cades Cove when a bear crosses the road.

Ask yourself. What is the number one cultural activity tourists engage in when they visit the mountains?

Ride go-carts? Spend a few hours at Dollywood? Play miniature golf? Watch handmade taffy being cranked out by machines? Shop at the outlet stores? Splash around in the motel swimming pool? Buy T-shirts with obscene slogans emblazoned across the front?

Those are all good guesses. Ye astute observers of that interesting species, *Tourii americanus,* are to be congratulated. But I threw a trick into the question. Please note I asked for their primary activity "when they visit the mountains." And that—a drum roll, please—is to stand in front of the Great Smoky Mountains National Park entrance sign and take stupid pictures of themselves.

You've seen these people, of course. Probably hundreds of times.

They line up like convicts in a firing squad and remain there—gawking, grinning, sticking out their tongues, waving "hi" and making the "We're Number One" sign as another member of the clan snaps the shutter or runs the video.

Then they swap out—in much the same manner as migrating geese shifting to the rear of the V—and take their place behind the camera while others in the group gawk, grin, tongue-stick, wave, and sign-make.

Over and over the procedure is repeated until they run out of film, the batteries go dead, or everybody's photo has been taken. Then they pile back into the car and return to the motel's swimming pool and video game parlor, their wilderness adventure having concluded.

All we gotta do, then, is charge 'em for the privilege. One dollar a shot, six shots for five bucks, something like that. The park service can even rent cameras and assign a ranger on site to help load film or reprogram digital models, as needed.

This is a win-win situation all around.

The locals, who have been mad as hornets ever since the idea of charging an admission fee to the park was suggested, will immediately pipe down. This won't affect them because they never stop to take such stupid pictures in the first place. The visitors won't know the difference because (a) they've been used to forking over cash since they left Toledo and (b) after they've dropped five hundred big ones at the factory outlet stores, an extra dollar will seem like the bargain of the century.

I'm so excited, I may treat myself to another box of homemade taffy, freshly imported from Chicago.

Sweaty Statistics

Something recently happened in church that I hadn't seen in years.

No, it didn't involve a juicy public confession, nor was there weeping, wailing, and gnashing of teeth. We Episcopalians tend to behave rather stoically in church. If the second coming occurred in our midst, our first reaction would likely be to consult the Book of Common Prayer to find the proper congregational response. Either that or appoint a committee to gauge the second coming's impact on the parish budget.

We did, however, get down to some old-fashioned sweat preaching. Sweat praying, too. This is what happens when the central air-conditioning system goes kaflooey on the first Sunday of summer.

Verily, we fanned. From the processional right up to the benediction, we looked like emergent butterflies testing new wings. By necessity, bulletins were the instrument of choice. They were a poor substitute for those floppy, wooden-handled funeral home fans that once were standard issue at every church in Dixie.

As I sat in my pew, furiously stroking my bulletin, I thought of forty-seven reasons to be thankful—starting with Phoenix, Houston, Miami, San Antonio, and Fort Myers. According to armpit experts at Old Spice, the aftershave and deodorant company, those are the top five sweatiest cities in the United States.

When you make your living studying body odor, you need a high threshold of stink tolerance—not to mention a weird sense of humor. I guess that's why the Old Spice staff conjured up such an aromatic list.

They took the height and weight of an "average" American male and female, factored in the average high temperature and average relative humidity for June, July, and August in one hundred cities, and then analyzed the sweat potential after Andy and Anne Average have walked for one hour.

The resulting data probably has as much credibility as an intelligence report on Iraqi weapons systems. But at least it's a lot more fun and, unlike Iraqi weapons, is available for inspection.

Knoxville ranked forty-eighth. We were quite cool compared with Memphis (seventeenth), Chattanooga (thirty-second), and Nashville (thirty-seventh). Only Bristol (sixty-ninth) was a drier Tennessee town.

Number one hundred in this roundup was San Francisco, preceded by Seattle, Spokane, Portland (Maine), and San Diego—leading me to wonder if towns beginning with the letter *S* are 80 percent more arid than the national average.

I'm not sure how this translates to deodorant sales. Maybe it means Old Spice will reduce its presence in cooler climes and concentrate on the odoriferous regions. Or maybe a burst of civic pride will inspire perspiring residents of the moist zones to practice a bit more personal hygiene.

But if the people at Old Spice are interested, here's a suggestion: Start offering a free church fan with every deodorant purchase. Sweltering congregations in all one hundred cities will surely appreciate the gesture.

Of course, before we Episcopalians do anything rash, we'll need to consult the Book of Common Prayer to see if Jesus was an Old Spice, Right Guard, or Mennen Speed Stick guy.

The Name Game

A 240-year-old boarding school in New England has been in the news recently because the folks in charge want to change its name.

They believe Dummer Academy is a turnoff to prospective students. Members of the board of directors are expected to vote on a new name soon.

The school, located in Byfield, Massachusetts, is named after its founder, Governor William Dummer. Hizzoner may have been BMOC in the 1760s, but here in the twenty-first century—particularly in light of hit movies like *Dumb and Dumber*—the name sparks laughs whenever it is mentioned.

"Rightly or wrongly, first impressions make a difference," headmaster John M. Doggett was quoted in the *Boston Globe*. "Certainly, when you go outside of the Boston region, the first impression sometimes doesn't convey what the school is all about."

The proposed change has ignited a firestorm of protests from many alumni. One of them, Thomas Driscoll, class of 1978, calls it "a horrible move."

As the Great Name Debate rages, I would suggest Dummer officials consult with a certain resident of Monroe County, Tennessee.

He, too, comes from New England. He, too, is an academician. He, too, knows something about weird handles.

And his suggestion?

"Be proud of your name."

This nugget of sage wisdom comes from Dr. James Noseworthy, president of Hiwassee College in Madisonville.

Yes, that's the same James Noseworthy who owns a protruding proboscis of prizewinning proportions.

We're talkin' a sensational schnozzle. A bounteous beak. A nucleus of nasal nicknames since Doctor Jim was in junior high.

"I was in about the ninth grade when my nose caught up with my name," he told me. "I've been 'The Nose' or 'The Schnoz' to a lot of my friends ever since. I even had a French teacher in high school who called me 'Monsieur Valeur Nez: worthy of the nose.'"

(For the record, I consulted with the prez about the propriety of penning prose poking fun of his prodigious—oh, stop it!—snout ahead of time. I would drop the matter if he objected. Happily, he agreed to play along. Clearly, the guy's got a nose for news.)

All the teasing has been in good fun, said Noseworthy, an ordained United Methodist minister who served churches in Iowa and North Carolina before turning his talents toward higher education.

"When I was in seminary, I became 'The Noble Nose,'" he added. "When I had a church in Davenport, Iowa, one of my clergy colleagues was Worthy Usher. Seriously, that was his given name. The papers out there had a ball with that."

What's in a name?

There's a road in rural west Knox County, down near the Loudon County line, that has seen more than its share of accidents involving beverages.

"Last year, a truck went off and spilled twenty-five-pound bags of cocoa everywhere," says Tom Campbell. "You could smell the chocolate for a week."

Shortly thereafter, another drinkable cargo was scattered, Campbell said. This time it was beer—850 cases of longnecks.

Both accidents occurred within three hundred feet of each other.

The name of this down-the-hatch thoroughfare? Buttermilk Road.

And just outside Newport in Cocke County, there's a gentle stream—hardly more than a trickle, really—named Dry Fork. But occasionally it's anything but dry.

In 2001, Dry Fork went on a rampage and covered its surroundings with more than five feet of water.

The English surname originated in the 1200s. It's not uncommon in the New England area, he said, even though it's rare in the South.

Noseworthy is the father of three adult children. His daughter Jane, who is pursuing a musical performance career in California, is a former Miss Nebraska who competed in the 2003 Miss America pageant.

As proud papa pointed out, "Fortunately, she didn't inherit my nose."

Riding Out the Storm

Hunkering down isn't all it's cracked up to be. Maybe it never was.

Hunkering down is what animals—domestic, wild, human, or otherwise—are supposed to do when the weather turns nasty, particularly in winter. Allegedly, some mysterious, sixth sense of survival is activated by tumbling temperatures and howling winds. It commands us to lay low till conditions improve. Then we can proceed with business as usual.

Blount Countian Melvin Giles, who always keeps me abreast of unusual signs, saw this one posted near a medical complex: "No Loitering After 7 p.m."

"I guess this means it's OK to loaf around over there before seven," he quipped.

Maybe there's an element of truth to this notion. Perhaps some biologist, physiologist, psychologist, or other "-ologist" could orate on the matter. Or could be that hunkering down has fallen out of favor since *Homo sapiens* abandoned caves and discovered the delights of Gore-Tex, four-wheel drive, and McFat Food. But for whatever reason, most modern-day humans don't hunker down worth a flip.

Oh, we might close schools for a day or two. Or shorten office hours. Or curtail certain government services. But all that does is give everybody a better opportunity to go sledding, skiing, shopping, even visit the dentist. Anything to avoid hunkering down.

I tried to hunker down a few days ago after Knoxville was slammed by snow and subfreezing temperatures. It was a frustrating experience.

Soon as it got good daylight, I took a walk in the woods in search of snow photos. Yes, it was cold. No, I didn't stay out for long. Yes, my bones, not to mention my teeth, were rattling by the time I got home.

It would make more sense to hunker down in January and take snow pictures on some sunny morning in May. But the odds of finding snow scenes in May aren't great. So I bundled up and trudged along, trying to focus through teary eyes with gloved, numb fingers.

While I walked, I realized many wild animals aren't good at hunkering down, either. The woods around my place were laced with tracks of coyotes, mice, rab-

That's Where I Come From

bits, and squirrels, plus birds by the dozens. Turns out my hilltop neighbor, Jim Colley, was avoiding hunkering down on the opposite side of the ridge at the same time. He added deer tracks and raccoon tracks to the inventory.

Back home by the fire, I tried in earnest to hunker down. The process was progressing at an excellent clip until (1) the coffee pot ran dry and (2) I finished both the morning newspaper and the book I'd been reading.

Then I started to fidget. Nothing ruins a good hunkering down faster than a dose of the fidgets.

I tried watching television but immediately became bored with pre-pre-pre-pre–Super Bowl hype and three consecutive broadcasts of the Weather Channel's local-on-the-eights forecast. Couldn't even find an *Andy Griffith* or *Three Stooges* rerun.

I'm forever intrigued by East Tennesseans' grasp of local geography. Knoxvillian Vera Roberts told me about the time, some years ago, when her husband was admitted to a hospital in Oak Ridge.

The admitting nurse asked where he was born, and he replied, "Right here."

"You mean Oak Ridge?" the nurse said.

"No, I mean right here," he repeated, pointing to the floor. "Right here is where our farm used to be."

I thought about cleaning out some old file folders but dismissed the notion just as quickly. Never know when I might need that stuff, I reasoned.

In desperation, I attempted to do honest work. I telephoned the office, retrieved my phone messages, and returned all my calls. I even—*gasp!*—worked up some notes that had been rattling around in my satchel for a couple of weeks. That put me two full columns ahead of schedule, which is light-years in the context of my normal production.

All of these hunker-down frustrations were exacerbated by the fact that my wife, a non-Type-A who can hunker down with the best of 'em, was consumed with computer duties.

The only time Mary Ann left her chair was to brew more tea or go to the fire and warm her "mouse hand." (Computer geeks, which is redundant, know what I mean.)

It finally got so bad that I unsheathed our twelve-month collection of receipts, writs, and cancelled checks and did the preliminary tabulations for our income tax return.

This is the earliest I have ever tackled this chore. Normally I wait until, oh, April twelfth or thirteenth. Then I sprint into Tax Guy's office, fling myself on his desk, sob hysterically, and beg for mercy. That I would begin this odious process in January shows the depths of despair to which a Type-A person will sink when trying to hunker down.

And failing miserably.

Selling Our Way out of Hock

What money crisis? Just because Knoxville is a cool ten million dollars in the hole, there's no need to panic.

Quite the contrary. It's time to party. Tell the Knoxville Symphony to strike up a snappy rendition of "Happy Days Are Here Again." Let us sing and make merry from Forks of the River to Farragut.

Why such gaiety? Simple. I've just realized how to free Knoxville from its economic quagmire. All we gotta do is let Warren Buffett buy the town, just like he did Jim Clayton's trailer empire.

In case you've been paying more attention to affairs in Baghdad than in Knoxville, you may have missed the biggest financial story to ever hit River City. Buffett, a kajillionaire investor from Omaha, Nebraska, bought Clayton's mobile home company. He paid $1.7 billion.

Repeat: That's *b*. As in "billion." In cash.

A pile of money that size is lost on most Knoxvillians. In matters of *b* purchases, we Joe and Jane Sixpacks typically think in terms of "baloney," "bread," "bacon," or "beer."

But to give you an idea how much $1.7 billion truly is, I sharpened my pencil and did some figuring.

(Since I have trouble adding two plus three, I also ran my calculations by Art Ridgway, the *News Sentinel*'s resident techie; Dr. John Conway of the University of Tennessee's math department; and Whitney Henderson of the AAA East Tennessee Automobile Club. They concurred. So if you spot an error, blame them. I'm still trying to balance my stupid %$#! checkbook.)

Consideration One: If you took Buffett's purchase price and reduced it to one-dollar bills (6.125 inches each), they would stretch 164,339 miles. If laid end to end at the equator, these George Washingtons would wrap around the world a little more than 6 1/2 times—assuming the wind doesn't blow and make a mess. Serious money, any way you cut it.

Consideration Two: If you took Knoxville's debt and reduced it to one-dollar bills, they would stretch a mere 967 miles. If laid end to end at Memphis, these bucks would reach to Mountain City and back to the Tennessee River in Perry County. Peanuts by comparison.

Consideration Three: Warren Buffett learned about Jim Clayton and his company after reading Clayton's autobiography, *First a Dream*. That led to talks between the two men, and before you could say, "Let's make a deal," Buffett was opening his wallet.

Consideration Four: There are several good books about our town. Among them are *Knoxville, Tennessee: A Mountain City in the New South*, by

Bruce Wheeler; *Heart of the Valley,* by Lucile Deaderick; *Knoxville!* by Betsey Creekmore; and *Knoxville: A Bicentennial Portrait,* by Cynthia Moxley.

Do you see where this is going? Of course you do. All we gotta do is put one or more of these books into Warren Buffett's hands, then sit back and wait for him to call the mayor's office and bail us out of hock.

"Buffettville, Tennessee."

Has a warm, margarita-ish ring to it, don't you think?

Chapter 8

The Wide World of Sports—
Afield, Afloat, and Athletic

I tend to write rather frequently about sporting topics. This habit came with the territory in 1985, when Harry Moskos, then editor of the *News Sentinel,* invited me to switch from outdoor columns to general interest and humor. I told Harry sports was my first love and that I needed to be able to fall back on sporting topics as a security blanket during the transition. He agreed.

Nearly twenty-five years later, I still spend quite a bit of time, not to mention *News Sentinel* travel money, on the road at sporting venues—outdoors and indoors. OK, so I'm slow at transitions.

I'm slow in other ways, too.

I've never been much of a runner—of either the long-distance or sprint variety. It's a genetic problem. Venables are engineered more along the lines of fireplugs than fireflies. When you are built as low to the ground as I am, you don't need to run away from trouble. You just duck or hide.

Nonetheless, I am forever amazed how fast a human being, present company included, can move when properly inspired. I was reminded of this phenomenon one day after hunting for wild turkeys.

Turkeys are usually found in steep country. To reach them you have to climb, often straight-up, hand-to-tree, slip-and-bust-knee. Perhaps climbing comes easily for dogs, cats, snakes, babies, and other critters. But it is an irksome chore for adult males, particularly when they are of the chubby variety and have weighted themselves further with an eight-pound shotgun and a hunting vest crammed full of snacks, maps, water bottles, and a dozen assorted calls the manufacturer swears will fool every turkey within a four-county radius.

Which explains why Larry Cook and I were ascending one of East Tennessee's Matterhorns before daylight, huffing and puffing and pulling ourselves along at the speed of garden slugs.

If, at that precise moment, you had told us there was a pair of thousand-dollar bills waiting for us at the top and all we had to do to claim them was jog up, we would have told you to keep your money. But as happened a few seconds later when a pair of turkeys gobbled at the crest of the ridge, we closed the distance like Olympic medalists. We plopped down at the base of a large white oak, I made some love music on one of my calls, and—testament to the horniness of spring gobblers, not my calling skills—both birds came strutting in, lust on their minds. They died with smiles on their faces.

Oddly enough, this swift-movement phenomenon repeated itself later that same day.

I drove home, cleaned my turkey, and started putting away my gear. I was dog-tired and aching of joint. I wanted to lie down on the sofa and catch up on my sleep.

But my camouflage clothes were muddy and wet, and I knew from past experience that muddy, wet camo clothes can turn into stinky, mildewed, camo clothes inside of twenty-four hours. Thus at the blurring pace of a refrigerated amoeba, I stumbled into the laundry room, shoved everything into the washing machine, added soap powder, and turned it on.

Approximately ten minutes later, I started searching for my billfold.

It was not with my pocket change and wristwatch. It was not on the truck seat, nor inside the glove compartment. It was not on the top of my dresser. Ever so slowly, my sleepy little gray cells began the arduous process of backtracking.

"Did His Rotundity leave his billfold at the country store when he and Larry checked in their turkeys?" the gray cells asked each other. "No, His Rotundity distinctly remembers putting it back in his camo pants pocket and buttoning the flap."

The gray cells flinched at the mention of the words "camo pants pocket."

"Camo pants pocket," they repeated. "Camo pants pocket! CAMO PANTS #@$%! POCKET! *Aaaaa-iiiii-eee!*"

Inspired once again, I reached the laundry room in just under .00726 second and rescued my billfold from soapy ruin.

Which brings me to yet another phenomenon I discovered that day: If you back your pickup truck into a sunny part of the driveway, spread all your drenched currency, licenses, notes, business cards, and other important papers across the seat, then roll up the windows and let them cook all afternoon, they will eventually dry out.

Thankfully, I'm not the only person who understands and appreciates the slow approach to the sporting life. While in the Fairfield Glade community one spring to address a Friends of the Library group, I met a fellow named Dan Jacober. Like many transplants to Tennessee (he's an Ohio native), Dan is retired. He has become an expert at doing nothing.

That's why he formed the United States Olympic Resting Team.

"Our logo is a chaise lounge, upon which rests the five rings, a symbol recognized the world over," he says. "To qualify, you have to be able to rest at the Olympic level."

"What's it like competing against the best?" I wanted to know.

"Sometimes it can get ugly," he answered. "Not long ago, we entered into an Olympic resting match with the North Korean team. Unfortunately, it didn't end up too well. We met over breakfast, and they slipped Sleep-Ease into the women's tea and Viagra into the men's coffee. The ladies were too drugged to compete, and the men were too agitated. We had to forfeit the entire game."

Bummer. But, hey, that's the breaks. You win some and you lose some and a few get snoozed out.

When Dan described the arduous training regimen he and his teammates undergo on a regular basis, I winced in pain.

Sometimes they actually stretch out and rest in the direct sunshine! When it's chilly, they have to reach for a blanket! And if they fall asleep, they might train three, four, five hours without a break! Oh, the humanity!

"You have to be committed to make this team," he said.

Naturally, Dan and his fellow teammates are professionals at resting. But he was willing to develop a program on the amateur, collegiate level.

Does his own expertise in this regard go all the way back to college?

"Well, no," he answered. "I never attended college. But I sure did a lot of resting in high school. Did a lot in the Navy, too. In fact, I had an old deck chief who used to notice that I always looked busy but nothing ever got done. I always told him I didn't want to start something I couldn't finish."

As Dan began to discuss the possibilities, the resting curriculum fell into place. He stressed that major universities, like Tennessee and other members of the Southeastern Conference, should accept nothing less than a five-star program, complete with state-of-the-art training facilities: beds, cots, mattresses, recliners, and box springs. Plus background music to help begin each difficult study session. And tutors, of course, for those less-than-gifted jocks who can't quite cut the classroom mustard.

Sounded great to me. And I'm certain this concept will be a hit on campuses throughout the region, if not the nation.

Just to show what a swell guy he is, Dan made me an honorary member of the resting team, right there on the spot. So if you'll excuse me—*yaaaawn!*—I gotta go practice. After all the potential my coach sees in me, I sure don't want to let him down.

Frightening Fishing

I have seen some classic warning labels in my life.

I've got an eight-foot aluminum stepladder at home that is covered with seven different labels, a rough average of one precaution every fourteen inches. Among them are such pearls of wisdom as "Do not use this product if you tire easily" and "Face ladder when climbing up and down."

Other people have noticed these silly things, too. A friend saw this manufacturer's gem posted on the panel of a small airplane a buddy of his was flying: "When landing, make sure you are on the ground before applying the brakes." A reader sent me these two pieces of sage advice on power tools in his workshop: "Not for indoor use" on the lawn mower and "Do not attempt to stop chain with your hand" on the chain saw.

But while shopping for fishing lures the other night, I discovered what surely will go down as the blue-ribbon warning label for all time. This admonition was on the back of a blister pack containing a three-inch-long plastic crankbait designed to catch bass.

"WARNING: This product contains lead, a chemical known to the state of California to cause cancer and birth defects and other reproductive harm," the label began.

Well, yes, I suppose there is some lead incorporated in this lure. Several tiny lead BBs are molded inside of it. They rattle when the bait is reeled through the water, creating a sound that allegedly attracts bass and other game fish. Of course, to expose the lead BBs to the air or the water or your own body, you'd have to smash the lure to smithereens with a hammer, ruining its effectiveness as a lure. But why dwell on logic when there was more comedy in the next sentence?

"Do not place your hands in your mouth after handling the product," it said.

Why would I want to put my hands in my mouth before or after handling a fishing lure? My hands would be occupied with operating the rod and reel.

The label continued: "Wash your hands after touching the product."

Huh? This is a piece of plastic, for Pete's sake, not strontium-90 or raw sewage or packing house waste. But just for the sake of argument, let's suppose I did follow the directions. Where am I supposed to wash my hands when I'm out fishing—in the foul waters of Fort Loudoun Lake, mayhaps?

Then I hit the mother lode, and I swear on a stack of Bibles I'm not pulling your leg: "Do not place the product in your mouth."

I turned the package back over and stared at the lure inside. Dangling fore and aft were two treble hooks—a total of six large, needle-sharp, barbed slivers of metal. Fishing lures have a habit of containing these things.

I purchased the crankbait and took it home and started to put it into one of my tackle boxes. But then—holy cow!—the seriousness of the situation hit me between the eyes like a two-by-four.

I have spent a lifetime accumulating bass lures. I own literally hundreds of them—crankbaits, surface plugs, spoons, jigs, flies, buzzbaits. They all contain sharp hooks. *And not one ever came equipped with a warning label telling me to keep them out of my mouth!*

Whew, talk about luck! It's a miracle I haven't eaten dozens of these deadly devices by now.

A Leg Up on Pests

I have just gotten off the telephone with Evan Bowers. He is one of the most skilled outdoor people I've ever met. Evan has spent most of his lifetime afield or afloat in the company of firearms, archery equipment, and fishing tackle. Any Tennessee critter that flies, swims, walks, crawls, runs, struts, or jumps is bound to have encountered this guy—and more than likely went home for supper. Evan's supper, that is.

Which explains why he and I were talking panty hose.

"The problem with most brands," he began, "is that they rip easily. I usually tear the first couple of pairs I try on every year. You have to learn how to wiggle into them."

The master woodsman was not finished dispensing tips: "Always buy the darkest kind you can find. They're made out of thicker material. The sheer ones are too thin."

The best place to purchase them?

"I always watch for sales," he replied. "The way I go through 'em, it helps to have a few extra pairs on hand."

I don't know what sort of thoughts are coursing through your mind right now. Whatever you and your brain want to think about a man who not only buys and wears panty hose but also talks about the experience is between you and your noggin. But permit me to set the record straight. The reason Evan traipses around in panty hose every spring involves neither fashion nor fetishes—unless you consider turkey hunting to be a fetish, in which case you would be wrong.

Turkey hunting is more than a simple fetish. It's a cult with tens of thousands of devoted Tennessee followers. Every April, these legions begin roaming the hills and hollows. They continue this insanity until the middle of May. Evan is among them every morning, and the reason he wears panty hose can be summed up in two horrifying words.

Seed ticks.

Like Evan and turkey hunters everywhere, I hate these awful vermin. Given the power, I would nuke them. If seed ticks were ever entered on the Endangered Species List, I would celebrate deliriously.

Seed ticks are the baby version of old-fashioned dog ticks. They are about the size of a pepper speck. They have teeth like a chain saw. If you're in the woods frequently, especially in areas where the deer population is high, you will most assuredly encounter them by the dozens.

Seed ticks are the meanest cootie in Mother Nature's ark of loathsome pests. They make chiggers feel like a mild case of heat rash. You will claw till you bleed. They start hatching in late spring and continue their evil deeds throughout the summer. Just the mention of them makes me start itching right now.

Turkeys start gobbling love sonnets about the same time the ticks start gobbling blood. Poke around in the boonies long enough in April and May and your body will become a walking smorgasbord.

I don't worry much about Lyme disease. It's the tick bite itself that drives me berserk. For reasons known only to dermatology, my skin is particularly sensitive to tick saliva—and I dearly hope you're not reading this essay over breakfast. Any time and every time a tick souses down on my flesh, it leaves a giant red welt that itches like a dozen chiggers rolled into one. Even worse, the itch remains long after the redness and swelling fade away.

I've been known to still be scratching an April tick bite in August. That goes for any kind of tick, your basic regulation dog tick all the way down to those murderous seed ticks.

Some years ago, Evan got to thinking that the body armor afforded by panty hose might repel seed ticks. He tried a pair one day—it was a solo outing—and could not have been happier with a twenty-pound gobbler.

A game warden friend, who shall remain anonymous for obvious reasons, recently told me about blue-lighting a pleasure boat that was plowing down the lake, throwing up a tsunami of water.

"The driver wasn't breaking any law that I could tell," the officer said, "but I knew by that huge wake he didn't have his motor tilted correctly. So I puttered over to him and hollered out, 'You need to trim 'er down a little bit!'"

Immediately, he realized that was the oh-so-wrong thing to say.

"I glanced to the back of the boat and saw his wife—or at least I assume it was his wife. Whoever it was, she was a big woman. I mean a biiig woman.

"'Your outboard!' I yelled as loud as I could. 'Trim your outboard down!' Then I turned and got out of there."

"Crazy as it sounds, they really will keep seed ticks off your legs and ankles," he said. "But they do take some gettin' used to. Even if you buy the largest size, they're still made for a woman."

No more they aren't. That's why I called Evan in the first place.

I had been listening to National Public Radio that morning and heard a story about an Ohio company that makes panty hose for men. The name of the outfit is G. Lieberman and Sons. The brand name is Comfilon.

I called up their Web site and printed out eight pages of information. Com-filons are marketed as a lightweight, full-length, support stocking—but with the added features of an expanded waist, more storage room Down Yonder, plus the all-important "discreet fly opening" in front. As the company brags, these are "not your mother's panty hose."

The fly business really caught Evan's attention. Learning to wiggle into the narrow legs and waist of women's wear is bad enough. Having to virtually disrobe in the forest for every round of coffee recycling tends to slow a fellow down.

These things aren't cheap. The thickest models run twelve dollars a pair. Nonetheless, I thought Evan was going to weep with joy.

Out there in the back country, where men are men, there's going to be an extra spring in a lot of steps this year.

Ah, to Be Young and Dumb Again

It's not every day that a traditional cultural event in a small European town makes the six o'clock news 'round the world. Then again, it's not every day that otherwise rational human beings throw themselves in front of several tons of four-legged death.

Meaning, of course, that it's time for the running of the bulls in Pamplona, Spain.

Surely there's nobody over the age of ten who hasn't heard about this spectacle. It occurs in July during the Fiesta de San Fermin. Every morning of the festival, bulls are released on the main street of town. At the same time, it is customary for thousands of daring young men to run in front of them.

This nuttiness has become a mainstay of summer reporting. Check out any newspaper, sports program, or news report during July—especially if significant trampling occurs—and you can watch the action up close and personal.

Talk about a photo op! This thing beats stadium and bridge demolitions all to pieces. Mainly because you never know who's going to get stomped to pieces.

Unless something goes horribly wrong during a planned demolition, the event is spectacularly, if boringly, predictable. Some guy off camera counts down the time, the dynamite goes ka-blooey, and the building implodes in a huge cloud of dust. Everybody cheers. Then trucks move in to transport the rubble to a landfill.

But with the running of the bulls, nobody knows what to expect—except that there's bound to be some gonzo footage of wild-eyed young men dashing madly about, like their crazy lives depended on it.

Uh, that's because their crazy lives *do* depend on it.

A couple of days ago, I made an Internet search of the Pamplona festivities and scrolled through page after page of details and tips about the half-mile-long melee. One paragraph in particular caught my eye:

"As well as the danger inherent in running in front of a bull—it's worth remembering this is an animal which weighs about thirteen hundred pounds and has two big rock-hard horns that can cut through practically anything, not to mention possible bruising from just being stepped on—there is also the problem of overcrowding in the run. So you have to be careful not to get bowled over or knocked down by other runners."

Do tell.

I realize I'm a doddering old nerd whose idea of flirting with danger is mowing the lawn without sun screen. These days, my heart gets a strenuous workout whenever I check the status of my 401(k). Nonetheless, I was young once, and I still remember what it was like to be stupid and bulletproof. As a proud redneck of southern Appalachian extraction, I speak with the voice of experience regarding one aspect of this insanity.

Even though it's been years since I took Spanish, and even though I couldn't "habla Español" on the kindergarten level, I'd be willing to bet a universal language is spoken by the vast majority of participants.

Roughly translated, it goes something along the lines of "Hey, Juan, hold my beer and watch this!"

Hard to Hide from a Camo Sale

I am eating serious crow. It is tough, stringy, and tastes somewhere between sun-dried carp and petrified polecat. But eat it I shall because I richly deserve this meal. By all rights I should go through the buffet line twice before hitting the desserts.

It's all because I used to laugh at the way women behave around sales. "Used" to laugh, I reiterate. My consciousness has forevermore been raised.

If you—I address persons of the male persuasion in this regard—have ever attended a discount event with wife, girlfriend, or other she-shopper, you know whereof I speak.

There is something about the words "reduced" and "bargain" that sets X-chromosomes on fire. We are talking hot flashes twenty-five degrees warmer than those of the Change. We are talking sweet smiles and cheerful dispositions replaced with fang and claw. We are talking femininity supplanted by brute force.

But shortly after nine o'clock the other morning, I saw the Y-chromosome version of this metamorphosis, and I'm here to tell you it's just as ugly. This is what happens when camouflage clothes go on sale.

At the stroke of nine, they opened the doors for Camo Day at Hammer's Discount Stores in Clinton, Maynardville, and Williamsburg, Kentucky. Since no obituary notices about the matter have been telephoned into the newspaper, I assume nobody died in the stampede.

I did not witness the mass of masculinity as it surged off the street and into the building. I am relying on those who were there and got sucked up in the melee. I didn't arrive at the Clinton store until fifteen minutes after nine o'clock, which proved about as timely as tuning into the Super Bowl during postgame analysis.

"You're too late!" came the voice from a brown-and-green mountain shuffling toward the cash register. "All the good stuff is already gone!"

Not that I could tell. Indeed, as I gazed toward the rear of the store, I was convinced 94 percent of the hunting and fishing license holders in East Tennessee were still present and accounted for. And grabbing.

There were men in blue jeans and tank tops. Men in suits and designer neckties. Men with beer bellies. Men with stomachs tighter than guy wires. Men with four days' worth of whiskers. Men freshly shaven and reeking of Old Spice. En masse, they looked like maggots reducing the carcass of a fallen elk.

"Grab something and just hold it, even if you don't intend to buy it!" one barked to me. "This is like a cocktail party. You gotta at least have a ginger ale in your hand!"

"Whatever you do, don't set anything down!" another advised. "It'll be gone!"

"Forget the racks!" came even more advice from the crowd. "Start tearin' into those boxes lined up on the wall!"

This spectacle came about, store owner Jeff Hammer later told me, because of a warehouse deal he had located in Texas. He bought the entire inventory, floor to ceiling, of a Walls and 10-X factory: boots, hats, gloves, rain suits, insulated bib overalls, jackets, coats, parkas. Translation for the outdoor-impaired: He tossed uncut heroin, at bargain-basement prices, to junkies.

In a little over two hours, the gorging was over—at least for the M, L, XL, and XXL sets. I assume a few selections remained for Mini-Me and the Jolly Green Giant. Otherwise, tough luck.

"I called Tom Wyrick, our store manager in Maynardville, and asked him what his camo selection was like," Hammer commented. "He said, 'You know on Animal Planet when two or three lions get hold of a zebra and start pulling? Well, our camo racks pretty much look like the zebra.'"

What did I buy? Not one blessed item. Cross my heart. Not so much as a camo hanky.

I'm still trying to analyze this inaction. I don't know whether it was due to shock, panic, or the fact that—like I suspect is true of many of the shoppers—I didn't actually *need* any more camo.

Which is no excuse, as any hunter, bargain or otherwise, will attest.

"Do you realize," I mused to one customer as the jerking and piling-on continued at a fever pitch, "that everyone in here is probably spending more money on camouflage than they've spent on dress clothes in the last five years?"

I might just as well have cussed aloud in church. The guy, double-arm loaded, stopped grabbing long enough to look at me in disgusted awe.

"So what's your point?" he asked.

Dangers on the Water

Starting in mid-February every year, I anxiously await the arrival of spring. This time around, however, I'm not so sure.

Spring signals the start of water activity, and based on what I've been reading lately, I want to distance myself from all bodies of water—large or small, fresh or saline. Indeed, if I only get close enough to water to splash a few drops into a cup of joy juice, so much the better.

Come to think of it, I oughta pour myself another helping of elixir before we go any further. Just imagining the horrible incidents that can occur on open water has given me a frightening case of the shakes.

My first concern was aroused by a snippet of information from the *Charlotte News and Observer*. A friend in North Carolina sent it to me. It was about a fisherman in Russia who caught a pike and, in his jubilation over boating the toothy beast, kissed it.

Don Cruze tells me he recently purchased a new Yamaha outboard motor. While inspecting it closely, he discovered his "Japanese" marine product was manufactured in France. Don said he has read the owner's manual cover to cover but still can't determine if he's supposed to use white wine or red in the fuel mix.

The pike repaid this show of affection by biting the fisherman. Hard. We are talking a chomp of bury-'em-to-the-gumline proportions. The man's friends killed the fish and cut off its head, but to no avail. It had to be surgically removed at a hospital.

Please understand that I, personally, have never kissed a pike. Or any other fish, for that matter. But I've seen it done on a number of occasions, particularly when I covered professional bass tournaments.

I remember one tournament in the early 1980s in which a fourteen-inch largemouth, caught during a sudden-death overtime, meant tens of thousands of dollars to the winner. Before he gently returned his prize to the fragrant waters of Cherokee Lake, the guy lip-locked that bass with all the passion of Rhett Butler on Miss Scarlett. Which shows what can happen when you've been on the water all day under a blazing sun.

Thus I appeal to my angling brothers and sisters to practice safe piscatorial sex, lest they wind up in the script of *ER* instead of an outdoor program on ESPN. If you must kiss fish, be sure to put a condom on your nose.

Don't think it's any safer in salt water, either. A buddy in Oak Ridge sent me a story from *Scuba Diving* magazine which discussed in great detail—I am not making this up—whale flatulence.

The story, written by marine biologist Richard Martin, described how whales, being mammals, have digestive tracts bearing many of the same characteristics as those found in cows. As you and I and most government scientists know, cows toot on a regular basis, a socially unacceptable act that contributes significantly to global warming.

Martin acknowledges a dearth of research on whale flatulence. But by taking documented information about human backfires and extrapolating the figures to a whale-sized animal, then expanding for the world's estimated whale population, he believes some forty billion gallons of gas are blasted into sea water every year.

I may never swim in the ocean again. If I do muster the courage to tiptoe back into the surf, you better believe I'll pay closer attention—and run like hell—if someone hollers, "Thar she blows!"

Even Their Brains Are Frozen

If you want a graphic illustration of recreational determination, not to mention dementia, consider what happened in Canada a few days ago when emergency teams tried to rescue some stranded ice fishermen.

The fishermen refused to leave. The fishing was too good.

According to news dispatches I read, this occurred on Lake Simcoe, near Barrie, Ontario. Hordes of people were fishing when a crack suddenly developed in the ice, leaving a gap of open water more than three-hundred feet wide in places. The crack eventually stretched for twenty miles. Six military helicopters were summoned. Several hundred anglers were plucked to safety, but dozens of others insisted on staying.

"They're determined ice fishers," is the way one police officer, Sgt. Dan Yoisten, described the scene.

And you thought Uncle Floyd was nuts to continue playing golf during that thunderstorm?

Actually, I'm not surprised. I have only ice-fished once in my life. This was during the mid-1970s when Fort Loudoun Lake froze bank to bank. I chipped a hole in the ice at Choto Dock and lowered a minnow, just to say I'd done it. But I've heard enough ice-fishing tales from David Etnier to realize the people Up There have a different definition of the word "frigid" than we do Down Here.

Etnier, a retired zoologist and fisheries expert at the University of Tennessee, grew up in Minnesota. Even though he has lived in Knoxville for more than thirty years and has witnessed some record-setting winters here, he's still waiting for the weather to turn chilly.

Etnier understood completely when I telephoned him with news about the abortive rescue attempt. He said ice fishing is one of the things he misses most since moving to Tennessee. When walleyes, bluegills, and yellow perch are being jerked through a hole in the ice, no serious participant would let something as trifling as a twenty-mile-long crack spoil the fun.

"You must remember that winter comes early and stays late," Etnier said. "If you really like to fish, you've got to do it through the ice."

It's a sport that goes to the core of the angling psyche.

"You get to watch a bobber go down, you get to yank a wiggling fish in by hand, and then you get to eat it," he said. "When I was in college, a bunch of my friends and I built an ice house and kept it on Lake Mille Lacs all winter long. We had bunk beds and a card table so we could play poker. We'd stay there every weekend. Caught some good walleyes, too. A lot of times, there would be entire communities out on the ice, complete with concession stands."

Fun, perhaps. But how do you stand the cold?

"You get used to it," he replied. "The whole time you're out there, you have to keep ice from forming in your hole. Many times, I'd just use my bare hands. Once, I remember coming home from a trip like that and noticing the temperature was eighteen below zero."

I think I just had a hot flash.

Fun at the Boat Ramp

If you want a hearty dose of seasonal humor, forget Leno and Letterman, cable TV, comedy clubs, or the latest rounds of political malarkey spinning out of Nashville and Washington. Instead, just mosey on over to the nearest boat-launching ramp some sunny spring afternoon and pull up a seat. Within thirty minutes, you'll be slapping your knees in mirth.

Doesn't matter which ramp on which lake. Try the Dandridge ramp on Douglas. Or Grainger County Park on Cherokee. Or the canal ramp at Tellico–Fort Loudoun. Or Kingston City Park on Watts Bar. Or any of the hundreds of put-in places up and down this side of the Tennessee Valley. The show will be equally entertaining.

You see, there's a fresh crop of skippers every spring. These folks have just plunked down a war pension on a shiny new ship, and they can't wait to hit the water.

Ah, but the only way they can earn their stripes is to screw up royally backing down the ramp like a drunk blacksnake or forgetting to insert the drain plug or flooding the engine or failing to unhook from the trailer or any of five thousand other opportunities to goof in front of everyone else.

I speak as an equal opportunity offender in this regard. Through the years, I have committed all these sins and more. So have 95 percent of boat owners from coast to coast. The other 5 percent are liars.

I recently listened as Jim Wilson told of a launch-ramp stunt he and his wife, Margie, pulled at Terry Point on Douglas Lake. It was a gem.

Please understand. I wasn't laughing *at* the Wilsons; I was laughing *with* them because they are seasoned boaters. Alas, it was just one of "those" days for them.

"I had backed the trailer down the ramp, almost to the water," said Jim. "Margie got into the truck to back me the rest of the way into the water. Then she was going to park the trailer."

So far, so good. The boat slid effortlessly off the trailer and into the drink according to plan. Jim fired the engine and hollered for Margie to pull out.

Unfortunately, Margie didn't hear him. She just sat there.

So Jim put the engine into reverse and started to back farther away. Unfortunately, he only thought he had it in reverse. And instead of slowly backing up, he soused down on the throttle. Big mistake.

The boat roared out of the water like a Nike missile. So fast, in fact, that it went airborne and— ka-thud!—landed sideways on the trailer. That's the precise moment Margie put the truck in gear, stomped the gas and started up the launch ramp.

"She didn't get too far," Jim sighed. "I finally hollered loud enough, and she backed me into the water again."

Contrary to Yankee myth, most southern Appalachians know how to tie shoes. Indeed, this is a skill many of us have mastered by the time we finish high school. Assuming, of course, we made it to high school in the first place.

But what I want to know is, how come the laces on athletic shoes are so long? When I lace up a pair of athletic shoes, I've dang near got enough string left over to fly a kite. This phenomenon remains constant despite the particular brand of shoe.

What are you supposed to do with the excess? Wrap it around your legs two or three times?

A suggestion to manufacturers: Why not cut back on the string and pass the savings on to us?

Well, yes. There was this little matter of a hole in the hull. But Jim got it patched, good as new. All's well that ends well.

"For a long time after that," he said, "all our friends would line the bank anytime we started to launch. They couldn't wait to see what we were going to do next."

Wendell Wyrick remembers being at Hickory Star Dock on Norris Lake one day when a crew of speed jockeys showed up to launch a racing boat.

Apparently they didn't have the bow properly secured. The truck driver backed down the ramp, hit his brakes sharply, and the whole shebang shot onto the pavement—to the accompanying grinding of metal and fiberglass and the shrieking of expletives.

And then there's the scene former news photographer Jack Rose described on Neyland Drive. Jack was coming to work via that route when he encountered a backup. Turned out police had blocked traffic near the ramp so a huge tow truck could merge onto the roadway. Jack figured a commercial tug boat had just been launched.

"But no," he recounted. "Attached to the big tow truck was your everyday-sized tow truck, dripping wet. Attached to the everyday-sized tow truck was a 1960s-vintage Ford pickup truck that was slowly draining half of Fort Loudoun Lake. And attached to the Ford pickup was a fourteen-foot aluminum fishing boat, still strapped to the trailer.

"I'm sure some old guy's wife was having a field day with that. And some poor tow truck driver was getting his butt kicked."

Then Jack added a zinger: "And some news photographer was cussing himself for not having his camera."

Thankfully, Jack wasn't present, with or without a lens, the other day when I backed my bass boat down the ramp at George's Creek, deposited it into the lake, parked the truck, walked back to my boat, and pushed off shore—only to be greeted by that most dreadful marine sound, the "grrr-rrrr" of a dead battery.

Hoo-boy. Pass the paddle, please. Also the Rolaids. Like I said, we've all been there.

Hidden Treasures

Crawling around on hands and knees is not the sort of thing I normally do for pleasure. But the more I read about finding fabulous treasures inside of ordinary houses, the more I'm ready to hit the floor and start mingling with the dust bunnies.

The latest bonanza occurred a few weeks ago when a vintage baseball bat turned up. It was the one Babe Ruth used to hit the first home run in Yankee Stadium. This stick has been authenticated by a sports memorabilia company in California. Soon it will go on the auction block. No telling how many gazillion dollars the thing will fetch.

This bat did not magically appear in some dusty locker in an isolated corner of the Yankee Stadium dressing room. It did not bob to the surface in the athletic archives of a university or college, either. Nor was it included among the sports souvenirs in the estate of a recently departed baseball player like Ted Williams.

Instead, it was found by an ordinary woman who looked under her ordinary bed. Cross my ordinary heart.

The identity of the woman has not been revealed. But according to Professional Sports Authenticators of Newport Beach, California, this is indeed the very bat swung by the Sultan of Swat on April 18, 1923, during a four-to-one New York victory over Boston.

Seems that sometime after the game, Ruth autographed the lumber and inscribed it to one Victor Orsatti, the winner of a youth home-run hitting contest.

Orsatti died in 1984, but not before giving the bat to the woman. She stuck it You Know Where—and it stayed there until she finally got around to doing some housework.

Ta-dah! Instant riches!

This phenomenon is not new. In fact, it seems like I read about similar discoveries every few weeks. Surely you have, too. Never fails.

Some Gomer swings by a garage sale looking for a cheap picture frame. He picks up a piece of trash priced at seventy-five cents, argues the owner down to a quarter, then takes it home and finds an original Van Gogh buried between the glass and the cardboard backing.

Another Gomer is trolling the county flea market for used tires. He finds a set with five thousand miles' worth of tread remaining, and during the ensuing high-dollar transaction (four bucks versus three), the owner throws in a worthless flower vase for boot. Gomer's ready to chunk the vase into the trash when he happens to catch a radio report about priceless pieces missing from some rare collection. And the next thing you know, he's driving a Lexus and smoking bootlegged Cuban cigars.

And now this Gomerette is combing through the pizza boxes and cat litter beneath her mattress and finds one of Babe Ruth's home run bats. Incredible.

How come it never happens to me?

The closest I ever came to something like this occurred in 1997. Mary Ann and I were cleaning out our subdivision house of twenty-seven years and preparing to move into a log home we'd built in the woods. Way up on a remote shelf in the garage, buried under several tons of assorted junk, was a portable duck blind I'd long since forgotten about.

Was this a duck blind once owned by Davy Crockett? Did Annie Oakley use it to bag her ten thousandth mallard? Of course not. It was nothing but a half dozen metal poles and some camouflage netting worth approximately $12.37.

But I have faith. I'm going to hit my knees and start crawling. I shall not be deterred. I shall rummage and dig and paw through all the dark, dusty hidey holes in my house. I'm going to find my share of this hidden treasure if it kills me.

Gulp.

Strike that word "kill." Get rid of the word "strike," too. And while we're at it, let's forget all about searching for priceless treasures.

The last time I was poking around in the crawl space beneath my house, I came face-to-face with an exceedingly large copperhead. Thank heavens he'd already gone on to that big snake pit in the sky. In point of fact, he was stuck to a glue pad I had put out for mice.

So much for artifacts. If that copperhead had been alive, and I'd just found one of Babe Ruth's baseball bats, I would've rendered it to splinters in approximately .0004 second. And considered it a bargain.

Making Scents

"It's cologne for my big date," I told the man at the checkout. "Think it'll help me score?"

The guy didn't say. Apparently he lacked both an opinion and a sense of humor. Either that, or he was too busy trying to hold his breath and use as few fingers as possible to transfer my purchase from counter top to bag.

You'd think a clerk in a sporting goods store would be used to these things by now. After all, fall is here. Deer season is nigh. And hunters are spending wads of cash on all kinds of trinkets guaranteed to outwit Bambi.

Why else would I be buying a bottle of raccoon urine?

No, it's not to dab behind my ears. It's dang-sure not to drink. Indeed, it's not for use anywhere on, or in, my precious bodily temple.

The reason I—and jillions of other generally sane people—buy this stuff is because it does such a good job of covering human scent. You see, Bill and Bubba may not be able to smell each other (unless it has been an extraordinarily long time between baths), but the critters in the woods certainly can.

Sporting goods manufacturers can, too. To them, it smells like money. And they're more than happy to keep ringing up those sales.

In cover scents, for instance, customers can choose among pine, cedar, acorn, apple, sage, and earth aromas, just to name a few.

Fine for some. But I'm a traditionalist. I'm a stickler for pee. All I ever buy is something to spray on my boots and give deer the impression I'm an incontinent fox or raccoon, wandering aimlessly through the woods in search of a tree.

Laugh if you want. Or gasp, as my wife usually does. All I can say is I have seen many deer bolt at the smell of a human; and, conversely, have watched them approach unalarmed when that same foreign scent is masked by some other woodland animal's Number One.

There are additional, nonhunting benefits, as well. Solicitors and other long-winded folks who "just drop by" usually don't stick around when you hem them in on the front porch next to a pair of urine-soaked boots, curing in the breeze.

The big push now in deer scents is for sexual attractants. They're designed to entice Mister Ten-Pointer into bow or gun range with a whiff of Eau de Floozie.

I have looked at many of these products on dealer shelves, but frankly, I nearly break into an embarrassed sweat when I read the labels. A number of them actually contain secretions from, uh, "certain glands" of female deer. Indeed, the Hot Scrape lure promises a "powerful sexual attractant to bring in bucks aroused."

Sorry, but that ain't my idea of a good time.

Still, business is business. Far be it from me to argue with success, in the store or in the woods. But one of these years, if I look on a sporting goods dealer's shelf and see something on the order of the Lewinsky Lure, I just may give up deer hunting forever.

In church a few Sundays ago, I noticed the prelude was a number called "Nun Bitten Wir," and it reminded me why my tush was nestled in the pew instead of the front pedestal seat of my bass boat. None were bitin'.'

Nobody Ever Quizzed the Worms

Sometime around 1959 B.C.—Before Codgerdom—I attended the science fair at the University of Tennessee.

Not as an entrant, you understand. No science project of mine ever made it beyond the classroom level, much less schoolwide competition. This is probably due to the fact that blue-ribbon science projects are clearly defined and painstakingly executed pieces of work—not half-cocked, ill-conceived, hastily assembled exhibits completed between lunch break and recess the afternoon they're due.

Nonetheless, I'll never forget two of the award-winning displays I saw that day. Both involved hamsters.

One proved beyond the shadow of a doubt that hamsters are inherently smart animals, capable of learning to memorize the route through an intricate maze.

A couple of aisles over, another project proved beyond the shadow of a doubt that hamsters are dumber than bowling balls, incapable of navigating from Point A to Point B if their stupid lives depended on it.

I came away from the science fair with two conclusions:

1. Individual hamsters are probably a lot like people. Some are brilliant; some are ignorant.

2. Until humans learn to speak hamsterese, we'll never know for sure.

I got to thinking about that science fair visit the other day when I read the results of two highfalutin research projects involving an age-old conundrum with fish. To wit: Do fish feel pain when impaled on a hook?

The first study was conducted by the Royal Society, Great Britain's national academy of science. It was reported by MSNBC and Reuters news service. It proved yes. Fish do hurt.

The second study was conducted by the University of Wyoming and published in the academic journal *Reviews in Fisheries Science.* I read a news brief about it in *Field and Stream* magazine. It proved no. Fish don't hurt.

Naturally, partisans on opposite sides of the sport fishing issue exclaimed, "See there? We were right all along!"

In reaction to the British study, a spokeswoman for People for the Ethical Treatment of Animals claimed this proves fishing is barbaric. Not surprisingly, a spokesman for Gone Fishing, a pro-sport association, said the findings are pure supposition.

In the case of the Wyoming study, the lead researcher, a professor of zoology and physiology, concluded fish "lack the specific regions of the cerebral cortex required to be aware of pain, fear or any other emotion." Not surprisingly, PETA claimed the scientist, an avid trout fisherman, was merely protecting his hobby.

I cling to the same opinions forged way back in 1959 B.C.:

1. Individual fish are probably a lot like people. Some have a high pain threshold; some have a low pain threshold.

2. Until humans learn to speak fishese, we'll never know for sure.

In the meantime, I think I shall retire to my bass boat for further study.

Problems with Pollsters

Anytime an election rolls around, I quickly tire of the political pundits, pollsters, prognosticators, predictors, projectors, play callers, and other practitioners of the not-so-exact science of voter analysis. These folks are no more accurate than meteorologists and stock analysts—and decidedly more boring.

Fortunately, these squawking heads pipe down after the campaigning concludes. But yikes, what would happen some fall weekend if they showed up at your friendly local college football stadium?

"Welcome to Knoxville and televised coverage of the Tennessee-Arkansas football game. I'm Nathan Numbers, your anchor for today's big event. It's still an hour before kickoff, but already we are projecting a runaway Tennessee victory, thirty-five to three. Here with details is our culinary correspondent, Clarence Count."

"Thank you, Nathan. I'm in the parking lot outside the stadium where tailgaters are feasting. We reached the thirty-five-to-three projection by conducting a survey of this audience, featuring partisans from both Tennessee and Arkansas. As you know, Nathan, barbecue is the barometer used in all game-day censuses. With the overwhelming predominance of barbecued pork on Tennessee tables, versus the less-robust barbecued chicken in Arkansas circles, it is certain the Vols will prevail by such a huge margin."

"Thanks for that report, Clarence. It is now fifty minutes until kickoff, and we must report that our projection has been altered slightly. Tennessee still has this game safely in the bag, but the margin of victory has slipped from thirty-five to three to thirty-five to ten. Apparently our pollsters did not take into account the fact that the Arkansas mascot is a razorback hog. Naturally, a number of Arkansas fans might opt for chicken instead of eating their own team's symbol. So we have changed our numbers to reflect this trend. Still, it is safe at this point to give Tennessee the victory, thirty-five to ten. We're now forty minutes from kickoff and—wait a minute! There's more breaking news! Let's switch to our on-field correspondent, Terrence Tally."

What's with the weird lids on sports drink bottles these days? Whatever happened to simply unscrewing the top and drinking from the bottle?

Maybe it's a generational thing, but I've never gotten used to squirting juice and soft drinks into my mouth the way it's pictured on television ads. Isn't this the way the Vietcong used to torture their captives?

"Thanks, Nathan. We have just completed a pregame poll of the degree of difficulty of stunts performed by the cheerleading squads of each school. Based on our determination that the extra flip the Arkansas cheerleaders have thrown into their routine, right after they scream, 'Suuu-weeee! Hogs!' we have amended the projected final score to be thirty-five to eighteen, Tennessee. Back to you."

"Excellent report, Terrence. This is one of the most exciting finishes we've ever broadcast, and it's getting closer as kickoff approaches. We've only got twenty minutes remaining, and the projected score is about to change again. For details, we switch to our roving reporter, Ann L. Ize."

"Big news, Nathan! We have been conducting the all-important peanut shell count on both sides of the stadium, and there's been a stunning change of events. Apparently the Arkansas fans have brought hundreds of pounds of imported peanuts with them to today's game. Never before have we seen this kind of reaction. I've checked with our team of statisticians, and they say all bets are off! This one's going to be too close to call decisively. They're projecting thirty-five to thirty-five at the end of regulation. Since games can't end in a tie, this is going to be a wild one. Back to you, Nathan."

"Amazing! Truly amazing! Ladies and gentlemen, you are about to witness one of the most stunning come-from-behind finishes in the history of college athletics. Just one hour ago, Tennessee had been projected to sweep this contest, thirty-five to three. And now, here it is, time for kickoff, and the best anyone can predict is an opening score dead even at zero to zero. We'd like to be able to stay with you the rest of the afternoon and broadcast this game as it develops, but there's breaking news in Florida. For the story, we switch to our Gainesville correspondent, Arthur Additup."

"Nathan, just as it did in the 2000 presidential election, something big is about to happen here in the Sunshine State. With less than two hours to go before kickoff of the Florida–South Carolina game, we are projecting a fourteen-to-ten upset by the Gamecocks. Our coverage of the Tennessee-Arkansas game will be suspended the rest of the afternoon so we can keep you abreast of these details as they develop."

Heaven help us. Horseshoes, anyone?

Redneck Riviera

'Twas three weeks before Christmas when flung wide the door
Of good ol' boy Mecca: the Bass Pro Shop store.
Bubba Joe in his camos, and I in mine, too,
Stared—slobber-jawed—as we took in the view.
Huntin' and fishin' and boat stuff piled high!
I joked to ol' Bubba we shore must'a died.

Where to start in this den was the first mystery,
So we each grabbed a buggy and took off to see.
He headed to Floor One, I opted for Two,
And we vowed to be broke when our business was through.

Not since my days clad in Uncle Sam's clothes
Hath mine eyes e'er witnessed so many gun rows!
Ruger, Benelli, Winchester, and Knight;
My budget had already done lost the fight.
I bought a new twelve gauge, some shells and four chokes,
Then gathered at decoys with dozens of folks.
Four woodies, two wigeons, eight teal, and six geese
Flew into my cart, plus a bow string release,
Not to mention a tree stand with scent pad compartment.
(Didn't tell you I'd moved on to archery department.)
A few turkey calls from my ol' pal Will Primos
Were also tossed in, plus a stainless steel thermos.

"Gore-Tex" and "Thinsulate" read many labels
Of jackets and coats mounded high on the tables.
I pawed through and tried on these foul-weather wares
While studying displays of snarling bears.
Selected a scope ground from optical glass
Plus a GPS trinket for finding my as-
Tro-nom-i-cal places afield
And bounties of game that they surely will yield.

Downstairs, Bubba Joe was a'workin' the aisles,
Packed with fishin' lures, nets, reels, and rods stretched for miles.
He grabbed crankbaits and spinnerbaits and tube jigs and worms,
All guaranteed to make bass come to terms.
He needed some line, got a bulk pack of Stren,
Then threw in three more—pound-test six, eight, and ten.
He stopped long enough to watch Dance on TV
And returned to his shopping with unbounded glee.

Uncle Josh pork rind and Rattle Trap plugs
Went into his cart, also Mossy Oak gloves,
Plus hip boots and long-johns and needle-nosed pliers
And high-tech devices for depth-finder wires.

We met down at Starbucks and marveled aloud
What our daddies would say 'bout this sporting goods crowd.
In their day you ordered from Monkey Ward's book,
Then waited three weeks or whatever it took.
And now one store offers a ton more of stuff,
(Although makin' the payments will surely be tough.)

"We ain't even started to see this great place!"
Bubba exclaimed with a tear down his face.
"They got bass boats and fish tanks, stuffed ducks, turkeys, deer!
"To do it all justice would take us a year!"
"Don't worry, ol' buddy," I said to my friend,
"We'll surely revisit, again and again."

Bubba gazed at the scene, and he sighed with deep bliss:
"Ha-yul-far . . .
"Life simply don't git any better than this!"

Stink Bait

I have two words of advice for the folks in Hueytown, Alabama, who are still reeling from a mess at their local post office.

Patent it.

File a claim immediately, before interlopers sweep in and steal all the profits.

In case you missed the news, a big stink arose in Hueytown when what postal authorities described as a "foul yellow liquid" was discovered leaking from a package. Before you could say "weapons of mass destruction," the office was evacuated, firefighters were summoned, and six postal employees were treated for breathing difficulties.

The source? Catfish bait components mixed with a cleaning compound applied to neutralize the spill.

"It was some sort of ammonia and garlic stuff a local man had ordered to make his own catfish bait," Hueytown Police Department dispatcher Joe Epperson told me. "It was pretty potent by itself, but when it came in contact with the cleaning agent, things got real bad."

Ask anyone who ever attempted to procure the main ingredient for a catfish dinner. The smellier the bait, the better the catch. Shad guts that have baked in the sunshine are a local favorite. So is rancid cheese. But this Hueytown concoction might blow 'em all off the stink-o-meter.

That's why I implore my angling brothers and sisters in Sweet Home Alabama to reconstruct the incident and smell the money.

I speak with a degree of authority in this matter. From the stink standpoint, that is. Thus far, riches—aromatic or otherwise—have eluded me.

Approximately twenty years ago, I too sent an odoriferous fishing package through the mail. It too was with the best of intentions. But that didn't help matters on the receiving end.

In those days, I had an acquaintance in New Hampshire who was an expert tier of trout flies. On a South Dakota hunting trip one fall, he mentioned the need for grouse feathers for some of the patterns he wanted to create.

"What kind of grouse feathers?" I asked. "Wings? Tails?"

"I could use the whole skin," he replied.

I filed his request in my mental Rolodex until the following winter when a buddy and I returned from a mountain outing with three fine ruffed grouse specimens. While cleaning the birds that evening, I remembered his wish. Good guy that I am, I boxed up the skins and mailed them to his house the very next day.

Yes, it would have been prudent to call first and let him know the parcel was on its way. But since it was dead of the winter anyway and I was shipping the skins to New-by-gosh-Hampshire, where the spring thaw arrives in time for Labor Day festivities, I assumed everything would be fine.

Bad assumption. *Very* bad.

You see, this transpired when (1) a freak warm spell hit New England and (2) my buddy was out of the country for two weeks. By the time he got back

A caller who identified herself only as "Susan from Illinois" left me a telephone message a few days ago. Susan said she is vacationing in East Tennessee with her husband. They've been fishing on Cherokee Lake.

"Are you aware of the activity that goes on in the lakes around here?" she asked. "In the last two days, we've seen a pontoon boat full of naked young ladies who were flashing other people as they motored by, plus another boat in which a couple were openly engaging in sex. We were shocked and surprised! This is outrageous!"

I should say so. All that commotion is bound to mess up the fishing.

Naturally, Susan didn't reveal the exact location of this activity. Fisherpeople always keep their secrets.

and found my gesture of goodwill, it was a runny, gooey blob of organic gel that reeked nauseatingly.

Too bad he was a Yankee trout purist rather than a Dixie catfish specialist. Instead of the royal cussing he unleashed, he'd still be singing my praises.

Trouble on the Golf Course

In a fit of delirium, I've agreed to participate in a celebrity golf tournament. The only reason I'm doing it is because it's a fundraiser for a charity I really like. Well, yes, and the fact it gets me out of the office all day.

I am not what you'd call an avid golfer. I am not even an occasional golfer. I maintain a strict policy of playing golf only once in any given decade.

I have nothing against the game, you understand. Some of my best friends are golfers.

Golf is an interesting exercise, not to mention a great excuse to drink beer. I've been around it long enough to know how to dress appropriately. I know how to drive a cart. I know how to cuss when a shot goes bad. Sort of.

Truthfully, I knew how to cuss long before I ever picked up my first club. But I still don't know enough about golf to tell whether a shot is good or bad. My rule of thumb is to wait until someone else in the foursome starts cussing—it happens nearly every time I swing—and then join the fray.

But one part of golf I've never mastered is how to keep a sharp lookout for killer kangaroos and dangerous brick paths.

Several months ago, a thirteen-year-old boy named Steven Shorten was seriously injured when a large male kangaroo attacked him on a golf course. Steven's cheekbone was shattered. Bone fragments had to be removed from behind his right eye.

And if you think that's scary, look what happened to a golfer named Dale L. Larson. He tripped and fell face-first into a brick pathway outside the clubhouse, breaking his jaw and shattering his teeth. Before he was pronounced healed, Larson underwent treatment for nine root canals and twenty-three dental crowns. In addition, his jaw had to be wired shut for several months.

Wow. All along, I considered a round of golf victorious if I broke one hundred on the front nine. Now, I've got all these potential health hazards to worry about, and I'm . . .

Huh? What's that? You say surely there's more to those stories than that? Something I may have omitted, perhaps?

Well, I never. If you absolutely insist on splitting hairs, I suppose there are a couple of teeny tiny details that might have fallen through the cracks. Such as:

Steven Shorten was playing on a golf course in the Outback of Australia when he was attacked by the kangaroo. And Dale Larson admitted in a Wausau,

Wisconsin, courtroom that he had just consumed thirteen alcoholic beverages before he made his ill-fated tumble to the bricks.

Like I said, those are trifling details.

You see, that's something else I have learned about golf. The details—like how many strokes it *really* took to reach the green—aren't all that important.

Winter Olympics in Dixie

Every time the Winter Olympics roll around, I do my best to get enthused.

I enjoy all the hype in the newspapers and television sports programs. For the first couple of days of competition, I attempt to keep track of the medals race. I also try to stay abreast of who's failing what test for steroids.

In the final analysis, though, this exercise is like trying to spray a can of paint on Teflon. Nothing sticks.

Yes, the opening ceremony is always impressive. Yes, those brash hot dogs on snowboards have nerves of steel and athletic grace beyond compare—then again, maybe they're just nuts. Yes, those "skeleton" riders take sledding to new heights of bravery—or depths of lunacy, as the case may be.

Beyond that, there's simply too much Dixie blood in my veins for the Winter Olympics to make my heart go pitter-patter. Frankly, my dear, I don't give a ding-diddly-darn.

Did you hear about the football player who was so dumb, he had to be rescued from the escalator after the power went off? It was the same player who, on the first day of class, was told to write a six-hundred-word essay on what he did over summer vacation. "Oh, not much," he wrote two-hundred times.

Recreating in the snow is a stretch in the first place. But doing it when jonquils are blooming, the crappies are biting, and every sunny dawn is pierced by the whistling of cardinals? Sorry. It just doesn't compute.

This isn't a refusal to athletically diversify. Instead, it's an acceptance of latitude and culture.

I was born and raised in the South. I think of winter landscapes in terms of barren oaks and waving tufts of brown broom sage, not drifts of fresh-fallen snow. Twenty-eight degrees Fahrenheit means a cold spell, not a heat wave. When I go fishing in the winter, the first thing I do is launch my boat in honest-to-gosh water, not drill a hole in the ice. I grew up walking down mountain slopes, not shushing along on skis. In short, the Winter Olympics say both "po-TAY-to" and "po-TAAH-to." I say "tater."

I hold no grudge toward people who enjoy watching or competing in speed skating, hockey, downhill skiing, and luge. I refuse to make fun of the skintight outfits—except to suggest this is the human expression of NASCAR panache. And I will resist the temptation to laugh at curling.

Quite the contrary. While I might dismiss most Winter Olympic sports with a yawn, I'm rather intrigued by curling. This is like shuffleboard on ice. Or maybe croquet. It seems like such a pleasant undertaking. Any minute I expect one contestant to drop his studious countenance and shout, "Hey, Oly! Isn't it your turn to buy the next round?"

That doohickey they call the "stone" looks more like Aladdin's lamp than any rock I ever lifted, but I do get a kick out of watching players scrub the ice to guide its direction and speed. I'd like to have the same capability to realign errant fly casts and grouse shots. Nonetheless, curling needs more excitement to keep me riveted to the tube. I'd pay more attention if those stones exploded upon contact, like watermelons dropped from a river bluff.

Saaay! Maybe that's the ticket! Maybe if the Winter Olympics offered a closer parallel to traditional southern culture, we crackers would show more of an interest.

That means deep-sixing the bobsled and luge right off the bat. You ever watched us southerners drive—I use the term loosely—after a two-inch blizzard has paralyzed our roadways? I rest my case. If we can lose control on level pavement at the blinding speed of twenty-three miles per hour, what hope do we have in a steep, banked tunnel when the G forces are strong enough to melt flesh?

Figure skating doesn't hold much promise, either—although I have seen some accidental axels on frozen sidewalks that would make French and Russian judges alike vote straight tens.

Some form of ski jumping? Hmmm. Now, you're talkin.' I'm not certain how you'd set up the course—inner tubes seem more applicable than skis—but I bet the good ol' boys would fight one another to participate in this high-flying adventure. Except you'd have to make them understand that Olympic protocol prohibits the ingestion of beer before every descent.

All things considered, though, a different twist to the biathlon offers the greatest potential. Maybe combine it with snowmobiling. Trust me. Once Dixie's finest realize there's a Winter Olympic sport that blends high-speed driving with gunfire, you can go ahead and chalk up the gold for Uncle Sam.

Members of the Golliher family of Knoxville were hunting quail on their farm in Rhea County. The dogs went on point.

"I was in the middle," said Steve Golliher. "My brothers Jeff and John were to my right, and our dad, Waldo, was to the right of the dogs. I kicked the bird up and it flew toward Dad. He killed it without firing a shot."

How?

"It flew straight into his gun barrel and fell stone dead at his feet. Absolutely true story."

Sounds like an excellent way to save on shotgun shells.

Chapter 9

Loose Screws and Other Leftover Parts

An interesting, yet totally predictable, phenomenon occurs every time an unsolicited parcel arrives at the *News Sentinel*.

If it's an economics survey bristling with statistics, percentages, graphs, and charts, it winds up on the desk of business editor Bill Brewer. If it's the inside dope on some hot-shot football prospect for the Tennessee Vols, it gets routed to sportswriter Dave Hooker. If it's a story about the latest innovations in fishing and hunting gear, outdoors editor Bob Hodge gets the call. If it's juicy fodder about gubernatorial candidates, Tom Humphrey in our Nashville bureau will be summoned.

If it involves flatulence, it comes to me.

I've never determined if this is due to my journalistic reputation or whether I'm regarded as an expert practitioner. I'm almost afraid to ask.

For instance: Once or twice a year back in the early and middle 1990s, we would receive news releases and testimonials about the Toot Trapper, a product I absolutely am not making up. This is a seat cushion filled with activated charcoal. It's designed for office workers afflicted with certain atmospheric problems of a highly personal nature.

Every time a Toot Trapper package arrived in the *News Sentinel*'s mail, it automatically ended up in my office. Didn't matter if it was addressed to the editor, file clerk, or the obituary department. I always got it, along with a hastily scribbled note from one of my colleagues. Usually something on the order of "This oughta be a real gas." Or "Go see if you can sniff out a column." Or "Since you don't know beans about anything else, maybe you can write about this." Everybody's a comedian.

All of which is a terribly long way of telling you the latest round of flatulence material just drifted in. It's about a product called Under-Ease. This is underwear with a mission. I quote directly from the company, Under-Tec Inc., of Pueblo, Colorado:

"Under-Ease is made from a soft, polyurethane-coated fabric with an 'exit hole' cut from the back of the air-tight material near the bottom for gas to be expelled. The exit hole is covered with a uniquely designed 'pocket' made from an ordinary porous fabric. A high-functioning, replaceable filter pad is inside the pocket, through which all gas passes. This multilayered filter pad contains, among other things, two layers of Australian sheep's wool and a layer of activated carbon."

The piece went on to describe how this product is just the ticket for individuals who suffer certain ailments of the digestive tract and are prone to involuntarily share their symptoms with everyone in the immediate area. It included reprints of newspaper stories from around the world, praising the innovative garment.

Not surprisingly, some of the headline writers at these publications obviously were handpicked for the task. Examples of their creative expertise: "Thunderpants" and "Softening the Blow." No doubt these people are held in the same professional esteem at their newspapers that I enjoy here in Knoxville. It's a burden we talented artists have grown accustomed to.

(I wanted to conduct extensive research on Under-Ease skivvies, but it simply wasn't possible for two reasons. First, there was this matter of patriotism and national pride. Why use Australian wool? According to the encyclopedia, Colorado is the fourth-leading producer of sheep in the United States, right behind Texas, California, and Wyoming. If a Colorado company was willing to ignore farmers in its own back yard in favor of sheep producers halfway around the world—well, it's like President Dubya keeps saying, "You're either with us or against us." Second, there were budgetary restrictions beyond my control. At that time, the *News Sentinel* was operating under intense austerity measures, not a dime to spare. There was no way to effectively examine this product without buying at least five hundred dollars' worth of pinto beans, pickled eggs, and cabbage.)

Stinky news has become such a part of my repertoire I have been designated the newspaper's official Disgusting Topics Editor. Hey, it's a living. Besides, this title came in handy when the Discovery Channel's *Discovery News* program reported some cutting-edge information regarding flatulence and doo-doo from animals.

All animals.

It's about time. For years, cows had been taking the rap for this crime. Scientists claimed cows were issuing jillions of tons of methane gas, a primary cause of the greenhouse effect and global warming. I'd always wondered why horses, mules, pigs, dogs, and human beings didn't have to shoulder some of the blame. But according to the scientists cited by the news program, the source doesn't matter because they had developed a compound that turns stink into a pleasant-smelling essence.

Seems an olfactory neuroscientist named Charles Wysocki and an organic chemist named George Preti concocted this substance. The Discovery Channel report said, "One part of the process takes advantage of a natural phenomenon known as olfactory cross adaptation, which happens when the nose adapts to one odor and then becomes less sensitive to a second smell that is perceptually or structurally different from the first."

Added Wysocki: "The cross adapting compounds in the patent are hypothesized to bind to their appropriate receptor sites and those for the bad-smelling molecule, thereby blocking the malodorous parent molecule from activating its full complement of receptor sites."

Sounded reasonable to me.

Thus these wise men experimented with various stinks—don't you know they have some great come-on lines at their local bar?—until they isolated "ethyl ester of three-methyl-two-octenoic acid," which "helps to turn dung into something that is 'quite innocuous—neither pleasant nor unpleasant.'"

The most obvious use for this innovation would be around stockyards, feedlots, and farms near urban areas. But I immediately thought of several other urban applications, not the least of which, harrumph, was the men's rest room at the *News Sentinel.*

There's more to being the Disgusting Topics Editor than flatulence, of course. You get to write about topics involving *any* type of bodily function, external or internal.

Wait a minute—did I say get "get to write"? I meant "are expected to write."

It's part of your job description to make wisecracks about human sexual practices (translation: condom columns galore), toilets, weird body parts, and anything connected to the groin region of the anatomy. As you will see in this chapter, the title also permits liberal license to make light of just about any institution, sacred or otherwise. In short, this is sophomoric silliness packaged as serious journalism.

The Disgusting Topics Editor trusts this clears the air.

A Few of My Favorite Things

I recently gave my office a thorough cleaning. I had no choice in the matter.

The *Knoxville News Sentinel* was moving from its ancient, patched-together downtown digs to a fifty-million-dollar, state-of-the-art new building out on the interstate. Since the wrecking ball was scheduled to swing, I had to grab my favorite things quickly.

First was my coveted Jar O'Vomit.

This was a quart of homemade chow-chow a reader gave me eons ago. Apparently the seal wasn't tight. Thus, as the jar aged on top of my file cabinet, its contents began to ripen. Art director R. Daniel Proctor coined the vividly descriptive name and printed a special label.

I put this vessel, complete with bubbling contents, on the giveaway shelf. It disappeared immediately. Whether it was adopted by one of my colleagues or confiscated by the Environmental Protection Agency remains a mystery.

I didn't throw away my favorite high school prom picture, however.

No, not the photo from my own prom. Cameras hadn't been invented back then. Instead, this one was from the 1997 Maryville High School dance. Laramy Gregory sent it to me after I wrote about the hot date he had that night.

Aaah, there stands proud, smiling Laramy, tuxedoed to the max, arm in arm with "Betty"—a blow-up doll.

Laramy's original she-date for the prom had gotten into trouble at home and was grounded by her folks. He couldn't find another girl. So he bought Betty at a trick shop. As it turned out, Betty was the queen of the hop. Every boy wanted a dance with her.

Another treasure I kept was a set of "neuticles." A Montana company named CTI sent them to me while I was researching a column on veterinary procedures.

Seems that an animal psychiatrist had determined male dogs suffer emotional distress after making that fateful snip-trip to the vet's office. So plastic neuticles were invented to take their place. The vet is supposed to install them—they come in pairs, you understand—when the originals are removed.

I should have offered these babies to members of the Tennessee General Assembly, who demonstrate nearly every session that such body parts are sorely missing in Nashville. But you never know when I might need them myself.

Let's see, what else? Oh, yes. My arrest mug shot from the Knox County Sheriff's Department, complete with serial no. 6969-101786.

During the Butcher banking scandal of the mid-1980s, I was working on a story at the jail one day when an officer friend suggested, ha-ha-ha, what a classic criminal face I have. He lined me up against the wall and snapped a few frames.

I own the original, but heaven only knows how many copies are still floating around law enforcement circles. Be assured no copper will ever catch me based on that photo, however. In it, my hair is dark brown, not gray and patchy like today.

Over the years, this photo proved to be quite a blessing. Whenever some office visitor who overstayed his welcome inquired about it, I just shrugged and said, "Oh, that's when I got picked up on the morals charge." That always brought idle conversation to a rapid conclusion.

Another photo coming off the wall truly has to be seen to be appreciated. It shows a bunch of my cousins and me, snapped when we were kids. Between our hand-me-down clothes, torn shirts, scuffed knees, rag-tag hair and orphan looks, we could pass for poster children of LBJ's Great Society campaign. Even today, I could probably send this gem to Washington and get a lucrative antipoverty grant by return mail.

There was a bunch more, far more than I've got room to describe. Yet I simply must pass on some words of journalistic wisdom that have been taped to my wall for decades. They're from legendary *New York Times* columnist Russell Baker: "The job of a columnist is to wait until the battle is over and the real reporters have done their work, and then go onto the battlefield and pick the pockets of the wounded."

This little sign is going to the new building. As it has done for years, it will keep me inspired to stay the course and finish the sacred mission of my chosen profession.

An Innovative Use for Toilet Tissue

When Joe and Jane Sixpack tour the toilet paper aisle at their friendly local supermarket, they probably do a bit of comparison shopping.

Maybe Joe's a Northern man. Maybe Jane prefers White Cloud. Despite their brand loyalties, odds are they'll glance at the other selections before making a choice.

Price is always a factor. Also, one-ply or two-ply is worthy of consideration. So is the number of sheets per roll. Can't forget softness—or lack thereof— either, especially if the Sixpacks immediately turn their cart down the hemorrhoid treatment aisle as soon as they leave TP. But I'll guarantee there's one facet of toilet paper application that never crosses Joe's or Jane's mind. Or any other part of their body, for that matter.

They never worry about how it holds up to highway traffic.

I've never thought about this, either—until I read about the latest developments in highway maintenance. In Saint Louis, Missouri, work crews are using You Know What as an integral part of asphalt repair.

I am not kidding. I hold a news dispatch from Saint Louis as we speak. It describes how members of the city's street crews go through hundreds of rolls of toilet paper a day—for road repairs, I stress. The story does not broach the subject of conventional toilet paper assignments.

Apparently someone in the maintenance department, who had way yonder too much time on his hands, not to mention a bizarre sense of adventure, determined that TP could be used to help patch the cracks in asphalt. This keeps the cracks from widening into potholes.

The time-tested way to accomplish this task is by filling the fissure with tar. Trouble is, fresh tar can be "tracked" by vehicles. It gets pulled up about as fast as it goes down. Anybody who's ever driven over a freshly tarred surface and heard the resulting *ssslllccckkk, slllccckkk, sssllllccckkk* knows what I'm talking about.

But, so the theory goes, if TP is rolled across the crack as soon as the tar is applied, the tar has a chance to dry. A few rainfalls later, the toilet paper disappears. The tar remains.

In Saint Louis, this is more than a theory. The story I read said road crews use so much toilet paper that deliveries of thousands of rolls are made on huge, flatbed trucks. Which points me toward one of three conclusions:

Someone in the administrative hierarchy of the Saint Louis city government is a civil engineering genius.

Someone in the administrative hierarchy of the Saint Louis city government did a lot of yard-rolling as a teenager and still has a mischievous sense of humor.

Someone in the administrative hierarchy of the Saint Louis city government is getting kickbacks from a relative who works in the toilet paper industry, and before long we'll be reading about criminal indictments in Charmingate.

No matter what the case, East Tennessee is far behind the curve.

I have just gotten off the telephone with service department representatives from the city of Knoxville, the county of Knox, and the Tennessee Department of Transportation. To the person, they disavowed any knowledge of using toilet paper in this manner—after they stopped laughing and saying stuff like, "Aw, c'mon man; what'd you *really* call about?"

> James Gill, the News Sentinel's librarian, just purchased a new reference book. It is—and I quote—The Pocket Oxford American Dictionary of Current English.
>
> This baby measures eight inches tall, five inches wide, and two inches thick and weighs just shy of two pounds.
>
> I hope James's pockets have reinforced thread.

Steve Roberts, deputy director of the Knoxville Service Department, even took the time to inquire around in his shop. "You should have seen some of the strange looks I got," he reported to me.

This is not surprising. Knoxville prides itself in staying behind the times. We never embrace a new trend until the rest of the country has grown weary of it

Loose Screws and Other Leftover Parts

and moved on to something else. Which could present a double problem in this instance. Even if the TP Treatment becomes standard policy for street repairs coast to coast, Knoxville will be exceedingly slow to adopt it.

Before we get around to trying toilet paper, we'll have to spend eight or nine years experimenting with corncobs and Sears Roebuck catalogs.

Condom Malfunctions

Brace yourself, America. Even though it's early, I can already tell this is going to be a long, hot summer with high tensions and short fuses among the restless youth of this country.

Because of social injustice, an absence of decent-paying jobs, the draft, and war in Southeast Asia? Heavens, no! That stuff went out of style after the long, hot summers of the 1960s. Instead, it's going to be an explosive summer because of an edict from the federal government.

Thousands of condoms are defective.

Officials of the U.S. Food and Drug Administration issued this warning a few days ago. They said the condoms, imported from Malaysia, were being sold in Tennessee and six other states—California, Florida, Michigan, New York, Rhode Island, and Texas.

According to the feds, the defective devices were manufactured by Dongkuk (no, I did *not* make up that name) Techno Rubber Industries and marketed under such brand names as Pamitex, Magic, Black Jack, Maxi, and Ginza.

The problem? A high percentage of them leak. Federal inspectors made this shocking discovery during routine water tests.

Uh-oh. Talk about a problem. With summer coming on and free time on their hands, teenagers are naturally going to buy lots of condoms. They're going to be mad as hornets if they pay good money for these things and they turn out to leak like sieves.

I don't blame these youngsters. I'd be mad too. How can you participate in a water fight with a leaky condom?

Surely you played these games when you were a kid. Indeed, youngsters have played them for decades.

You and your buddies sneak out (sneaking was required in the old days, not today) and buy a dozen condoms, fill them at the spigot, and spend the rest of the afternoon blasting each other with humongous water bombs. This is a time-honored, all-American sport that teaches kids important phases of real warfare, like stealth and surprise, while letting them stay cool in the process.

Oh, sure. Sometimes condoms in the hands of wild teenagers can lead to more serious trouble. They've been known to fill a couple of these babies with water, climb to the top floor of a tall building, open a window, and drop elongated grenades on unsuspecting pedestrians and motorists below.

Not this summer. Whether they have fun fights or mischief on the mind, teenagers in Tennessee and six other states will have to make new plans this year, thanks to slipshod workmanship in Malaysia.

Oh, by the way, the Food and Drug Administration's warning also said something about not having—*sshhh!*—s-e-x with these condoms because they aren't effective against—*sshhh! again*—pregnancy and disease.

Big deal. As any member of the Religious Right will tell you, youngsters don't know about this use for condoms. So forget I mentioned it.

He Has a Real Head for Awards

In my never-ending quest to chronicle the latest international events, I'm pleased to announce a new ear-hair king has been crowned. His name is Radhakant Bajpai. He lives in Pradesh, India. According to the *Guinness Book of World Records,* the mane flowing from his ears measures 5.19 inches at its longest point.

I'm staring at a picture of the champ as we speak. He has a standard-issue haircut—on his noggin, I mean—and a standard-issue moustache. But his ears look like someone glued a pair of mutton-chop sideburns on them. Or else Lassie is digging for a Milk-Bone lodged somewhere near the guy's hypothalamus.

(Pardon me for a second. I've just been overtaken by an incredible urge to shiver violently and moan "Uuuugggghh" like we used to do as kids when bearded Aunt Bertha from Boston showed up at family reunions and demanded a hug and kiss. There. I'm better now.)

To win this award, Bajpai uprooted the defending titlist, B. D. Tyagi of Bhopal, India, by a full 1.18 inches. Among ear-hair contestants, that's a thorough thrashing.

I know what you're thinking right now, especially if you have follicle issues: How fast can I get to India and drink some of their water?

But the rest of us have a different thought: What good is five-inch ear hair besides winning the record?

Does this stuff have marketable value? Can it be regularly harvested, like cotton or wool, and spun into cloth? If so, what do they make out of it? Rugs? Welcome mats?

What's more, is there a training regimen involved? Aerobic exercises, perhaps? A strict diet high in fiber?

And since we're dealing in athletic competition, is the new champ immediately drug-tested to ensure he hasn't received ear-canal applications of Rogaine on the QT—or the Q-tip, as the case may be?

My mind continues to wander and wonder: Is Bajpai barred from using revolving doors? When he swims in creeks, do minnows and eels get caught in those side-mounted nets of his? Or, in swimming pools, is he required to wear itty-bitty ear caps, lest fallout clog the filtration system? In Weather Channel broadcasts from India, does his ear hair show up as precipitation? And from a cultural standpoint, do codgers in India sit around a pot-bellied stove and idly comb their ear hair the same way old-timers in southern Appalachia create curls of cedar shavings with their pocket knives?

Pundit drivel aside, Bajpai is quite proud of his accomplishment.

"Making it to *Guinness Book of World Records* is indeed a special occasion for me and my family," the winner told reporters after claiming the crown. "God has been very kind to me."

Excellent. More power to this fine, furry fellow. But if I looked in the mirror and saw that much hair spewing from my ears, I'd grab the clippers and not stop cutting until I reached the Milk-Bone myself.

Heave-ho for the Hyphen

A major event just occurred at my newspaper. We got rid of our hyphen.

We ceased being the *Knoxville News-Sentinel*. Instead, we became the *Knoxville News Sentinel*.

Let me say that again: No more *News-Sentinel*. From now on, we are the *News Sentinel*.

See the difference? Our name sounds the same. We just don't have a hyphen.

Don't ask me why. This is a metamorphosis that corporations and politicians undertake from time to time. It's like changing hairstyles or going from pleated trousers to plain fronts. This is how U.S. Senator Lamar Alexander became Lamar! during one of his campaigns.

It's also why we moved. I think there's a rule in the journalism code that says you have to change locations anytime you change your name. Just look at the sign on our old downtown building, 208 West Church Avenue, and compare it to the sign on our new digs off Western Avenue. At the old place, we were the *News-Sentinel*. Here, we're the *News Sentinel*. At 2332 News Sentinel Drive, no less. We got a brand new facility out of the deal, plus we're buying new presses. Such is the awesome power of a hyphen.

Unfortunately, I didn't realize we were moving so soon. I found a great deal on hyphens several months ago and bought thousands of dollars worth of them. Lord knows I've been trying to use them up. I've spent the past few weeks building columns around hyphenated words like "self-evident," "hard-core," "half-baked," and "dirt-cheap."

I have deliberately crafted sentences so the words break awkwardly at the end of each line, necessitating the lavish use of even more hyphens.

I have gone out of my way to point out that *News-Sentinel* columnist Sam Venable's career with the *News-Sentinel* began long before he was hired by the *News-Sentinel* in 1970; indeed, throughout much of his childhood, he had a *News-Sentinel* route in south Knoxville, delivering the *News-Sentinel* to more than fifty *News-Sentinel* subscribers every day.

But it's no use. I'm overwhelmed. I feel like I'm trying to dry up the ocean with a sponge. I just checked the hyphen storage bin on my computer, and it's still crammed full of the hateful things. I couldn't dent this vast inventory with a coal shovel, let alone a keystroke.

So here. Have all you want. Take plenty for yourself and all your friends
----

---.

There's more where those came from.

It Was a Tour of "Dooty"

The first thing you need to know before crawling through a colon is where to start. There's nothing more embarrassing than getting down on all fours to begin winding through this gastric chute and suddenly realizing—holy hemor-rhoid!—you're going the wrong way.

Such was my dilemma recently at the Healthy Living Expo. Baptist Health Systems had brought in a forty-foot-long, four-foot-tall replica of a human colon, allegedly to illustrate the importance of cancer screenings, regular colon checkups, proper nutrition, and boring stuff like that.

The real reason, of course, is to give smart-aleck columnists the opportunity to write poop-related double entendre. This is our sacred dooty, hoo-ha, and we're happy to be the butt of these lame wisecracks, even if they really stink. But I digress, so let's cut the crap and get down to business: I had a colonoscopy last year. If you haven't, get your doctor to schedule one for you. Don't put this off. It's important. It could save your life. And that's no shtick.

I dearly hope a license plate I spotted recently doesn't portend gloom and doom. The car sped by me so rapidly I couldn't get the numbers. But I definitely saw the three-lettered prefix: FLU.

The plate was attached to a sport utility vehicle, not a VW Beetle. Otherwise, I'd be warning you about a FLU Bug that's on the loose in our midst.

Fortunately, several Baptist staffers were working the display. In addition to handing out brochures about colon health, they showed me the proper orifice to enter.

Loose Screws and Other Leftover Parts

Once inside, I began touring a rogues' gallery of bowel ailments. Among them were Crohn's disease, diverticulitis, precancerous polyps, and the awful killer itself—colon cancer, the second leading cause of cancer death.

It was quite an education. Then again, since this was my first peek inside a colon, human or human-made, I really didn't know what I was seeing. If not for interpretive signs along the path, I might have come to some strange conclusions.

Polyps, for instance, looked like melons. Cancer resembled the surface of a burnt cheese pizza. (Note to self: strike melons and cheese pizza from any and all future menus.)

This was not a solitary journey, by any means. In the ten minutes or so of my colon crawl, many children came rumbling through. I scooted over as best I could—even with four feet of maneuvering room, a colon has its limits—and let them pass. But as they bumped and bounced along, I couldn't help but think this is what my own colon experiences after a session of three-bean chili.

At about the midway point, I hit a blockage. There was a person of the adult female persuasion in front of me and, quite frankly, I didn't know how to address the situation. I mean, it's not like running into the office secretary at happy hour.

"Come here often?" didn't seem appropriate. So I just smiled and said, "This colon isn't big enough for both of us." Thank goodness, she agreed and crawled ahead.

Back on the outside, I breathed a sigh of relief, thanked the Baptist folks for their assistance, and gathered my coat, notepad, and other belongings. But before leaving, I purposely reentered from the wrong direction and crawled a short distance.

That way, I can agree with disgruntled readers when they call to voice objections over something I've written.

"Yes, sir; you're right," I can now say. "I *do* have my head firmly planted up there."

My Own Personal Money

Today's lesson is How to Win Huge Dollars Playing the Tennessee Lottery.

I am superbly qualified to teach this course because I'm a huge winner. I invested five dollars in the state's new gambling scheme and earned seven dollars, netting a tidy two-dollar profit for roughly thirty seconds of work.

Do the math. Two bucks every half-minute translates to $240 an hour. Over the course of a forty-hour workweek, that comes to $9,600—or $499,200 per year. I can live on that.

Well, yes, that's assuming I continue my winning ways. Details, I say. Mere details. Somewhere in all those transactions, I'm sure to hit for even more than seven bucks. I just know that's going to happen. All lottery players know it. It's what keeps the fools coming back for more. But I'm smarter than the other fools. I've learned the secret to success. And if you'll quit interrupting, I'll tell you how it happened.

My trip down Easy Street occurred on the opening round of lottery ticket sales. I drove to a convenience store on Campbell Station Road. For the next thirty to forty-five minutes, I interviewed players as they filed through the store. Satisfied I'd gathered enough material for a column, I officially declared myself off the *News Sentinel*'s clock.

I stuck my pen and note pad in one pocket and extracted my own personal money clip from another. I peeled off my own personal Abe Lincoln and purchased one Tennessee Treasure ticket (two dollars) and three Lucky Sevens (one dollar each).

The cards I bought were of the scratch-off variety. To reveal the hidden numbers, you take a hard object—fingernail, edge of a coin, knife blade, anything like that—and scrape off the covering.

There was a community quarter on the store counter. Players had been using it, off and on, all night. So I picked it up and started scratching.

That stupid quarter was jinxed. I know this for a fact because I used it to scratch my two-dollar card—for naught. I also used it to scratch two of my one-dollar cards—again for naught.

Finally, a light bulb flickered in my brain.

"You numbskull!" I exclaimed to myself. "You're not winning because you're using an unlucky scraping device! Try something else!"

I put the community quarter aside, reached into my pocket, fished around in my own personal charge, found my own personal penny, and started scraping the remaining one-dollar card with it.

The University of Tennessee's "big orange" color is perfect for multitasking. You can wear it to the football game on Saturday, to the deer stand on Sunday, and to the job site on Monday. Try that with chartreuse or purple.

And that, dear children, is when the truth was revealed. My penny was charmed!

Using the lucky penny to reveal the last numbers, I came up with a seven-dollar winner. Then I tucked my own personal lucky penny back into safe keeping, marched to the cash register and smiled while the clerk counted out seven George Washingtons into my own personal outstretched palm.

What's that? You want to know why I'm being so persnickety about whose money belongs to whom?

Simple. I don't want the newspaper's bean counters to start claiming a piece of the action. This was my own personal money, not theirs. The only way it would have been their money is if I had lost.

In which case, of course, I would've been forced to camouflage it on my expense account.

Preventing Tooth Decay

I've been leery about the interior of toothpaste dispensers ever since reading about an alleged incident that occurred to a man in Shelton, Connecticut. According to documents filed in Connecticut Superior Court, Joseph DeMarco is suing Colgate-Palmolive because of some extra protection that came packed in his paste.

In his lawsuit, DeMarco says he purchased a tube of Colgate's Great Regular Flavor Toothpaste in 1999. DeMarco claims he used the toothpaste several times without any problems. But then one morning—or maybe it was evening; my information is incomplete—he says he pushed the pump handle for a squirt of paste and out popped a used condom.

I'm serious. I've taken this information straight from an Associated Press story about the lawsuit. Although the AP report did not specify the time of day DeMarco allegedly dispensed the condom, it did point out the toothpaste instrument involved was a "six-ounce, stand-up" model. Just the facts, ma'am.

As you can well imagine, this was a bit more disconcerting than finding a fly doing the backstroke in your soup.

DeMarco claims the incident eventually led to a heart attack and high blood pressure. He says he suffers from sleep deprivation, has developed rashes on his torso, and fears he might contract a sexually transmitted disease. He also must be suffering from a serious lack of oral care, for as his lawyer put it, DeMarco "can't brush his teeth or he'll gag."

No telling how it'll turn out in court. In the meantime, however, this unsettling situation does make me scratch my chin, recheck the list of ingredients on my own dispenser of toothpaste, and start asking a whole bunch of questions. Among them:

Is there another additive besides fluoride that has been keeping my teeth so protected all these years?

Is this the reason why some brands of toothpaste have an odd taste?

Is this the sort of component the toothpaste people were talking about forty years ago when they advertised the "invisible (knock-knock) protective shield"?

Is there any particular way to squeeze the tube to avoid this problem—like maybe starting in the middle and working to one end or the other?

Is there an oral cootie we should be concerned about in addition to the villainous D. K. Germ?

Y'know when you really think about it, dentures might not be such a bad idea.

Rest Stops by the Quart

Based on official state pronouncements and my own unofficial research, it appears Tennessee drivers are much more sanitary than motorists in other regions. Meaning they avail themselves of restroom facilities along the way.

Honest-to-gosh porcelain restroom facilities, you understand. Not portable plastic ones they fling out the window after use.

Frankly, I'd never given much thought to this matter until someone sent me a clipping from the *Akron Beacon Journal* describing a study by the Ohio Department of Natural Resources. Columnist Bob Dyer reported that many bottles containing human urine are dumped on the state's roadsides each year.

Specifically, 972,372. The department counted.

The column was a riot to read. Truthfully and enviously, I wish I'd written it myself. ("Do you get the same score for filling a seven-ounce Little Kings Cream Ale as you do for filling an empty quart of Bud?" he asked.) But while I laughed at Dyer's take on the study, I couldn't help but think: Is Ohio the only state with asphalt sewers?

Apparently not. I found a report on a travel service Web site that chronicled similar studies in other states. With similar results. Iowa officials found 147 bottles of urine along a sixteen-mile stretch of interstate. Also, a crew in Spokane, Washington, collected three-hundred of the same sort of vessels in one week.

"The bottles are predominantly plastic beverage containers," the report said. "Capped and thrown from a moving vehicle, some retain their seal. In the summer heat, urine bottles build up heat and, when nudged by a clean-up crew, may explode, or be spun into the air by lawnmower blades."

Bleech!

But surprisingly, Tennessee drivers (who seem to believe roadside littering is not only a constitutional right but a requirement for citizenship) are a bit more modest.

"We haven't made an inventory like other states, but it's not a big problem," said Kim Keeler, spokeswoman for the Department of Transportation in Nashville. "Our crews go through safety training and are instructed to contact the Department of Environment and Conservation if they find anything that might be considered hazardous waste. This includes needles, bodily fluids, medical waste, any unknown substances."

Then I conducted my own survey, albeit highly unofficial. I drove from Knoxville to Crossville and back on Interstate 40, counting what appeared to be "restroom milk jugs" along the shoulder and in the median. No, I didn't stop to inspect them. On steep-banked areas, it was impossible to see into the ditch.

The tally for 126 miles, round trip, was thirteen jugs en route to Crossville, 23 coming home. Leading me to surmise that eastbound travelers gotta go at a much higher rate than their westbound comrades.

Of course, much of this highway is forested. Given our southern Appalachian shyness, maybe we are more inclined to take our business straight to the trees.

Smoke Signals from Above

With all due respect to Benedict XVI, I can't help but wish the pope selection process had wound on for awhile.

No, not for theological reasons. As a non-Catholic, I understand very little about the workings of the church. Fine by me if members of the College of Cardinals want to iron out this decision in secret.

But I've been intrigued by that business of smoke signals. Specifically, how the media and general public inspected and dissected every puff that may—or may not—have indicated a new pope was chosen.

As everyone this side of Mars knows by now, the color of smoke tells what's going on inside. When the cardinals can't reach a decision, the smoke is black. When their choice is final, it's white. Sounds good on paper. But apparently smoke follows no script. Thus the results were quite confusing.

Perhaps in 1378 or 1590, smoke language was high-tech stuff. These days, however, it can't even hold a flame to fossilized methods like the crank telephone and Morse code.

Think about it. We live in the most technologically advanced era since the dawn of creation. Around-the-world communication takes place in fractions of a second. Thanks to the wonders of electronics, you could live in Nome or Norway and stay abreast of the happenings at Vatican City the very instant they're announced. Hundreds, maybe thousands, of print and electronic journalists have been hanging out in Saint Peter's Square, anxiously waiting some minutiae of news to disseminate to millions.

And yet what was there to disseminate for several days except the color of smoke wafting from a chimney?

It's as if the great botanists, biologists, physicists, and medical experts of the world had gathered in one place to work on an epic piece of scientific history, and all the media could discuss is whether the sandwiches at lunch were turkey or ham.

Surely you heard about the starts and stops.

The first day, a Vatican Radio announcer glanced at the plume of smoke and said, "It seems white. No, no, it's black!"

It got worse the next day. I quote from an Associated Press dispatch: "When the smoke went up shortly before six p.m., it seemed white but no one was sure. People said 'white' and 'black.' Then some began to chant, 'it's white, it's white.' . . . As the minutes ticked by the uncertainty grew, and at 5:55 p.m., Amy Turnipseed [I swear on a stack of Bibles I didn't make that name up] from California, said: 'It looks really white, but I'm not sure.'

"There was a brief flutter when the bells rang at 6 p.m., but the cheers died down when they stopped ringing. Minutes later, they began in earnest and the crowds erupted. 'Oh my gosh; this is insane,' Turnipseed said."

I'm quite the stickler for tradition. In many instances, the old ways are the best ways. But in this particular situation, don't you think, say, a digital bulletin board would work better? A fax machine, maybe? Flag signals? A cell phone? This is a question that needs to be addressed.

And speaking of weighty questions the media is no doubt going to ask: Did the cardinals drank regular coffee or decaf while they debated?

The Old Columnist

Key West, Florida—Apologizing profusely to the memory of Ernest Hemingway, the Old Columnist settled into a chair at Sloppy Joe's Bar, 201 Duval Street.

The Old Columnist felt obligated to drink at Sloppy Joe's. It is the duty of all writers who visit Key West. Sloppy Joe's was Hemingway's favorite watering hole in the 1930s, before he moved on to Cuba.

To remain pure to the Hemingway tradition, the Old Columnist should have ordered a shot of scotch. But the Old Columnist does not like scotch. He asked for a beer.

Not just any beer. It was an Original Sloppy Joe's Beer. The Old Columnist put the bottle to his lips and drank. The waitress asked the Old Columnist's opinion. The Old Columnist pronounced the contents acceptable. The Old Columnist, it should be pointed out, adheres to a theory about these matters: There ain't no bad beer, just some a little better than others.

The waitress asked if the Old Columnist wanted an Original Sloppy Joe's sandwich. The Old Columnist said, "No, thanks; I've just eaten."

The Old Columnist's wife laughed. She said, "When did that ever stop you?" The Old Columnist ignored her crude attempt at humor.

The Old Columnist took his Original Sloppy Joe's beer and began to explore the interior of the bar. The bottle was cold. Beads of condensation rolled down the neck and onto his hand. It was cool to the touch. This was a stark contrast to the heat of Duval Street and its hustlers and its row upon row of tacky T-shirt shops.

The first thing the Old Columnist noticed was the noise. It was deafening. Pot-bellied, pasty-skinned tourists like the Old Columnist sat and stood everywhere. They all talked loudly. On stage was a singer. He was slapping at a piano. He sang and played into a microphone, greatly amplifying his efforts. The Old Columnist asked a passing waitress who the singer was.

"What?" the waitress yelled back.

The Old Columnist pointed to the stage and shouted, "Who is that guy?"

"Barry Cuda," the waitress answered.

The Old Columnist continued his journey.

On the side wall, he found many framed photographs of Hemingway lookalikes. They come to Key West every July for Hemingway Days. The Old Columnist studied each photo. Some of the subjects bore an amazing resemblance to Ernest Hemingway. Some were merely ruddy-faced, fat-cheeked, and whitebearded.

On another wall, he found a huge poster from the motion picture *The Old Man and the Sea*. The movie was based on Hemingway's 1952 classic book. As a boy, the Old Columnist had read the book and seen the movie. He remembered enjoying the book more. But now, decades later, the Old Columnist could only gaze at the movie poster and think all manner of envious thoughts about how six-figure contracts continually manage to evade him.

On yet another wall, the Old Columnist found many photos of Hemingway. In some of them, Hemingway posed with dead fish and dead animals. The Old Columnist also found framed articles about Hemingway and his association with Sloppy Joe's. He found a framed case holding a wooden bat, "Skinner's Peacemaker." The text below the case indicated the bat had been deployed by bouncers to teach manners. The bat appeared well used.

The Old Columnist soon found something else. It was a room that read MEN on the door. The Old Columnist stepped inside. He saw a line of condom machines on the wall. The Old Columnist, who has been in a bar or three in his life, had never seen such an array of condom machines. Later, when he visited other tourist sites in Key West, he would see even more condom machines on the restroom walls.

The Old Columnist is not an economist, but he thought to himself, without bars, tacky T-shirt shops, condom machines, and street hustlers, Key West would go broke.

The Old Columnist spent the next day in the solitude of the Everglades, looking at alligators, turtles, herons, and egrets. He much preferred the Everglades to Key West.

What? No Centerfold?

Down through the years, the pages of *National Geographic* have depicted pain through a variety of riveting photos. You've probably seen examples of them yourself.

The frost-framed face of an arctic explorer comes to mind. So do the cracked, leathery hands of a Chesapeake Bay commercial fisherman. The spoke-ribbed belly of a South American street urchin, perhaps. Not to mention various African tribal warriors, fresh from ceremonies welcoming them into manhood, their lacerated flesh still oozing blood.

But for gut-stomping, toenail-pulling, eyeball-gouging anguish, it's hard to beat the cover of the *National Geographic* swimsuit issue, now available at a newsstand near you.

The excruciating photo—oh, how I wince at the thought!—shows Australian model Hanna Hobensack wearing what the magazine calls "nature's own bikini"—two scallop shells Up Yonder and one scallop shell Down There, each held in place by a leather thong.

At least I think it's leather. Gimme a magnifying glass. Hmmmm. Yes, definitely leather. No, wait. Let me look again. Hmmmm. I'll have to get back to you.

In any event, can you imagine how painful it would be to actually swim in this garish outfit? Every time poor Hanna made a stroke with her arms or kicked her legs, those shells or the strap would surely pinch and cut her delicate—let me have that magnifying glass one more time.

But before you (I speak to persons of the testosterone persuasion here) break into a cold sweat, be advised this swimsuit edition isn't your standard cheesecake material. We're talking *National Geographic,* not *Sports Illustrated.* You won't see certain female body parts referred to in boorish, locker-room terms like "hooters" and "chamungas." In *National Geographic,* they use only scientific terms—like "hooteri maximus" and "chamungae americana."

I tease, of course. But I don't tease when I tell you this is, in fact, a quaint look at swimsuit culture over the course of a century, gleaned from *National Geographic's* bounteous archives. Whether the subject happens to be one of those hideous long-john coveralls Granny was forced to wear or an itsy-bitsy teeny-weenie orange polka-dot bikini from the Sizzlin' Sixties, what we have here is a slice of human history from around the globe.

Why swimsuits instead of, say, gloves or hats? Duh. Because only seventeen people would fork over ten bucks to look at glove and hat fashions from the last one hundred years, that's why.

National Geographic officials clearly had an eye on the bottom line, if not the common denominator, when they launched this project. As editor Bill Allen noted in his introduction, "Taking ourselves less seriously is a big part of life's big picture. The glimpses of skin in these pages might elicit a few more of those nudges and winks at parties, but I know what the images bring out in me: a sense of fun and wonder—as well as total astonishment at what some people will wear in public."

Precisely. What I particularly like about these photos is that they illustrate, graphically, the notion that swimsuits and swimming aren't the sole property of bodacious, bronzed Beautiful People.

The magazine is rife with images of Al and Amanda Average, complete with their pasty guts and sagging cellulite. Check out that Michelin man on page 90, cleverly disguised as a sun worshipper in Brazil. Or the matronly "Russian picnicker" on page 98. Yee-ouzers! No potato salad for me, thanks.

But like it or not, that's the way we humanoids really are. Run down the inventory at any swimming pool or beach: For every finely chiseled body, you'll see a hundred pieces of scrap metal. I speak with extensive experience in this regard. Not only have I logged more than twenty years as a lap-swimmer, I am personally acquainted with that glorious size known as XL.

Yet as compelling as this particular magazine may be, I'd just as soon the concept stops here. Between the *Sports Illustrated* swimsuit edition and the *National Geographic* swimsuit edition, I'm up to my nose clips with this idea.

If *Field and Stream* starts featuring deer hunters in thongs or *Progressive Farmer* trots out the latest in agricultural fashions from Speedo, I may give up reading altogether. Not to mention swimming.

The Perfect Pill

The world of medicine is about to achieve the pinnacle of success. A pill for stupidity is in the works. I'm serious. I'm reading a Reuters news service dispatch from Germany as we speak.

It quotes Hans-Hilger Ropers, director of the Max Planck Institute for Molecular Genetics in Berlin, who "has tested a pill thwarting hyperactivity in certain brain nerve cells, helping stabilize short-term memory and improve attentiveness." The scientist claims this is "the world's first anti-stupidity pill."

Ropers cited positive memory test results on mice and fruit flies. Alas, no word on other primitive forms of life like politicians, TV preachers, and radio talk-show hosts.

(Shame on me. That was a cheap shot. I hereby apologize to mice and fruit flies.)

Nonetheless, I remain absolutely ecstatic over the possibility that this medication might one day be available to all of humanity. Among the loathsome diseases of the world, stupidity ranks near the top of the list—and there's every indication it's spreading in pandemic proportions.

Can you imagine how marvelous life would be if stupidity joined scurvy, smallpox, syphilis, and other ailments for which treatment is now available? Just pop a pill and—poof!—you're a rational, clear-headed genius.

This thing offers tremendous possibilities for heads of state, diplomats, military leaders, and business executives. But it could also work wonders for your average Joe and Jane Sixpack. In fact, I can rattle off any number of situations where stupid pills should be ingested ASAP to avoid pending disaster.

Such as:

"You want to see my driver's license, officer? OK, but turnabout is fair play. I'll show you mine if you show me yours. You go first."

"Good news! That dreamy chartreuse, blue, and brown leisure suit I've been eyeballing down at Frickelsson's department store has finally gone on sale!"

"Yeah, I know the doctor said I'm dangerously overweight, but that quart of double-fudge ripple ice cream in the freezer is callin' my name."

"I'm tired of selling insurance for a living. I've always wanted to be an exotic dancer, and now's the time to start."

"Sure, what's one more drink for the road going to hurt?"

"Wonder what would happen if I plugged in this old lamp I found in Uncle Herb's attic?"

"Did I ever show you my famous back flip off the high board?"

"Naah, no need for a contract. I've always been a good judge of character. You look like an honest person."

"I know the gauge says empty, but we can go at least fifty more miles before we need to stop for gas."

"Look at that cute little raccoon! Let's see if he'll eat this cracker out of my hand."

"Sounds like a sure-fire investment. Here's my thousand bucks. No, on second thought, make it five thousand."

And the number one instance where these pills should be swallowed by the double-handful:

"What do you think I am—stupid or somethin'?"

Painfully Plentiful "Pun"-ishment

NORRIS—During the joint meeting of the Brotherhood of Unruly, Lowdown, Lying Hillbillies Observing Creative Knowledge Every Year (BULLHOCKEY) and the Society of Appalachian Saintly Sisters (SASS) at the Museum of Appalachia's annual Tennessee Fall Homecoming, the following business was transacted:

• Dr. William Foster, chief medical officer, announced the sad news of an angry professional spat between two of the organization's most prominent physicians.

"After years of practicing medicine together, they've gone their separate ways," Dr. Foster said. "Now each is accusing each other of stealing patients and have brought lawsuits alleging alienation of infections."

Dr. Foster was directed to file his report in triplicate and forward it to the Insurance Committee for processing and payment.

• In his crime report, Chief Deputy Ray Rutherford noted that a recent murder was still under investigation.

"The victim was beaten with a bowl, milk was poured all over his body, and a banana was stuck into each ear," he said. "We suspect a cereal killer."

On a voice vote of "Cheerios!" Rutherford was urged to close the case as soon as possible, before humidity damages the evidence.

• Bonnie Peters, chairwoman of the Committee on Aging, said, sadly, that her memory isn't as sharp as it used to be.

"Also," she added, "my memory isn't as sharp as it used to be."

Several members made notes to be sure to write that one down.

• Floyd Anderson, chairman of the Sitting Committee on Dairying, took the floor to pose this question: "Why does a milking stool have three legs instead of four?"

When no answer was forthcoming, Floyd said, "The cow has the udder."

Immediately, there arose a cry of "Aw, what a bunch of bull!" But Sergeant-at-Arms Allen Longmire ruled the impromptu protest out of order since male bovines have a relatively minor role in dairying operations.

• Royce Beaty, chairman of the Domestic Relations Committee, announced the arrival of a new divorce lawyer in the community.

Said Royce, "His motto is 'Satisfaction guaranteed or your honey back.'"

• When a loud crash was heard outside the meeting hall, Charlie Mead was dispatched to investigate. Upon return, he said a large truck loaded with thesauruses had skidded off the road and smashed into a massive oak tree.

Asked if anyone was hurt, Mead replied, "No, thankfully, but the witnesses were astounded, shocked, taken aback, surprised, startled, dumbfounded, thunderstruck, and caught unawares."

• Larry Mathis and Mike Snider gave personal testimony about poverty.

"We were so poor," said Mathis, "the only thing Mama could do for supper was read recipes to us. My sister was hard of hearing, and she nearly starved to death."

Snider said things weren't much better in his hometown: "The closest thing we had to heavy industry was a four-hundred-pound Avon saleslady."

- Ernest Payne, chairman of the Language Arts Division of the Geography Committee, said that to be best of his knowledge, the capital of Arkansas is A.

By voice vote, the majority agreed.

- Ernest's report prompted Gene Purcell, chairman of the Veterinary Research Committee, to announce that if you remove the wings from a fly, it becomes a walk.

- And speaking of animals, Carlock Stooksbury, chairman of the Avian Syntax Committee, reported the results of a six-month project to use the words "defense," "detail," "defeat," and "deduct" in the same sentence:

"Defeat of deduct went over defense before detail."

A love offering was taken to fund further research by Carlock's committee.

> Jim Mann, a reader from Waynesville, North Carolina, sent me this nugget of wisdom, which pretty much sums up the history of humankind:
>
> "We always try to make things idiot-proof, but the world keeps making better idiots."

- Andrea Fritts announced she recently joined a fitness club and reported for her first aerobics class.

"Talk about strenuous!" she exclaimed. "I bent, twisted, gyrated, jumped up and down, and perspired for an hour. But by the time I finally got my leotard on, the class was over."

- John Patterson, chairman of the Enclosures Committee, asked if anyone knew how a bikini and a barbed-wire fence were alike.

When nobody answered, John said, "They both protect the property, but you always get a good view."

Sergeant-at-Arms Longmire put Patterson on official notice that the correct pronunciation was "bobwar."

- Connie Adams reported that her husband's birthday was approaching, and he'd been dropping hints for "something fancy that would go from zero to two-hundred in four seconds."

Proudly, Connie said, "I bought him some expensive bathroom scales."

Several other wives in the crowd took notes.

- John Rice Irwin, chairman of the Music Committee, said a band called the Prison Players had recently come by for an audition.

When pressed about the group's odd name, Irwin said, "They're always behind a few bars, and they can't find the right key."

When asked what genre of music the band plays, Irwin replied, "It's a new style, somewhere between country and rap. I think they call it crap."

- Billy Joe Cooley, chairman of the Library Committee, announced the shocking news that all nine copies of the recently acquired book, *How to Commit Suicide,* had been checked out and were long overdue.

- Ben Adams reported that a preacher friend of his had been quite worried lately about a woman in the congregation who was becoming overly friendly with several of the deacons.

The reverend finally approached the wayward woman before services one Sunday morning, took her aside, and whispered in her ear, "I prayed for you all last night."

Whereupon the woman whispered back, "Why didn't you just telephone? I could've been here in ten minutes."

Four ministers in the audience immediately remembered duties in their respective parishes and exited the premises.

- Carolyn Cornelius asked permission to tell the joke she'd just heard about a snail that was headed to town but ran a stop sign and was hit by a turtle, and when the cops arrived and tried to quiz the snail about the accident, the snail said, "I can't remember; everything happened so fast."

Permission was denied.

- Jimmy White reported that his fiftieth birthday was a joyous occasion but that things had gone steadily downhill ever since. Not only was his hair beginning to turn gray, he was also experiencing chronic stomach pain.

"I can't understand it," Jimmy said. "My wife bought me a bottle of Grecian Formula to remedy the situation. But it hasn't helped, even though I've taken a tablespoon every morning."

The matter was referred to the Committee on Aging with the recommendation that Jimmy try doubling the dosage.

- David Irons announced that a good friend of his recently died and was cremated. Instead of the traditional urn, however, his wife deposited the ashes in an hourglass.

"That way, David noted, "she could finally get some work out of him."

Several members asked for an explanation.

- George Vincent, chairman of the Spreading Spores Committee, told of the mushroom that walked into a bar and asked for a beer. The bartender refused, saying mushrooms weren't welcome in his place of business.

"But why?" the mushroom asked, "I'm a fun guy."

- Several rounds of high-octane refreshments were served, and a second love offering was taken to cover bail for the Refreshments Committee.

- There being no further business, the meeting was adjourned. Refreshments continued well into the night. A good time was had by all.

Someday I May Find Honest Work was designed and typeset on a Macintosh computer system using InDesign software. The body text is set in 10/13 Minion and display type is set in Myriad Pro and Minion. This book was designed and typeset by Kelly Gray and manufactured by Thomson-Shore, Inc.